Complete Modern Persian (Farsi)

Narguess Farzad

First published in Great Britain in 2004 by Hodder Education. An Hachette UK company.

First published in US in 2004 by The McGraw-Hill Companies, Inc.

This edition published in 2010 by John Murray Learning

British Library Cataloguing in Publication Data: a catalogue record for this title is available from the British Library.

Library of Congress Catalog Card Number: on file.

Paperback ISBN: 978 1 444 10354 0

eBook ISBN: 978 1 444 13171 0

9

The publisher has used its best endeavours to ensure that any website addresses referred to in this book are correct and active at the time of going to press. However, the publisher and the author have no responsibility for the websites and can make no guarantee that a site will remain live or that the content will remain relevant, decent or appropriate.

The publisher has made every effort to mark as such all words which it believes to be trademarks. The publisher should also like to make it clear that the presence of a word in the book, whether marked or unmarked, in no way affects its legal status as a trademark.

Every reasonable effort has been made by the publisher to trace the copyright holders of material in this book. Any errors or omissions should be notified in writing to the publisher, who will endeavour to rectify the situation for any reprints and future editions.

Cover image © Oliver leedham/Alamy

Typeset by MPS Limited, A Macmillan Company.

Printed and bound in Great Britain.

John Murray Learning policy is to use papers that are natural, renewable and recyclable products and made from wood grown in sustainable forests. The logging and manufacturing processes are expected to conform to the environmental regulations of the country of origin.

Hodder & Stoughton Ltd
338 Euston Road
London NW1 3BH
www.hodder.co.uk

Also available in ebook

Contents

Meet the author

When I left Iran, ostensibly like many of my fellow countrymen intent on pursuing a science-based university education such as engineering, that would equip me for employment in most corners of the world, as well as with rosewater, pistachios and saffron, my suitcase was laden with books of Persian prose and poetry, modern and classical, intriguing, romantic and spiritual.

And they offered me respite whenever I needed to get away from differential equations and inorganic chemistry! Love of Persian poetry in particular eventually led me to take an academic interest in the subject and to explore and re-evaluate the beauty of the Persian language itself, its historic development and its resilience in the face of more than a millennium of onslaught by so many invaders who were all ultimately absorbed into the Persianate world.

I have been teaching Persian language and literature at SOAS and other institutions for nearly twenty years and the thrill of watching my students progress from those hesitant early steps to confident users of the language never loses its magic. Observing their learning process and challenges helped me create what I consider to be a very user-friendly and comprehensive guide to learning Persian. And perhaps that early mathematical training came into its own in structuring this book.

Only got a minute?

Persian is one of the oldest living languages of the world and one of the few whose millennium-old prose and poetry is perfectly understood by its modern native speakers and by those who learn it properly as a second language.

Persian is an Indo-European language and therefore speakers of European languages will find it a lot easier to learn than say a Semitic language such as Arabic or a Sinitic language such as Chinese. As a speaker of a European language you already know several Persian words that share a common ancestry with languages such as English or German, and I do not mean European words such as 'tāksi' (taxi), 'terāctor' (tractor), 'sinemā' or 'restorān' (restaurant) but rather words such as 'barādar' (brother), 'abrou' (eyebrow), 'dokhtar' (daughter), 'setāre' (star) or phrases such as 'nām-e man' (literally meaning 'name of mine', or 'my name'). Many English words such as 'band', 'beggar', 'builder', 'check-mate', 'pyjamas', 'chinaware', 'tulip', 'taffeta', 'orange', 'lemon', 'spinach', 'aubergine' and 'cash' have their origins in Persian.

Persian is the official language of Iran, the sixteenth-largest country, in the world; as Tajiki, written in the Russian, Cyrillic alphabet, it is the official language of Tajikistan and as Dari it is one of the two official languages of Afghanistan.

As Muslim armies began to conquer their neighbouring lands in the 7th century, the local languages of conquered Iraq, Syria and Egypt, for example, were gradually wiped out and superseded by Arabic. Iran was the only country in that region whose language, Persian, was not replaced by Arabic. Although Persian started to be written in what became the Perso-Arabic script, it retained its solid grammatical features and indeed, after it became a Muslim empire in its own right, it took the Perso-Arabic script and numerous Persian loanwords further east to many parts of the Indian subcontinent, the Malay Archipelago, Brunei (Jawi script) and to the borders of China (Uyghur). Until the 18th century, Persian was the official court and administrative language of India.

Learning the script may strike you as daunting but be assured that it is more difficult for a speaker of Persian to learn English than it would be for you to learn Persian.

5 Only got five minutes?

Many westerners' first encounter with Iran or the word 'Persian' is often through a whole host of media, old and new. These days hardly a day passes when some reference to Iran, positive or negative, is not covered by global news outlets. However, for many, the image of Iran, or Persia, is conjured through the study of ancient history and wars with the Greeks, travel books, works of literature, films and, of course, the spectacular examples of Islamic architecture.

In the 1588 play *Tamburlaine* Christopher Marlowe intrigued his audiences with accounts of conquests of the great central Asian emperor of the same name as he wrote: 'is it not passing brave, to be a king, and ride in triumph through Persepolis?', and in 2007, the Academy Award nominated film, *Persepolis*, based on Marjane Satrapi's autobiographical graphic novel, once again brought the name of the seat of the ancient Persian empire, to audiences across the world.

Persepolis, this most spectacular of ancient desert cities and a UNESCO World Heritage site, known as *Takht-e Jamshid*, throne of Jamshid in Persian, is about 850 km south of the Iranian capital Tehran and was founded at around 515 BCE by Cyrus the Great, the founder of one of the greatest empires, both in size and influence, that the world has ever known. The cuneiform tablets, rock-reliefs and other archaeological finds in this city give us examples of Old Persian, the first phase in the development of the modern language of Iran (known to its local speakers as *Farsi*), large sections of Central Asia (known as *Tajiki*) and Afghanistan (known as *Dari*).

Robert Byron, in his critically acclaimed book *The Road to Oxiana* (1937), gives a magical and entertaining account of his ten-month travels in Iran and Afghanistan in 1933 and 1934, including a journey to Persepolis. This book has captured the imagination of, and inspired many later travel-writers. He interlaces his observations on Persian architecture, gardens, customs and officialdom with references to the language too:

The day's journey had a wild exhilaration. Up and down the mountains, over the endless flats, we bumped and swooped. The sun flayed us. Great spirals of dust, dancing like demons over the desert, stopped our dashing Chevrolet. Suddenly, from far across a valley, came the flash of a turquoise jar, bobbing along on a donkey. Its owner walked beside it, clad in a duller blue. And seeing the two I understood why blue is the Persian colour, and why the Persian word for it means water as well.

The Persian word for water is 'āb', formed from the first two letters of the Persian alphabet, 'ā' and 'b', written in the Perso-Arabic script (read from right to left) as بآ. Wherever there is 'āb', or water, there will be prosperity and the first steps in development of human settlements. You find the Persian word 'ābād', a euphemism for city, in many central and south Asian city-names such as Ahmadabad, Hyderabad, Ashgabat and Islamabad. Does the Persian word 'ābād' not remind you of the English word 'abode'? This is only one example of the numerous words that, thanks to their common Indo-European ancestry, Persian and English share.

The Persian words for several colours are formed by adding an -i sound (pronounced as *ea* in *easy*) to an object or fruit that is that colour. Therefore, as Robert Byron discovered, Persian for 'blue' is 'ābi', that is 'āb' (water) + i. Similarly, the colour described in English as 'khaki' comes from the Persian 'khāk' (dust, earth) + i. Brown is: 'qahve'i' which is made up of 'qahve' (coffee, or, closer still, think of café) and 'i'. Can you guess what colour 'nārenji' is? Think of the Italian pronunciation of a particular citrus fruit.

Numbers

Persian numbers originate from the Hindu-Arabic numeral systems, developed by Indian mathematicians and then adopted by the Persian mathematician Khawrazmi in 825 CE. After further modification by Arab mathematicians these numbers spread to the western world in the 11th and 12th centuries. You can see, for example, that if you rotate the Persian number ٣ by 90° anti-clockwise, you will arrive at the European, 'Arabic' number 3. The table below shows the Arabic and Persian numbers:

Western Arabic numbers	1	2	3	4	5	6	7	8	9
Persian numbers	۱	۲	۳	۴	۵	۶	۷	۸	۹
Arabic numbers	١	٢	٣	٤	٥	٦	٧	٨	٩

The Persian numeral 5 is 'panj' and is written as ۵ looking like an upside down heart. The Indian State 'Punjāb' is really the Persian 'panj-āb' literally meaning 'five waters', that is the land of five rivers. The shape of the numeral five is derived from the print of the palm of one's hand, where the five fingers point upwards and the middle finger is the tip, while the lower part reflects the heart-shaped base of the hand.

Persian numbers are written from left to right and on the whole, and compared to some other combined number systems such as the French for example, are remarkably easy to learn.

I hope that this brief overview of the Persian language and writing system has whetted your appetite for the main course that follows in this book. Enjoy the journey!

Introduction

Persian, known to native speakers as *Farsi*, is the official language of modern-day Iran and is spoken in many parts of Afghanistan and the central Asian republics of Tajikistan and Uzbekistan. Historically, it has been a much more widely understood language in an area ranging from the Middle East to India. Sizeable minority populations in other Persian Gulf countries (Bahrain, Iraq, Oman, the People's Democratic Republic of Yemen and the United Arab Emirates), as well as large diaspora communities in Australia, Canada, Europe, Turkey, and the USA, also speak Persian.

The Persian spoken in Afghanistan is known as *Dari*. The dialectal variation between *Farsi* and *Dari* has been compared with that between European French and Canadian French, or between UK English and English spoken in Australia or South Africa.

The Persian language of Tajikistan is known as *Tajiki*, which is written in Cyrillic. *Tajiki* had minimal contact with other Persian-speaking countries during the Soviet era and contains a large number of Russian and archaic Persian words.

Modern Persian, also known as New Persian, is the linguistic continuation of Middle Persian, itself a successor to Old Persian, the language of ancient Iran up to about 330 BCE. Old, Middle and New Persian represent one and the same language at three stages of its history and development. Persian has its geographical origin in Pārs (now known as Fārs) in central Iran with its famous city of Shiraz, homeland of some of Iran's most famous poets, enchanting rose gardens and lush 'paradise on earth' orchards; this region is, historically speaking, the true home of Persian, although dialectical features of Persian vary as you travel throughout Iran.

About Iran

Iran is one of the few countries that has had a continuing influence in shaping contemporary history and also played a prominent role in the early history of civilization.

Iran's history as a nation of people dates back to the second millennium BCE. In succession to the empires of Assyria and Babylon, Iran became the major power in the Middle East in the sixth century BCE, when the Persian Empire of Cyrus, Xerxes and Darius stretched from the shores of Greece to the edge of India. In the fourth century BCE Iran's hegemony was briefly interrupted by the short-lived dominion of Alexander the Great and his successors, but under the Parthian and Sasanian rulers Iran was again a dominant political power.

Iran's ancient religion, Zoroastrianism, is considered one of the earliest monolithic religions. It has probably influenced mankind more than any other faith, for it had a profound impact on Judaism, Christianity and Islam. Strong adherence to Zoroastrian beliefs and

rituals continues among its modern followers in Iran, India and throughout the world.

Historically, the Silk Road, a trade route that made economic exchanges between the West and the East possible and allowed this delicate commodity to reach the markets in Rome, passed through Iran which acted as a major junction between these trading nations.

Iran is also an immensely fascinating modern state. One of the more significant countries of the Middle East with a predominantly young population of nearly 70 million and 16th in size among the countries of the world, Iran is located at one of the most strategically important parts of our planet, linking Central Asia and the Indo-Pakistani subcontinent to Europe.

Iran's role as a trading partner with the countries of the European Community is rapidly increasing. One of the founding members of the Organization of Petroleum Exporting Countries (OPEC), Iran is the third largest oil-producing country with one of the largest natural gas reserves and oil tanker fleets.

For veteran travellers in search of the new and the under-explored, Iran is an exciting tourist destination, offering breathtaking contrasts of nature as well as a wealth of ancient and medieval sites. Of the world's 12 places recognized and registered in the 'Index of World Human Heritage' by UNESCO, three are located in Iran making it seventh in the world in terms of possessing significant world heritage sites.

Iran is the home of miniature paintings, calligraphy, exquisite carpets and vibrant glazed tile works and its art remains a popular area of research and study for artists and students alike.

In recent years the success of Iranian films at international festivals, winning hundreds of prestigious awards, worldwide retrospectives of Iranian directors and popular screenings in many major capitals, has placed Iranian cinema firmly on the map, inviting comparison with Italian neo-realism and similar movements in the past decades.

Linguistic development

It is estimated that the Iranian tribes came to settle on the plateau of Iran at the beginning of the first millennium BCE. However, the most ancient traces of Old Persian date back to about 600 BCE. Examples of Old Persian are found in the form of inscriptions of Cyrus the Great and Darius I at Bisitun and Persepolis in Iran, sites that feature as highlights of archaeological tours of Iran.

By 400 BCE Old Persian was heading for extinction and a new system of linguistic expression with relatively greater simplicity was established as the *lingua franca* of the Persian Empire. Middle Persian became the official, religious and literary language of Iran in the third to seventh centuries CE.

By the end of the tenth century CE, some 300 years after the Islamic conquest, New Persian came to be written in the much clearer Arabic alphabet that replaced the old, Aramaic ideograms. Before long, New Persian became spread over a much larger area extending to Xinjiang and to Central and South Asia.

Phonetically and grammatically, the degree of evolution from Old to Middle Persian is considerable, the differences being comparable with differences between Latin and French, for example. On the other hand, New Persian remains in many respects quite close to Middle Persian. For example, more than 60% of Persian vocabulary is identical to the Middle Persian words. This means that most educated speakers of Persian would have some idea of what their forebears of more than a millennium ago might be saying, in the event of a chance meeting. Another distinctive difference is that Old Persian was written from left to right, but both Middle and New Persian are written from right to left.

Does learning Persian help with learning other languages?

In a word, yes! Until recent centuries, Persian was culturally and historically one of the most prominent languages of the Middle East and the Indian subcontinent. Persian is the second language of Islam and was instrumental in the spread of the faith during the reign of the Moguls in the Indian subcontinent. For example, it was an important language during the reign of the Moguls in India, where knowledge of Persian was cultivated and held in very high esteem. To a lesser extent it was instrumental in bringing the Arabic script, known as *Jawi*, to Malaysia. Nowadays, 'Jawi' is less commonly used and a Romanized Malay writing script has gained more of an official status. However, Jawi is written in the Perso-Arabic script. The use of Persian in the courts of Mogul rulers ended in 1837 when it was banned by officials of the East India Company, but not before the development of a Persian–Indian vernacular. Persian poetry is still a significant part of the literature of the Indo-Pakistani subcontinent.

Very close links between Persian and Urdu, and the presence of numerous Persian words in Turkish, offer a high degree of mutual intelligibility to speakers of these languages and the study of Ottoman Turkish literature without a knowledge of Persian would be meaningless. Malay also contains countless Persian words and for scholars of Malay literature a classical Persian dictionary is often among their most used reference books.

If you are interested in learning other modern Iranian languages, such as Baluchi or Kurdish, knowledge of Persian and the Perso-Arabic script helps. For example, all the languages in the following list are written in this script or were written in it until very recently: Assyrian, Southern Azeri spoken by 20 million people in Iran, Hausa (gradually superseded by Romanized script), Kashmiri, Punjabi of Pakistan, Pashtu, Sindhi and Uyghur until very recently, although there are now efforts underway to use an adapted Latin alphabet for writing in this language.

How difficult is Persian to learn?

New Persian, that is the language of modern Iran, is written in the Arabic script, but as a language it belongs to the Indo-European family of languages, which includes Sanskrit, Greek, Latin and English. This may in part explain why speakers of European languages find learning Persian relatively easy to begin with. Moreover, some basic vocabulary that is comparable to English, added to similarity of syntax, compensates for the initial strangeness of the alphabet. Words such as *barādar* 'brother', *pedar* 'father', *mādar* 'mother', *setāre* 'star', *tārik* 'dark', *lab*, 'lip', *abru* 'eyebrow', *dar* 'door', and many more illustrate the common Indo-European genealogy that English and Persian share.

Persian is not a very difficult language for English-speaking people to learn, in contrast to many other major languages of the Middle East or some European languages and is regarded as extremely sonorous and beautiful to listen to.

New Persian contains quite a few foreign words, the majority of which are Arabic, which reflects the extent of cultural and intellectual exchanges between Iran and its neighbours and, of course, the impact of Islam since the seventh century CE.

The mixed character of modern Persian vocabulary is a basic feature of the language. A comparison can be made between Persian and English: the Arabic element in Persian has a similar status to that of Latin and Romance languages in relation to the original Anglo-Saxon of English.

In the first quarter of the 13th century Iran began to experience the unimaginable havoc caused by the brutal invasion of the Mongols. They ruled Iran for more than one hundred years without challenge but over the next century they began to gradually lose their supremacy to independent local rulers. During the years of Mongol rule a large number of Mongolian and Turkic words made their way into Persian. These are mostly words of a military or administrative nature.

From the 18th century, political and commercial contact with Europe increased and many of the Iranian elite travelled to Europe, mostly to Russia, France and Britain, encountering ideas, situations and objects for which there were no Persian names. In the opposite direction, many European visitors, mostly missionaries, merchants and military advisors, arrived and settled in Iran. These exchanges meant that Persian has also borrowed many loanwords from European languages that are fully embedded in the everyday vernacular of Iranians.

Most of these words are originally French and are uttered with a French pronunciation, ranging from the simple *merci* for 'thank you' to names of European items of clothing such as *robe de chambre* for 'dressing gown', *cravate* for 'tie', *deux pièces* 'ladies' two-piece', *imperméable* 'raincoat' or 'rainproof outerwear', *manteau* 'thin overcoat' (the staple outerwear of women in Iran today), *sac* 'bag' (pronounced *sāk*), *papillon* 'bow' and many others. Other European words invariably accompanied the arrival of modern technologies or utilities in Iran, e.g. words such as telephone, television, radio, film, cinema, theatre, bus, pieces of machinery, decimal units of weights and measures, names of particular European dishes and some medical and modern scientific terminology. Again the majority of these terms are pronounced the French way.

Persian is the official language of Iran and although there are large areas of Iran where Persian is not the mother tongue, e.g. in Azerbaijan, Kurdistan or Luristan, it is *spoken* or understood by most of the urban population, and for at least half the population (70 million) of Iran, Persian is the native tongue. In Afghanistan, *Dari* enjoys official status along with *Pashtu*.

Study of Persian in Europe

Apart from the early familiarity of a handful of British scholars with the names and works of some medieval Iranian scientists and philosophers, the first steps towards the study of Persian in Europe were taken in the early fourteenth century. Moreover, European travellers, merchants, missionaries and, of course, the envoys and officers of European courts increasingly encountered Persian in the huge geographic sphere where it was spoken or existed as the *lingua franca*.

'Systematic' study of Persian in Europe, however, started in the seventeenth century with a steady increase in the number of Europeans interested in the orient and the literary treasures it offered.

In Britain alone this has resulted in the publication of numerous books of grammar, dictionaries and readers over the past 300 years written by diverse personalities ranging from envoys to adventurers, missionaries and traders, as well as the established scholars and orientalists. Some of these earlier books make for surprisingly good reading and provide windows not only into the linguistic conventions of the time and general approach to study of foreign languages but offer fascinating descriptions of national characteristics of both the Persians and the visitors. The sketches offered in books to assist language acquisition, for example, tell a lot more about the circles in which the European emissaries moved and their main preoccupations than the usefulness of the manuals as a tool for learning Persian.

The importance of immersion in the real language as spoken by its native speakers, however, was recognized early on. The Reverend William St Clair-Tisdall (1859–1928), for example, who served as the Secretary of the Church of England's Church Missionary Society in Esfahan in Iran and who has likened Persian to '*the Italian of the East*', refers to his own difficulties in communicating with Persians. Having studied and learnt to speak Persian in the Panjab in India he found, in the course of attempted conversations with the Persians he met in Bombay, that he was 'almost if not quite unintelligible to them, since many of the words, phrases and idioms he had learnt from the pages of the poet Sa'di and other classical Persian authors had become obsolete and had been superseded by others in the modern language as spoken in Persia itself'. He writes in his introduction to *Modern Persian Conversation Grammar* (1923): 'It was as if a foreigner, having discovered some corner of the world in which English was still spoken by the learned, just as it occurs in the Elizabethan writers and with the pronunciation of that distant day, had learnt the language from them and then tried to converse with the English people of today.' The Reverend St Clair-Tisdall concludes that the conversation of such a novice 'would seem at once stilted and vulgar, and it would amuse everyone with whom he came in contact'. It is therefore essential for learners of modern Persian to try and have as much contact with native speakers or at least make use of the innumerable websites that allow the learner near immersion in the culture, music and media of Persian-speaking countries, as well as ever-increasing numbers of sites that offer on-line teaching resources that complement grammar books and readers.

Basic characteristics of Persian

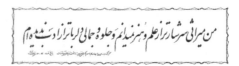

من میراثِ شرسارِ تراعلم و هنر نمیدانم و جلوهٔ حالیِ الربا تراز دست مده ام

Nastaligh calligraphy. Quotations from Imam Ali Ibn-Abi Talib

Persian is written from right to left in the cursive, that is joined-up, Perso-Arabic script. This script can be most ornamental and, in this respect, Iranians more than others who use this script have made the art of calligraphy and refined penmanship their own. Towards the end of this introduction I say a little about some of the traditional instruments that are used for Persian calligraphy. The so-called Perso-Arabic script has innovations that accommodates sounds such as *ch*, as in 'chair' or *p* as in 'Paris' that do not exist in Arabic but are part of Persian.

The Persian alphabet has 32 letters. All of these, with the exception of the first letter, *alef* ‎ا are consonants. However, two of the letters of the alphabet have a dual existence and can function as symbols for long vowels too. These are the letters 'v' ‎و and 'y' ‎ی that can respectively represent the long vowels 'u' and 'i'.

It is important, however, to point out early on that seven letters of this alphabet are best described as one-way letters and when it comes to writing down the words, they behave differently from the other 25 letters. I shall go over this point in much more detail later on as we start learning the script.

There are *no capital letters* in the Perso-Arabic script.

For reasons of simplicity I shall suggest that there are six vowels in Persian: three long and three short vowels.

Unlike English, the three short vowels are not written down. However, to help you learn to read properly all short vowels will be marked in the initial units of this book by using a system of diacritics or 'pointing' with small indicating signs. All long vowels are and must be written in with the use of the 'ā', which is the first letter of the alphabet or the other consonants that represent 'i' and 'u'.

Persian is remarkably simple in terms of formal grammar. There is no gender, no noun inflection, no adjectival agreement and no irregularity in verbal conjugation. However, rather like English in this respect, what Persian lacks in inflection it more than makes up for in syntactic and idiomatic complexity. If you know any Iranians, you will know that they hardly ever use straightforward, simple prose in English so you can imagine what it must be like when they speak Persian! But do not despair: acquiring a sound, basic foundation in the language will enable you gradually to expand and develop your knowledge of Persian and appreciate the ornate vernacular, which is adored and used to great effect by all Iranians.

This brings us to the second major hurdle, which is the acquisition of vocabulary, but that is true of any language where the students start from the absolute beginning – remember as an Indo-European speaker you have a head start with quite a lot of vocabulary.

Look at the following examples of commonly used Persian and English words with Indo-European connections:

English	Persian
better	*behtar*
bezoar	*pādzahr*
body	*badan*
candy	*qand*
cow	*gāv*
dark	*tarik*
dental	*dandān*
door	*dar*
drug	*dāru (*orig: *dārug*)*
graft	*gereftan*
group	*gorouh*
intern	*andarun*
iron	*āhan*
juvenile	*javān*
physician	*pezeshk*
star	*setāre*

By taking a certain few rules into account you will see a closer similarity still between the words above. The first rule is that, unlike English, no Persian word begins with two consonants. Therefore, a Persian speaker would find the English words such as 'brown', 'script' or 'stop' quite odd. The order of appearance of vowels and consonants in Persian are either vowel–consonant–vowel, e.g. '*above*', consonant–vowel–consonant, e.g. '*got*' or vowel–consonant–consonant, e.g. '*act*'. So, to the Iranian ear the word 'must' is OK but 'star' is not. However, if you separate the 's' and the 't' of 'star' by the vowel 'e' you will get the equivalent Persian word *setāre*, which is how the word is pronounced.

The other observation is that over the course of the development of Indo-European languages certain letters in one group have been changed by another. For example, 'f' and 'v', or 'd' and 't' seem to replace one another in words that evidently have a common root. For example, the English 'dark' becomes even closer to the Persian *tārik* if we replace the 'd' with the 't'.

First steps

To begin with, this course will emphasize the written element of Persian until the user comes to grips with the letters and reading the script and feels able to follow the fundamental, elementary aspects of grammar. However, this will not be done at the expense of the spoken tongue, i.e. the colloquial language that reflects the day-to-day exchanges of all levels of society in Iran. I have attempted to familiarize the user of this book with educated contemporary, standard Persian as written and spoken in Tehran and broadcast to the world in radio, TV and used in many Iranian films.

Intonation

One of the hardest things about learning a new language is trying to copy the voice pitch and the intonation of the native speakers. I think it would be fair to say that learning to speak like an Iranian is nowhere near as difficult as learning to speak like an Italian, but one or two hints may be helpful.

In most Persian words the stress is on the last syllable. In affirmative sentences there is usually a rise in the pitch just before the verb, but in negative sentences the pitch rises on the negative verb.

Question words in Persian, 'how', 'who', 'where', 'why' and others, normally carry the stress which is opposite of what happens in English. In fact, stress on the question words in English can sound threatening and gives the impression of aggression. In Persian, however, it is not unusual to put the stress on the interrogatives.

Script

Nastaliq, the style of writing most popular in Iran, is an art in which laws of mathematics and nature are obeyed. It enables the artist to create a beautiful piece of calligraphy by using several forms of the same letter or by employing various forms of the words and using them in different compositions. With its mystifying beauty, nastaliq has closely accompanied Persian poetry and has played an important role in communicating the poetic concepts to the readers. Looking at the works of calligraphers, both modern and traditional, reveals that nastaliq has served both literature and mysticism. In fact, compared to other poets, the poems of Hafiz and Rumi have most often been used by artists. In Persian culture and art, poetry, traditional music and calligraphy are intimately related and are complementary elements.

The most basic tools of a calligrapher are his reed pens known as *qalam* and his ink. The pens are traditionally carved from the reeds taken from the reed beds of southern Iran, on the shores of the Persian Gulf. Calligraphers then use their penknives or very sharp blades to cut the nib and to trim it until the desired shape of the pen is achieved. The pens range in length from 20 cm to almost 30 cm and are 1–1½ cm thick.

Calligraphers develop a profound knowledge and almost an instinct of how to spot the best cane suitable for a good pen, how to trim the nib and, finally, to create the perfect writing instrument. A good pen is treasured and rarely is it lent to another person as its use over the years almost moulds it to the demands and expectations of its owner.

Inks can be in many colours including black, brown, yellow, red, blue, white, silver and gold and, with the aid of new technology and changing trends in writing styles, more vivid coloured inks are also being developed. In the old days, many calligraphers refined the formulas of making the best ink but their recipes, based on complex chemical experiments, were usually carefully guarded secrets.

The arrival of paper in Iran from China in the mid-eighth century was a turning point in the art of writing. Paper was made from cotton and occasionally from silk.

Geometric principles play an essential role in Persian calligraphy, which adheres very strictly to the rules of dimension and proportion. The *alef* provides a unit of measure for all the other letters of the alphabet.

The size of the dot is also of crucial importance. The dot is a diamond or square impression made by pressing the nib of the pen on to paper.

Depending on the calligrapher and the style of the script he is working on, the height of the *alef* can vary from three to 12 dots. The width of the *alef* is usually equivalent to one dot.

You will, of course, find that your initial attempts at handwriting will look shaky and uncertain. Perhaps the letters you write down may not always look the same or uniform, but don't lose heart. It will take a while before you achieve a good, legible style of writing. Even those Iranians who pride themselves in having nice handwriting will baulk at the prospect of writing with traditional writing tools, which is the ultimate test of being able to write accurately and beautifully.

This is perhaps as good a place as any to return to the purpose of writing this book, tempting as it is to go on about the artistic aspects of the written language. This is perhaps an appropriate moment also to remind the readers that this book does not promise to teach its users all the complex aspects of the Persian language. That would be a foolish promise to make and to my knowledge no book has ever achieved it. Later sections of the book give you glimpses of the complex grammar, and the 'Taking it futher' section will point you in the direction of further academic studies of Persian. My aim is to whet your appetite sufficiently and to give you enough of a solid grounding to persuade you that Persian is really not a very difficult language to learn and to entice you to use this book as the basis for a more fundamental study of the language.

The following icon ◀ indicates that the material is on the recording.

The opening lines of the preface that Alexander Finn (1847–1919) wrote for his *Persian for Travellers* in 1885 as an aid 'to those holding intercourse with the natives', offers an apt ending for this introduction: 'This is a work of no pretensions.' However, I hope it will equip you on the start of a journey of discovery into one of the East's most enchanting languages and the immense body of writing that is written in this language.

Writing and pronunciation

How to write Persian

Before we even look at the alphabet let us first try the following exercises:

Can you draw straight, horizontal lines from right to left?

Can you draw semi-circles and parts of triangles going clockwise?

Try sketching a railway line by drawing the tracks from right to left and then a series of connecting sleepers, vertically from top to bottom and from the bottom to the top.

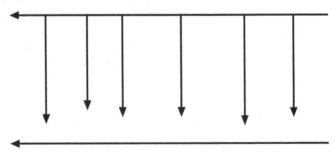

Can you do back slashes and the mirror image above the line and can you draw lines meeting at an angle in one sweep of the pen, like the tip of an arrow?

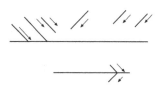

How about a series of small, connecting semi-circles, again going from right to left as in the edges of a doily?

Can you make a combination of the above movements without taking your pen off the paper?

If you find these exercises easy, then you are ready to start learning the alphabet.

To begin with, you should try to write the full, unconnected form of the letters and don't worry about other forms until you are confident about copying these full shapes. Luckily, the Perso-Arabic letters of the alphabet fall into patterns and different number of dots distinguish one letter from another in the same pattern.

Start with the opening letter which is the vertical letter ا, ﺍ, the *alef* which is drawn downwards. Next, try copying out the 'horizontal' group of letters that look like 'plates' with tiny curved edges: ث, ت, ب, پ. To write these out first try to draw horizontal lines from the right to the left. Then repeat this movement but this time start with a tiny downward stroke for the right-hand edge of the 'plate', about two millimetres in length, and continue horizontally along the lines of the paper for about seven or eight millimetres and finish the letters with an up-swoop for the left-hand edge, equal in size and mirror image of the right-hand edge. The movement of your pen should be clockwise.

Don't forget the dots!

Now try your hands at the next pattern of letters that look like 'hooks':

ح، ج، ج، خ

To write these out you should start with drawing the two sides of a tiny triangle or joining a forward slash on to a backward slash, moving your pen in the clockwise direction. This will help you to get the top of the 'hook' right. As you see the two sides need not be of equal length:

Once you have mastered this movement try combining this shape with the curved bottom which looks like a capital 'C' letter. The letter 'C' shape has to be drawn in an anti-clockwise movement, as it is in English. The size is over-exaggerated to make it easier for you to follow the movement:

The four 'hooked' letters of the Persian alphabet are a combination of clockwise and anti-clockwise movements. The next 11 letters are all written with a clockwise movement until you get to the two Arabic letters ع and غ. These two letters that look like a lower-case letter 'c' sitting on top of a capital 'C' are written with an anti-clockwise movement. After these two letters, the rest of the alphabet is written in the clockwise direction.

_____

Learning the order of the alphabet

There is no magic formula for remembering the names of the Persian letters in order. However, occasionally they do fall into a familiar 'European' pattern as in the sequence of ل, م, ن, (و) that is similar to 'l', 'm', 'n', (o), if you take و in its guise as the vowel 'o' and not the consonant 'v'.

Once you have familiarized yourself with the full forms of the letters, try copying out the initial versions. All you need to do to get the initial form is to 'chop' the tail end off the full forms, from the left-hand side. The initial forms are those that appear at the beginning of a word. However, don't forget to leave the identifying dots intact.

For example, if you cut the tail end off the letter ب you will get بـ . Similarly after cutting the tail end off the letter چ you should be left with چـ . The initial form of a letter such as ک should look like کـ .

For the letters ض، ص، ش، س you will lose the deep final curve and should replace this with an extra 'tooth':

سـ ← س
ضـ ← ض

Reminder

1 Never forget to put in the all-important dots, otherwise the letters will be meaningless shapes.

2 Seven letters of the alphabet never change their shape as nothing can be attached to their left side. I refer to these letters as 'one-way' letters. They are: آ or ا (ā), د (d), ذ (z), ر (r), ز (z), ژ (zh), و (v or o/u).

These letters can be connected to a preceding letter from the right side, but will not join on to any letter that comes after them. For example you can have a word like ﺑﺎ (bā) but in a word like ﺍَﺏ (āb), the ﺏ (b) cannot be joined to the left-hand side of ﺍ (ā).

3 No Persian word begins with two consonants. Now you know why most Iranians – and many Arabs for that matter – who start learning English find it hard to pronounce words like 'start', 'brown', 'plastic', 'try', 'street', 'square' or 'bus stop' and instead have to say *estar, pelastic, teray, esquare* or *sequare* or *bus-estop*. A sequence of consonants can only appear after an initial vowel or in the middle or at the end of a word.

◀) **CD 1, TR 1, 00:35**

The following table gives you the full list of the Persian alphabet including the names of the letters and the phonetic pronunciation.

Take your time and spend a good few days just tracing the letters of the alphabet to get the shape right and then try to remember which consonant they represent.

		Connected	Connected	Connected	Final, full form
Sound in English	**Name of letter**	**End of word or attached to previous letter**	**Middle or in between two letters**	**Initial or followed by another letter**	**Unconnected, standing alone**
ā and initial vowels *a, e, o*	*alef**	ﻟ...	ﻟ...	ﺍ	ﺍ or ﺍ̃ *
b	*be*	ﺐ...	...ﺒ...	...ﺑ	ﺏ
p	*pe*	ﭗ...	...ﭙ...	...ﭘ	ﭖ
t	*te*	ﺖ...	...ﺘ...	...ﺗ	ﺕ
s	*se*	ﺚ...	...ﺜ...	...ﺛ	ﺙ
j	*jim*	ﺞ...	...ﺠ...	...ﺟ	ﺝ
ch	*che*	ﭻ...	...ﭽ...	...ﭼ	ﭺ
he	*he*	ﺢ...	...ﺤ...	...ﺣ	ﺡ

kh or x	khe	...خ	...خـ...	...خـ	خ
d	dāl*	...ـد	...ـد	د	دٔ
z	zāl*	...ـذ	...ـذ...	ذ	ذٔ
r	re*	...ـر	...ـر...	ر	رٔ
z	ze*	...ـز	...ـز...	ز	ز
zh (as in 'measure')	zhe*	...ـژ	...ـژ...	ژ	ژٔ
s	sin	...ـس	...ـسـ...	...سـ	س
sh	shin	...ـش	...ـشـ...	...شـ	ش
s	sād	...ـص	...ـصـ...	...صـ	ص
z	zād	...ـض	...ـضـ...	...ضـ	ض
t	tā	...ـط	...ـطـ...	...طـ	ط
z	zā	...ـظ	...ـظـ...	...ظـ	ظ
' (a)	'ain	...ـع	...ـعـ...	...عـ	ع
gh	ghain	...ـغ	...ـغـ...	...غـ	غ
f	fe	...ـف	...ـفـ...	...فـ	ف
q	qāf	...ـق	...ـقـ...	...قـ	ق
k	kāf	...ـک	...ـکـ...	...کـ	ک
g	gāf	...ـگ	...ـگـ...	...گـ	گ
l	lām	...ـل	...ـلـ...	...لـ	ل
m	mim	...ـم	...ـمـ...	...مـ	م
n	nun	...ـن	...ـنـ...	...نـ	ن
v, w, u and o	vāv*	...ـو	...ـو	و	ؤ
h	he	...ـه	...ـهـ...	...هـ	ه
y, i	ye	...ـی	...ـیـ...	...یـ	ی

*The seven letters with an asterisk next to them are called 'one-way' letters in this book and this means that no letter of the alphabet can be joined on to their left-hand side.

Insight

Try writing on lined paper and with a pencil rather than with a biro and such like until you get a sense of the proportion of the letters.

The grid below is provided as a 'tracing template' so that you can practise writing the individual letters of the alphabet.

ا	ا	اً	اَ	اَ	آ	آ	آ
ب	ب	ب	ـهٔ	ـهٔ	ـه	اُ	اُ
ث	ث	ت	ت	پ	پ	بـ	بـ
چ	چ	ح	ح	ثـ	ثـ	تـ	تـ
حـ	حـ	چـ	چـ	خ	خ	ج	ج
ز	ز	ر	ر	ذ	ذ	د	د
سـ	سـ	ش	ش	س	س	ژ	ژ
ضـ	ضـ	ض	ض	ص	ص	شـ	شـ
ع	ع	ظ	ظ	ظـ	ظـ	ط	ط
فـ	فـ	ف	ف	غـ	غـ	غ	غ

گ	گ	ک	ک	قـ	قـ	ق	ق
مـ	مـ	م	م	لـ	لـ	ل	ل
ه	ه	و	و	نـ	نـ	ن	ن
یـ	یـ	ی	ی	هـ	هـ	هـ	هـ

Exercise 1

Can you write the following letters as one word?

١ ا + ب + ا + ب

٢ ر + ا + ز + ا + ب

۳ پ + ر + س + ت + ا + ر

٤ آ + و + ا + ز

٥ م + ا + ش + ی + ن

٦ ه + ز + ا + ر

۷ م + ر + ج + ا + ن

۸ ن + ا + ظ + م

۹ ا + ژ + د + ر

۱۰ م + ق + ی + ا + س

۱۱۱ س + ت + ر + ا + ح + ت

۱۱۲ ج + ا + ق

۱۳ و + ر + ا + ث

۱٤ک + و + چ + ک

۱٥ خ + ی + ا + ب + ان

۱٦ گ + ا + ر + ی

۱۷ م + و + ق + ع

۱۸ س + و + س + ک

۱۹ ل + ا + ک + پ + ش + ت

۲۰ م + و + ش + ک

۱۲۱ ص + ف + ه + ا + ن

۲۲ ض + ر + ر

۲۳ ظ + ه + ر

۲٤ ط + ا + و + و + س

۲٥ ی + و + ا + ش + ک + ی

۲٦ک + ت + ا + ب + خ + ا + ن + ه

۲۷ ه + م + س + ا + ی + ه

۲۸ ق + ه + و + ه

۲۹ ر + ا + د + ا + ر

۳۰ س + ف + ی + ر

Example of 'chalipaa' style of Persian nastaligh calligraphy

◀️ 〰 1, TR 1, 03:30

Try reading the following words that contain examples of Persian vowels. This is just an exercise to help you read the Persian words and familiarize you with the sound of the vowels, so don't worry about the meaning of the words.

Try reading them first and then listen to the recording and repeat. Remember to read the words from the right to the left!

Long vowels

Let us start with the long vowels.

Long vowel *u*, و

The first long vowel in the following words is the *u* sound as in 'woo' or 'zoo' or the long *u* in 'rude'. This long vowel is always written in the script and is denoted by the letter و, the 30th letter of the alphabet. This vowel is written as *u* in English transliteration, to demonstrate its pronunciation.

Long vowel *u* in the middle of a word

lace *tur* تور ◀—— blind *kur* کور ◀——
joy/salty *shur* شور light *nur* نور
force *zur* زور burning *suz* سوز
ant *mur* مور long *dur* دور

Long vowel *i*, ـِ (ی)

Next is the long vowel *i* as in 'deep' or 'seat'. This vowel must be written in the script and is denoted by the last letter of the Persian alphabet which is ی. In this section, we are looking at the long vowels as they appear in the *middle* of the word so the middle form of the letter ی, which is ـِ, is used for this medial 'i' sound. We use the letter *i* to transliterate this Persian vowel in English.

Long vowel *i* in the middle of a word

arrow *tir* تیر ← twenty *bist* بیست ←
apple *sib* سیب it's not there *nist* نیست
wire/silver *sim* سیم half *nim* نیم
before *pish* پیش made of silver *simin* سیمین

Long vowel *ā* , ا

Finally, let us look at the long vowel *ā*, as in the English words 'father', 'cart' or 'sarnie'. Like the other two long vowels, the long *ā* must be written in the script by using the middle form of the first letter of the alphabet ا, which is ا. The long vowel ا is shown as *ā* in English transliteration.

Long vowel *ā* in the middle of a word

unclear *tār* تار ← work *kār* کار ←
(boy's name) *dārā* دارا snake *mār* مار
machine *māshin* ماشین (girl's name) *sārā* سارا
last year *pār-sāl* پارسال year *sāl* سال

Now let us look at examples of long vowels appearing at the beginning of a word. This means looking at words with the *initial long vowels ā, i*, and *u*.

Initial long vowel *ā* , آ

The following words all start with the vowel *ā*. Some contain the long vowel *ā* in the middle of the word, too. The long vowel *ā* that appears at the beginning of the word must always be written as آ, that means it has to have its little hat:

sun *āftāb* آفتاب ← water *āb* آب ←
free *āzād* آزاد that *ān* آن
gentleman *āqā* آقا harm *āzār* آزار
prosperous *ābād* آباد they *ānhā* آنها

Insight

Persian long vowel ā, as in the English word 'car', is a little difficult to copy but is distinctly different from an 'o' or the short 'a'. Listen to the recording or native Farsi speakers to get the right sound.

Initial long vowel *i*

The initial long vowel *i* sounds like the 'ea' in 'eat' or 'ease' or the 'ee' in 'seen'. In the Persian script the initial long vowel *i* is written in as ـايـ:

here *injā* اينجا ←   this *in* اين ←

Iran *irān* ايران   stop *ist* ايست

(boy's name) *iraj* ايرج   faith *imān* ايمان

they *ishān* ايشان   to provide *ijād* ايجاد

Initial long vowel *u*

Well, luckily for all learners of the Persian language I can think of only one word that begins with the long vowel *u*, as in 'ooze' or 'oodles' – you see there are not many English words beginning with 'u' sound either. The initial long vowel *u* is written as او in the Persian script. This one and only common Persian word that is written with an initial long vowel *u* happens to be just that: او which is a third person, singular pronoun, meaning 'he' or 'she':

he, she *u* او ←

There are three clear *final long vowels* in Persian that must be written in the script and are represented by the letter ا *ā* as in 'papa' or 'Toyota', ى *i* as in 'see', 'me' or 'happy' and و *u* as in 'shoe', 'you' or 'goo'. These vowels can be attached to the previous letter or they may stand alone, depending on which letter precedes them.

Final long vowel *ā* ا

air/weather *havā* هوَا ←   father *bābā* بابا ←

alone *tanhā* تنها   up/high *bālā* بالا

they *ānhā* آنها   here *injā* اينجا

acceptable *ravā* روَا   to watch *tamāshā* تَماشا

Final long vowel *i* ى

who *ki* كى ←   tea-pot *quri* قورى ←

play/game *bāzi* بازى   what *chi* چى

carpet *qāli* قالى   greyhound *tāzi* تازى

tray *sini* سينى   taxi *tāksi* تاكسى

Final long vowel *u* و

knee *zānu* زانو ←——
blanket *patu* پتو
drug *dāru* دارو
conversation *goftogu* گُفتگو

upper arm *bāzu* بازو ←——
lady *bānu* بانو
scent *bu* بو
broom *jāru* جارو

Short vowels

The three Persian short vowels are not usually written in the script; however, to make it easier for learners to read the words, or to avoid ambiguity later on, a system of markers known as diacritics is used and these symbols are placed either above or below a consonant, such as *n*, to indicate whether this consonant is read as, for example, *na*, or *ne* or *no*.

Short vowel markers

The marker used to indicate the short vowel *a*, as in 'at' or 'apple', is a tiny forward slash (ـَ) placed above the consonant that comes before the vowel, i.e. placed above the letter of the alphabet that carries this vowel. For example, *na* will be written as نَ, while *nā*, with a long vowel will be written as نا. Try reading the following examples of words that contain the short vowel *a* ـَ:

Short vowel *a* in the middle of a word

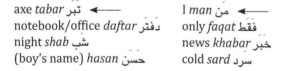

axe *tabar* تبَر ←——
notebook/office *daftar* دَفتَر
night *shab* شبَ
(boy's name) *hasan* حَسَن

I *man* مَن ←——
only *faqat* فَقَط
news *khabar* خبَر
cold *sard* سرَد

Short vowel *e*

The short vowel *e* as in 'egg', is also indicated by a small marker in the shape of a tiny forward slash, however, the *e* is placed *underneath* the letter of the alphabet (ـِ) that carries its sound. So if a consonant such as *n* is followed by an *e* this will be indicated in writing as: نِ *ne*.

Short vowel *e* in the middle of a word

Examples of words where the short vowel *e* appears in the middle position:

like *mesl* مثل ←

redcurrant *zereshk* زِرِشک

heart *del* دل

winter *zemestān* زِمِستان

heavens *sepehr* سِپِهر ←

red *qermez* قِرمِز

worm *kerm* کِرم

eyes *cheshm* چِشم

Short vowel *o*

The third short vowel is *o*, pronounced as in 'old', 'hope' and 'boat'. This vowel is marked by placing a tiny comma sign (ُ) above the letter that carries it. For example the letter *n* followed by the vowel *o* looks like this in Persian: نُ .

Short vowel *o* in the middle of a word

Here are some examples of words that contain the vowel *o* in the medial position:

full *por* پُر ←

bird *morgh* مُرغ

camel *shotor* شتُر

fistful *mosht* مشت

big *bozorg* بُزُرگ ←

large *dorosht* دُرشت

morning *sobh* صبح

he/she said *goft* گُفت

We have looked at the short vowels appearing mid-word, but what about words that begin with a short vowel? How are these *initial short vowels* indicated?

One very important point to remember is that although short vowels are generally not represented in the Persian script, the initial short vowels must be written in. The three initial shorts vowels in Persian are:

اَ *a*, as in 'apple' or 'aspect'

اِ *e*, as in 'egg' or 'end'

اُ *o*, as in 'old' or 'open'

Try reading the following examples of words beginning with short vowels.

Initial short vowel *a* اَ

(boy's name) *ahmad* اَحمَد ←

is *ast* اَست

frown *akhm* اَخم

eyebrow *abru* اَبرو

clouds *abr* اَبر ←

horse *asb* اَسب

origin *asl* اَصل

brocade/Atlantic *atlas* اَطلَس

Initial short vowel *e* اِ

exams *emtehān* امتحان ⟵   name *esm* اسم ⟵
this year *emsāl* اَمسال ́   tonight *emshab* امشَب
kindness *ehsān* اِحسان   contact *ertebāt* ارتِباط
possibility *emkān* امکان   today *emruz* امروز ́

Initial short vowel *o* اُ

hope *omid* اُمید ⟵   bus *otobus* اُتوبوس ⟵
camp/Urdu *ordu* اُردو   master *ostād* اُستاد
room *otāq* اتاق   pattern *olgu* الگو
steady *ostovār* اُستوار   he/she/it fell *oftād* اُفتاد

Insight

The written form of *all words beginning with a vowel* in Persian
will start with the vertical sign for the letter alef 'ا' which will
either be followed by an 'ـ' or an 'و' or will have a '~' for a hat
to denote 'i ـاٖ' or 'u او' or 'ā آ'; or, will have one of the three
short-vowel markers 'اِ ، اُ ، اَ' to denote 'a', 'o' or 'e' vowels.
These short vowel-markers are never used in writing by native
or advanced speakers and will gradually be omitted as learners
progress.

If a word in Persian ends with a *final short vowel*, then this vowel must
be represented in the script. The final short vowels are not written by
using the usual markers of ـ; instead we 'borrow' two letters of the
alphabet to show that the word ends with an *a*, an *e* or an *o*. We use
the final forms of the letter ه/ـه, representing also 'h', to indicate the
presence of a vowel *a* or *e* at the end of the word. Final short vowels
'a' and 'e' are not too common in English, except in words such as
'visa' or 'cobra' (and perhaps a casual pronunciation of 'footballer'
where the 'r' is almost omitted!). But Italian pronunciation of words
like 'donna' and 'casa' or 'bene' and 'nome' may give you some idea of
what the final short vowels *a* and *e* sound like in Persian.

To show the presence of the vowel *o* at the end of the word, we 'borrow'
the letter و 'v' and pronounce it as something between an 'o' and an
'ow'. Final short vowel 'o' sounds like 'go' or 'hello' or 'woe' or 'toe'.

Final short vowel *a* ‿

Fortunately, in the educated Tehran accent that has been used as the model in this book, there is only one common word that ends with the sound 'a', and that is the informal word for 'no': نَه *na*. (Bear in mind that in many rural and regional dialects many words that end with an 'e' sound in Persian are pronounced with an 'a' ending.)

Final short vowel *e* ‿ (ه ‿ـه)

Note that in the following examples, I have used the marker ‿ at the end here to indicate the presence of the short vowel *e*, but this is not usually done in writing:

house *khāne* خانه ←	letter *nāme* نامه ←
fruit *mive* میوه	cooked *pokhte* پُخته
child *bache* بچه	simple *sāde* ساده
greenery *sabze* سبزه	small garden *bāghche* باغچه

Note: The 'helper' letters ه ‿ـه (*h* acting as *e*) and و (*v* acting as *o*) are only read as final short vowels *e* and *o* when they come after a consonant; however, if they follow a vowel, they are then read as proper consonants *h* and *v*. Example: باده *bāde* (final short vowel *e*) but ماه *māh* (proper 'h' ending). Similarly, گو *gu* (و acting as vowel *u*) but گاو *gāv* (proper *v* ending).

Final short vowel *o* ‿ (و) (almost an 'ow')

There are not many common words in Persian that end with this *o* sound:

you (sing.) *to* تو ←	vine *mo* مو ←
two *do* دو	barley *jo* جو
pilau rice *polo* پلو	don't go! *naro* نرو
listen *beshno* بشنو	become *sho* شو

Exercise 2

◀) CD 1, TR 1, 16:17

a Read the following words out loud:

پا – بارو – سوپ – کاشی – کِتاب – کوچِه – میخ – صابون –

مَریَم – آقا – شیراز – اَفغان – اِمروز – ایزَد – اَشک – طاقچِه –

کوشِش – آرامگاه – کاغَذ – اِصفَهان – ایجاب – عُقاب

b Copy out the words used in this unit to practise your writing skills further.

Exercise 3
Write the following words in Persian, paying attention to the vowels. Remember, short vowels are not written unless they appear at the beginning or the end of a word. Try to indicate their presence, however, by using the three little markers.

1	*fardā*	**14**	*zard*
2	*palang*	**15**	*havā*
3	*boshqāb*	**16**	*emshab*
4	*āchār*	**17**	*irland*
5	*ātash*	**18**	*shirin*
6	*vājeb*	**19**	*dokhtar*
7	*namak*	**20**	*bist*
8	*kuchak*	**21**	*bimārestān*
9	*akbar*	**22**	*shomā*
10	*zohr*	**23**	*hadaf*
11	*gusht*	**24**	*'amu*
12	*khāne*	**25**	*khāle*
13	*qahve*		

Things to remember . . .

- Persian script is more rounded and curvaceous, compared with Arabic writing, which can look somewhat jagged. Don't forget to put in the dots of the letters that need one, two or three dots. It is very common for beginners to forget the dots of the Persian letters.

- In words that are made up of several letters, which can be joined up, try writing the whole sequence without taking your pen off the paper, rather than writing each letter individually. This will go some way in making your handwriting look nice and closer to a native hand.

- A huge number of Persian words end with the sound 'e' as in 'café'. In writing, this sound is transcribed using the attached or standalone form of the penultimate letter of the alphabet 'h' 'ه or ه'. Therefore 'khāne' 'house' is written as خانه in Persian or 'setāre' 'star' is written as ستاره.

- There is no gender in Persian so the context alone distinguishes between 'he' and 'she'.

1

Greetings and meeting people

In this unit you will learn how to
- *Greet people*
- *Say goodbye and goodnight*
- *Say 'thank you', 'you're welcome' and 'please'*
- *Say the days of the week and seasons*

Listen to the following informal and formal ways of saying 'hello' and 'goodbye'.

◄) **CD 1, TR 2**

hello, dear Maryam	*salām maryam jān!*	سَلام مَریم جان!
hello, darling	*salām 'azizam*	سَلام عَزیزَم
good morning, Babak	*sobh be-kheyr bābak*	صُبح بِخیر بابَک
good day, madam	*ruz be-kheyr khānom*	روز بِخیر خانُم
goodbye, Mrs Farhadi	*khodā-hāfez khānom farhādi*	خُداحافِظ خانُم فَرهادی
goodbye, till tomorrow	*khodā-hāfez tā fardā*	خُداحافِظ، تا فَردا
goodnight, my son	*shab be-kheyr pesaram*	شَب بِخیر پِسَرَم
goodnight, (dear) mum	*shab be-kheyr māmān jān*	شَب بِخیر مامان جان
goodbye, children	*khodā-hāfez bache-hā*	خُداحافِظ بچه‌ها
farewell, safe journey	*khodā negahdār, safar be-kheyr*	خُدانِگهدار، سَفَر بِخیر

Learning a few basic, polite phrases in Persian could not be easier and it will earn you a lot of Brownie points.

> **Insight**
>
> The greeting *salām*, سلام 'hello', lit. *peace*, can be used at any time of day or night and if necessary can be followed by a more time-specific greeting.

'Yes' and 'no'; 'hello' and 'goodbye'

◀) CD 1, TR 2, 01:04

Try out these phrases on your own and then listen to the recording:

بَله	*bale*	yes (formal)
أره	*āre*	yup, yes (informal)
نَه	*na*	no (informal)
نَخِير	*nakheyr*	no (formal)
سَلام	*salām*	hello, hi! (can be used any time of day or night)
دُرود	*dorud*	hi! greetings!
صُبح بِخِير	*sobh-bekheyr*	good morning
روز بِخِير	*ruz-bekheyr*	good day (formal or on TV and radio)
عَصر بِخِير	*'asr-bekheyr*	good afternoon (used in formal settings)
شَب بِخِير	*shab-bekheyr*	goodnight (when it's time to leave or bedtime)
سَفَر بخیر	*safar-bekheyr*	safe journey (bon voyage)
خُداحافظ	*khodā-hāfez*	goodbye, farewell
خُدانِگَهدار	*khodā-negahdār*	goodbye (God keep you safe)

| تا فَردا | tā fardā | till tomorrow (informal) |
| می‌بینَمِت | mibinamet | see you (informal, addressed to one person) |

Always listen out for other native speakers greeting you first. You can then just imitate them. If you know a person's name you should use it or otherwise prefix your greeting by 'mister' or 'madam' on more formal occasions:

سَلام مَریَم.	salām Maryam	Hello, Maryam.
سَلام. صُبح بِخیر پَرویز.	salām, sobh-bekheyr parviz	Hi! Good morning, Parviz.
عَصرِ‌بِخیر آقا.	'asr-bekheyr āqā	Good afternoon, sir. (addressed to a man you do not know)
شَب بخیر عَزیزَم.	shab-bekheyr 'azizam	Good night, my dear.
خُداحافِظ خانُم.	khodāhāfez khānom	Goodbye, madam. (Miss or Mrs)
خُدانِگَهدار خانُم سَلیمی.	khodā-negahdār khānom-e Salimi	Goodbye, Mrs Salimi.

By now you may have worked out that the phrase بِخیر bekheyr means 'good, well or pleasant' as in 'good morning' or 'good journey'.

Insight

The huge number of greeting-terms in Persian are a direct illustration of the emphasis the culture places on observing rituals of formality and showing and receiving respect. No other language, to my knowledge, has so many different ways of asking after other people's state of being, wishing them good health or bidding them farewell or safe journeys. It is important for learners to learn a few useful ways of saying hello, goodbye, please and thank you, and not be alarmed at the amount of time given by Persian native speakers to these ritualized social exchanges.

Exercise 1

How would you greet a female shopkeeper in the morning; neighbour's little boy Ahmad; your friend's grandfather in the afternoon? Say 'goodbye' to Maryam; 'goodnight' to Babak, 'safe journey' to Mr Shams.

Listen to the following semi-formal exchange of niceties:

🔊 **CD 1, TR 2, 02:30**

Hello sir, good morning.	salām aqā, sobh-bekheyr.	سلام آقا، صبح بخیر.
Hello madam, may I help you?	salām khānom, befarmāid.	سلام خانم، بفرمایید.
Thank you, a coffee with milk, please.	motshakeram, lotfan yek qahve bā shir.	مُتَشکِرَم، لُطفأیک قَهوِه با شیر.
Here you are, coffee with milk and sugar. Anything else?	befarmāid, qahve bā shir va shekar, digar amry nist?	بفرمایید، قَهوِه با شیر و شِکَر. دیگر اَمری نیست؟
No thanks; thank you very much.	na mersi aqā, kheyli mamnun.	نَه مِرسی أقا، خیلی مَمنون.
You are welcome.	khāhesh mikonam.	خواهِش می کنم.
Goodbye.	khodā-hāfez.	خداحافظ.
You're welcome (i.e. nice to have had you in the shop), goodbye.	khosh āmadid khānom, khodā negahdār.	خوش أمدید خانم، خدانگهدار.

As explained in the introduction, Persian places a lot of emphasis on self-deprecation and humility. There are endless words and phrases in Persian for saying 'please' and 'thank you' to show various degrees of appreciation. Here are a few common examples:

خواهِش مى كُنَم *khāhesh-mikonam* please (lit. I request from you)

بى زَحمَت *bi-zahmat* please (if it's no trouble)

لُطفاً *lotfan* please (if you'd be so kind)

🔊 **CD 1, TR 2, 03:30**

In Persian as in English or French (*pardon*), the same word for 'sorry' or 'excuse me' can be used to apologize or to seek information. The changing of the stress changes the meaning. Listen to the recording:

بِبَخشيد! *bebakhshid* excuse me (if you want to ask a question, get someone's attention, get through or to say sorry; lit. forgive me)

بِبَخشيد؟ *bebakhshid* sorry?, excuse me? (if you want someone to repeat what they have just said)

Another similar expression:

مَعذِرَت مى خواهَم! *ma'zerat mi-khāham* sorry (lit. I beg your pardon)

مَعذِرَت مى خواهَم؟ *ma'zerat mi-khāham* pardon?

And another:

بِفرماييد *befarmāid*, a word that you will hear a lot in a Persian conversation, can mean 'here you are', 'please help yourself', 'what can I do for you' and 'what would you like to order' as in a restaurant, for example.

Insight

Intonation and stress positions in Persian can make a word that is usually a compliment sound like an insult or vice versa. That's why you should pay close attention to the tone used by native speakers or in the recordings.

There are endless ways of saying 'thank you' in Persian. Here are some of the common and less idiomatic expressions:

مُتشکِرَم *motshakram* thank you (lit. I'm grateful)

مَمنون *mamnun* thanks!

سپاسگزارم *sepās-gozāram* I'm grateful

مِرسی! *merci!* Thanks! (originally French but commonly used in cities in Iran)

Persian uses two different words to express *welcome*, as in 'welcome to the city' and as in 'you're welcome' in reply to 'thank you'. In the latter case, a number of different words and expressions can be used:

خوش آمَدید! *khosh āmadid* Welcome. (to our house, for example)

خواهِش می کُنم. *khāhesh-mikonam* Welcome. ('you're welcome' in response to 'thank you')

You may have noticed that خواهش می کُنم *khāhesh-mikonam* is exactly the same as the word used for 'please' (see earlier). This is because in response to gratitude a Persian speaker should show humility and imply 'please don't even mention it'. Therefore, in Persian 'please' = 'you're welcome' = خواهِش می کُنم *khāhesh-mikonam*.

Two more useful expressions:

حَتماً *hatman* sure, definitely

باشَد *bāshad* (*bāshe* informally) OK, all right

Insight

Some languages have specific terms of endearment, appearing in the form of suffixes that are put on a name. Japanese, for example, has a large number of these terms such as the suffixes *-chan* or *-san*. Persian has one very common, everyday suffix of endearment: 'jān', جان, that is put after the names of close friends and relations, e.g. 'Maryam jān', lit. 'Maryam my soul', or 'Dāriush jān'. 'jān', meaning life-essence or soul, goes with names that are more than one syllable long but sounds odd if used with one-syllable names. Therefore you can say 'Thomas jān' or 'Katie jān' but it sounds odd to say 'Tom jān' or 'Kate jān'! You'll see the word 'jān' used in many dialogues in this book.

Exercise 2

(a) Translate the following into Persian:
1 Good morning Mehri, welcome!
2 Yes please, tea if you don't mind.
3 I am sorry, Babak.
4 No thank you, Pari.
5 Safe journey, Reza and thank you.
   Don't mention it

(b) Translate into English:

١   سلام آقا، بفرمایید.

٢   لُطفاً ی   چای و ی   شیرینی دانمارکی.

٣   بِبَخشید خانم، خیلی مَعذِرَت می خواهَم.

٤   نه مِرسی بابَ   جان.

٥   خواهِش می کُنَم، خدانِگهدار.

Days of the week, months and seasons

Don't despair if you find the endless expressions of greetings and showing gratitude in Persian confusing. Let's try learning some other useful and relatively easy vocabulary: days of the week in Persian.

Days of the week

◆ CD 1, TR 2, 05:10

The Persian names of the days of the week are very easy to remember.

The Persian week or هَفته *hafte* (lit. of seven) begins on Saturday, شَنبه *shanbe*, the ancient Sabbath. Thereafter, the following days are identified by numbers one to five added to the word شنبه *shanbe*, with the exception of Friday, which has its Arabic name to denote the day of communal prayers i.e. جُمعه *jom'e*.

Listen to the name of the days of the week:

Saturday (1st day of the week)	شَنبه	shambe
Sunday (one day after Saturday)	یکشنبه	yekshambe
Monday (two days after . . .)	دوشَنبه	doshambe
Tuesday (three days after . . .)	سه شَنبه	seshambe
Wednesday (four days after . . .)	چَهارشَنبه	chahārshambe
Thursday (five days after . . .)	پنْجشَنبه	panjshambe
Friday	جمعه	jom'e

The weekend in Iran is Thursday and Friday; پنجشنبه و جمعه.

You will have noticed that the word شَنبه *shanbe* is pronounced as *shambe*, with an 'm' instead of an 'n'. This is because when an 'n' precedes a 'b' it is pronounced as an 'm'.

Some pocket diaries and calendars carry the Persian name for Friday too which is آدینه *ādine*. However, the use of this noun in everyday or informal conversation and writing is very rare.

The Persian calendar

The everyday Persian calendar is based on the solar calculation of the Muslim era. This means that although the Persian calendar goes back a very long time, the starting point of the current calendar is the morning after the flight of Mohammed, the prophet of Islam, from Mecca to Medina (in Saudi Arabia) on 16 July 622 CE. The Persian months and the start of the New Year, however, are still based on the pre-Islamic Persian traditions.

The Iranian New Year, celebrated by Persians, Afghans, Tajikis, Kurds, Parsis of the Asian subcontinent and many more, falls at the beginning of the vernal equinox which coincides with 20 or 21 March. The first day of the New Year is on the first of the month of farvardin, the first month of the Iranian year. The Royal Observatory at Greenwich is a very good source of when the earth passes through the four equinoxes and the website can give you the precise time when the Iranian New Year begins!

The months

The names of the Persian months can be quite a mouthful as they are mostly the names of Zoroastrian archangels. It is quite interesting that the Persian months correspond exactly to the signs of the zodiac. For example, if you are born on 18 June, then your birthday, according to the arrangement of the Persian months, will be on 28 *khordād*, which is the 28th day of the sign of Gemini.

The names of the 12 Persian months and the corresponding zodiac signs follow. They are quite a mouthful to pronounce. Listen to the name of the months and follow the script as they are being read:

فَروَردین	*farvardin*	Aries	starts 21 March
اُردیبِهِشت	*ordibehesht*	Taurus	starts 21 April
خُرداد	*khordād*	Gemini	starts 22 May
تیر	*tir*	Cancer	starts 22 June
مُرداد	*mordād*	Leo	starts 23 July
شَهریوَر	*shahrivar*	Virgo	starts 23 August
مِهر	*mehr*	Libra	starts 23 September
آبان	*ābān*	Scorpio	starts 23 October
آذَر	*āzar*	Sagittarius	starts 22 November
دی	*dey*	Capricorn	starts 22 December
بَهمَن	*bahman*	Aquarius	starts 21 January
اسفَند	*esfand*	Pisces	starts 20 February

The first six months of the Persian year have 31 days each, the next five have 30 days each and *esfand*, the last month of the year, is 29 days long.

However, every fourth year, in a leap year, known as *kabise*, کبیسه، *esfand* also is 30 days long.

All public institutions and almost all daily newspapers note the Persian, Muslim and the Christian calendars. In this way, religious festivals and important anniversaries can be observed and the business and academic community can keep up with dates used in the West.

The seasons

◆ CD 1, TR 2, 08:20

The four seasons in Persian are:

بَهار	*bahār*	spring
تابستان	*tābestān*	summer
پاییز	*pā'eez*	autumn
زِمِستان	*zemestān*	winter

Exercise 3
1 Put the following in the correct order:

۱   پَنجشَنبِه، یکشنبِه، جُمعِه، سه شَنبه

۲   زِمِستان، تابِستان، بَهار

2 What are the last two Persian months of autumn?
3 What are the Persian summer months?
4 What Persian months correspond to 14 April, 21 July, 8 January and 30 October?
5 How many days are there in the Persian summer months?

_____

Things to remember . . .

- Persian has a lot of complimentary responses that are features of its very complex socio-cultural system of communication. For example as well as the straightforward 'thank you' and 'please' you can use 'may your hands not hurt' (*daste shomā dard nakonad* دستِ شما درد نُکند) instead of 'thank you' and the response to this would be 'may your head never ache' (*sar-e shomā dard nakonad* سر شما درد نکند).

- Politeness with regard to people's status, whether male or female, close friend and relative or more distant and formal, is flexible in Persian. Terms such as Mr, Miss and Mrs can be used both with first names and surnames and, unlike in English, you can call your friends and close relations 'Mr' or 'Mrs', such as *Maryam khānom*, lit. 'Miss' or 'Mrs Maryam', or *Hasan Agha*, lit. 'Mr Hasan'. In a formal setting 'Mr' and 'Mrs' precedes the surname as in *Khānom-e Salimi*, 'Mrs Salimi', or *Aghā-ye Rastegār*, 'Mr Rastegār'.
- The Persian week starts on a Saturday, *shambe*, the old Sabbath, and the days of the weekend are Thursday and Friday. To learn your days of the week learn the numbers 1 to 5 in Persian. Friday is the day of 'assembly', coming together for ritual worship, and has its own name: *Jom'eh*, or a Persian name used less commonly, *Ādineh*.
- The Persian calendar is solar and is organized according to the timings of equinoxes and solstices in the northern hemisphere. Every New Year starts when the earth moves through the vernal equinox at a precisely measured time. This is usually on 20th or 21st of March.
- Persian months run in perfect tandem with the months of the Zodiac. The first month of the year is *Farvardin* and corresponds to Aries and the last is *Esfand* which is exactly in parallel with Pisces.
- Iranian media, academic institutions, the commercial sector and Persian newspapers use the Gregorian and Islamic calendars, too, but the Persian calendar is the calendar that is used most widely.

Can you answer these questions? They have all been covered in this unit.

1 What is the most common greeting in Persian?
2 How do you greet someone in the morning?
3 What is the formal 'yes' in Persian?
4 How do you address a woman you have just met?
5 Is there any difference in phrases for 'please' and 'you are welcome'?
6 What is the most common soubriquet or term of endearment used with names in Persian? How would you say 'dear Isabel'?
7 What is the first day of the Persian week?
8 What's the significance of Vernal Equinox for Iranians?
9 What is your birth sign if you are born on the 16th of the Persian month of Ābān?
10 Can you work out your Persian birthday if you were born on 5th May 1968?

2

....

Numbers

In this unit you will learn how to
- *Use and write cardinal and ordinal numbers and qualifying nouns*
- *Form plurals*
- *Use 'this', 'that', 'these' and 'those'*

Persian numbers

◄◙ **CD 1, TR 3**

Persian uses Arabic numerals and these are written numerically from left to right (in the opposite direction to the script). The following are the cardinal numbers from 1 to 20. Listen to how they are pronounced:

یِک *yek* ۱ 1	دو *do* ۲ 2
سه *se* ۳ 3	چَهار *chahār* ۴ 4
پَنج *panj* ۵ 5	شش *shesh* ۶ 6
هَفت *haft* ۷ 7	هَشت *hasht* ۸ 8
نُه *noh* ۹ 9	دَه *dah* ۱۰ 10
یازده *yāzdah* ۱۱ 11	دوازده *davāzdah* ۱۲ 12
سیزده *sizdah* ۱۳ 13	چَهارده *chahārdah* ۱۴ 14
پانزده *pānzdah* ۱۵ 15	شانزده *shānzdah* ۱۶ 16

هفده *hivdah* ١٧ 17   هجده *hizhdah* ١٨ 18

نوزده *nuzdah* ١٩ 19   بیست *bist* ٢٠ 20

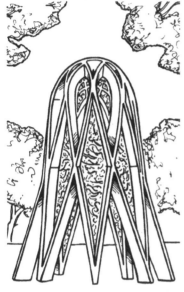

'Zero' is صفر *sefr* (٠) in Persian.

In numbers greater than 20, the different elements follow each other as they do in English with the larger number coming first; in pronunciation they are joined together by the sound -*o*, meaning 'and'. So, for example, 21 (٢١) is:

بیست و یک *bist-o yek*.

Similarly 136 (١٣۶) is:

صد و سی و شش
saḍ-o si-yo shesh

2,574 (٢۵٧۴) is:

دو هزار و پانصد و هفتاد و چهار
do hezār-o pānsad-o haftād-o chahār.

Mausoleum of Omar Khayyam, north-east Iran

Bear in mind that there are irregularities and differences in the way some numbers are written and pronounced. For example, 17 and 18 are not pronounced as they are written. Seventeen (١٧), is written as هفده *hefdah*, but is pronounced as *hivdah*; similarly, 18 (١٨) is written as هجده *hejdah* but pronounced as *hizhdah*.

The tens of numbers have some element of the unit in them but are, on the whole, irregular.

The round units of ten, from 20 to 90, are:

بیست *bist* ٢٠ 20   سی *si* ٣٠ 30

چِهِل *chehel* ۴٠ 40   پَنجاه *panjāh* ۵٠ 50

شصت *shast* ۶٠ 60   هَفتاد *haftād* ٧٠ 70

هَشتاد *hashtād* ٨٠ 80   نَوَد *navad* ٩٠ 90

Formation of the hundreds is almost regular, with the exception of 100, 200, 300 and 500. Again, you will spot the presence of the unit number in the two, three and five hundred. Listen to the recording as these numbers are read out:

صَد *sad* ۱۰۰ 100   دویست *devist* ۲۰۰ 200

سیصَد *sisad* ۳۰۰ 300   چهارصَد *chahārsad* ۴۰۰ 400

پانصَد *pānsad* ۵۰۰ 500   ششصَد *sheshsad* ۶۰۰ 600

هَفتصَد *haftsad* ۷۰۰ 700   هَشتصَد *hashtsad* ۸۰۰ 800

نُهصَد *nohsad* ۹۰۰ 900

There are *no* irregularities in forming the thousands:

هِزار or یکهِزار *hezār* or *yek-hezār*	۱۰۰۰	1,000
دو هِزار *dohezār*	۲۰۰۰	2,000
پَنج هِزار *panj-hezār*	۵۰۰۰	5,000
دَه هِزار *dah-hezār*	۱۰۰۰۰	10,000
سی و هَفت هِزار *si-yo haft-hezār*	۳۷۰۰۰	37,000 and so on

The cardinal numbers always come *before* the noun, object or the person that is counted, which is similar to English:

دو روز   *do ruz* two days

سه کتاب   se *ketāb* three books

بیست و پنج مُسافِر   *bist-o panj mosāfer* 25 passengers

Remember that quantified nouns always stay in the singular in Persian. This means that, unlike in English, nouns in Persian stay in the singular after numbers.

Exercise 1

1 Write the following numbers in Persian in digits: 6, 12, 25, 34, 7, 0, 107, 358, 819, 48, 987, 1046, 26, 903.

2 Write these numbers in words in Persian:
forty-two, eleven, eight, thirteen, forty, sixty-nine, one hundred and fifty-one, two hundred, one thousand six hundred and twenty-five.

3 Say these numbers out loud in Persian, and write them in English:
  ۷ – ۱۲ – ۲۳ – ۱۹۸ – ۵۹۱ – ۱۸۳ – ۹۲۱۲.

4 Translate into Persian: three books, one boy, eight cars, two men, 14 days.

Insight

Persian numbers originate from Hindu–Arabic numeral systems, developed by Indian mathematicians and then adopted by the Persian mathematician Khawrazmi in 825 CE. After further modification by Arab mathematicians these numbers spread to the western world in the 11th and 12th centuries. You can see, for example, that if you rotate the Persian number ۳ by 90° anti-clockwise, you will arrive at the European, 'Arabic' number 3. The following table shows the Arabic and Persian numbers:

Western Arabic numbers	1	2	3	4	5	6	7	8	9
Persian numbers	۱	۲	۳	۴	۵	۶	۷	۸	۹
Arabic numbers	۱	۲	۳	٤	٥	٦	٧	٨	٩

Counting words or qualifying nouns

One major difference between Persian and English is that usually a singular, sometimes idiomatic, qualifying word is inserted between the number and the counted noun. Depending on the reference book you choose, these qualifiers are also known as 'counting words', 'classifiers', 'numerative words' or 'counters'. These qualifiers are rarely used in English but to give you the idea, consider these examples:

300 *head* of Jersey cattle
four *items* of clothing

three *batches* of loaves
two *rounds* of golf
two *dozen* eggs
four *pairs* of shoes
ten *volumes* of poetry

The words *head, items, batches, rounds, dozen, pairs,* and *volumes* typically precede a certain type of noun.

The following may also help to explain the point further, although the words *shoal, herd* and *flock* are 'collective nouns' in English and usually refer to large numbers of the following noun:

a *school* or *shoal* of fish
a *herd* of cattle
a *flock* of geese

Persian has many more qualifying words than English and uses them a lot more extensively. Indeed, to an Iranian, it feels odd to hear a singular noun linked to a number without the buffer of some qualifying word.

Many South Asian languages have these classifiers that must come after cardinal numbers, to the extent that some Tibeto-Burman languages have many classifiers used for round things, metal things, animals and birds, etc. In comparison with these languages, Persian has fewer classifiers for you to learn, you'll be pleased to know!

The most common of the Persian qualifying nouns is تا *tā*, roughly translated as *item* and it can accompany almost any counted noun (but has to be more than one) with the exception of expressions of time. Units of time such as hour, minute, day, month, etc. already act as specific qualified nouns.

تا *tā* is the most widely used classifier of nouns in the spoken language:

سه تا خاله	*se tā khāle* three aunts (maternal)
دَه تا کلاه	*dah tā kolāh* ten hats
پنج تا کتاب	*panj tā ketāb* five books
دو تا خانم	*do tā khānom* two ladies
صد تا دانشجو	*sad tā dāneshju* 100 students

Note: Remember that you *cannot* say کتاب تا یک *yek tā ketāb* 'one book'. تا *tā must* follow numbers of two or more.

Other common qualifying words

The other most common qualifying or classifying words in Persian are:

نَفَر *nafar* person (used for living beings)

دانه *dāne* grain, seed (used for 'things', i.e. concrete but small objects varying from one grape to an emerald; it is occasionally used in the colloquial for cars or houses to denote the rather small or insignificant size)

عدَد *adad* item, number (used mainly for small objects)

جِلد *jeld* volume, copy (used mainly for books)

دَست *dast* lit. hand, can mean 'set' too (used for clothes as in 'a suit'; also 'suite' for furniture)

جُفت *joft* pair

All units of weights and measures, such as متر *metr* 'metre', کیلو *kilu* 'kilogram', لیتر *litr* 'litre' are used as qualifying words. Note that the French pronunciation of these metric units is used in Persian:

سه متر پارچهٔ اَبریشمی *se metr pārche-ye abrishami* three metres of silk cloth

دو لیتر شیر کَم چَربی *do litr shir-e kam charbi* two litres of low-fat milk

یک کیلو و نیم گوشت چَرخ کَرده *yek kilo o nim gusht-e charkh karde* one kilo and a half (lit.) minced meat

Word order of numbers and nouns

The cardinal number precedes the singular noun that it refers to. If, as is mostly the case, a qualifying or classifying noun is also used then the word order is as follows: number *followed* by qualifying word, *followed* by the noun in its singular:

چَهار نَفَر ایرانی *chahār nafar irāni* four Iranians (lit. four 'persons Iranian')

پَنج جُفت کَفش *panj joft kafsh* five pairs of shoes

یک دانه سیب و دو تا موز *yek dāne sib va do tā mowz* one (seed/
item) apple and two (item) bananas

دَه روز تَعطیل *dah ruz ta'til* ten days holiday or break

Ordinals

🔊 CD 1, TR 3, 04:15

Ordinal numbers in Persian are generally formed by the addition of
the suffix مـ *-om*, to the cardinal number. In English, the ordinals are
made by adding *-st, -nd* or *-rd* to the first three numbers and to their
compounds thereafter, e.g. 21st, 22nd, 23rd, and by adding *-th* to the
subsequent numbers, e.g. fifth, tenth, 20th, 126th.

Although the suffix *-om* is added to *all* cardinals, the first three
ordinals in Persian are slightly irregular. This is because the Arabic
word اَوَّل *avval* 'first' is much more commonly used in Persian than
the equivalent Iranian word یِکُم *yekom*.

The Iranian یِکُم *yekom* is, however, used in all the compounds, such as
بیست و یِکُم *bist-o yekom* 21st or سیصد و هفتاد و یِکُم *sisad-o haftād-o
yekom* 371st.

Moreover, the subsequent numbers دو *do* 'two' and سه *se* 'three' in
Persian end in the short vowels 'o' and 'e'. Therefore, we have to
compensate for the two short vowels (one at the end of the numeral
and the other at the beginning of the suffix *-om*) coming together by
the addition of a 'v' between the vowels 'o' and 'e':

دوُم = مـُ + دو   *do + om* = (not *do-om* but) *dovom* second

سوُم = مـُ + سه   *se + om* = (not *se-om* but) *sevom* third

Hence the change of 'o' and 'e' to 'v'.

This formation will be carried through the compounds as well, such as:

بیستُ سوُم   *bist-o sevom* 23rd

چِهِل و دوُم   *chehel-o dovom* 42nd

صَد و شَصت و سِوُم   *sad-o shast-o sevom* 163rd

Look at the following comparison table:

Cardinal	Ordinal
۱ یک yek	(یکم yekom) اَوَّل avval much more common
۲ دو do	دوُّم dovvom
۳ سه se	سوُّم sevvom

The ordinals after the first three, however, are very regular, as they are in English. So, in English the ordinals of numbers from four to 100,000 and beyond, with the exception of any compound number ending in one, two or three, are formed by the addition of *th*. In Persian, too, the ordinals of all numbers from ۴ چهار (four) upwards are formed by the addition of ـُم -*om* to the last element of number (see following table of comparison).

Cardinal	Ordinal
۴ چهار chahār	چهارُم chahārom
۵ پنج panj	پنجُم panjom
۲۰ بیست bist	بیستُم bistom
۲۱ بیست یک bist-o yek	بیست یکُم bist-o yekom
۲۷ بیست و هفت bist-o haft	یست و هفتُم bist-o haftom
۱۰۰ صد sad	صدُم sadom
۱۰۰۰ هزار hezār	هزارُم hezārom

and so on thoughout the number system.

- -

Insight

Persian zero looks just like a dot (٠). The decimal point is shown by a slash sign (/). 35.72 is therefore written as ۳۵/۷۲. Persian uses 'million' for 'million' but the French 'milliārd' for 'billion'.

- -

Summary

1 In case of compound numbers ending with the numeral 'one' such as 231 for example, the suffix -om of *yekom* is attached to the end of the entire group and *not avval*. Therefore, the Persian equivalent of 231st, for example, will be:

دویست و سی و یِکُم *devist-o si-yo yekom*

2 The Persian ordinal of compound numbers ending in two or three will have the same irregular suffixes of *-vom* for 'second' and 'third', e.g. 52nd will be پنجاه و دوُم *panjāh-o dovom* and 63rd will be شصت و سوم *shast-o sevvom.*

3 Ordinal numbers behave as adverb–adjectives. As adjectives they will follow the noun as in:

هَفتةَ چَهارُم *hafteh-ye chahārom* the fourth week

اُتوُبوس سوُم *otobus-e sevvom* the third bus

فیلمِ اوَل *film-e avval* the first film

Insight

Persian uses a large number of 'counting-words' or qualifying nouns such as '*tā*', or '*nafar*', etc. These are similar to the more specific English counting words such as 'loaves' or 'head' or 'round' or 'rasher'. The counting words follow the number and come before the noun. The universal counting word is '*tā*' and is used with number 2 and above.

Exercise 2

🔊 CD 1, TR 3, 05:07

1 Write these numbers in Persian, and say the ordinal and cardinal forms: 2, 6, 10, 11, 23, 41, 125, 94.

2 Translate into English:

چَهارُم – بیست و شِشُم – شَبِ سِوُم – هِزارُم – یازدَهُمِ فَروَردین،
اولِ خُرداد، سی و یِکُم

Plurals

Listen to the recording where the nouns 'book' كتاب *ketāb* and 'boy' پسر *pesar* are used, first in the singular, then quantified with numbers, in combination with 'this' and 'that' and, finally, in the plural:

book	*ketāb*	کِتاب
two book(s)	*do ketāb*	دو کتاب
five book(s)	*panj ketāb*	پَنج کتاب
five (items of) book(s)	*panj tā ketāb*	پَنج تا کتاب
those (lit. that) five book(s)	*ān panj ketāb*	آن پَنج کتاب
these (lit. this) two book(s)	*in do ketāb*	این دو کتاب
books	*ketāb-hā*	کتاب ها
these (lit. this) books	*in ketāb-hā*	این کتاب ها
boy	*pesar*	پِسَر
one boy	*yek pesar*	یک پِسَر
two boy(s)	*do pesar*	دو پِسَر
two (numbers of) boy(s)	*do tā pesar*	دو تا پِسَر
that boy	*ān pesar*	آن پِسَر
those (lit. that) boys	*ān pesar-hā*	آن پِسَرها
these (lit. this) two boy(s)	*in do pesar*	آین دو پِسَر

Insight

Demonstratives 'this' and 'that' also remain singular if accompanied by numbers and/or plural nouns as in 'this two girl' or 'that boys'.

Forming the plural

There are several ways of making plurals in Persian.

1 The most common way is by adding a ها *hā* to the end of a noun. This is almost the equivalent of adding an 's' to English nouns to form the plural and is most commonly used with non-living, inanimate things:

books کتابها or کتاب ها = ها + کتاب book کتاب

flowers گلها or گل ها = ها + گل flower گل

houses خانه ها = ها + خانه house خانه

2 By adding the plural ending ان *ān*. However, the plural ending ان is only ever used for animate beings (including the nouns for growing things such as trees or herbs) or nouns and adjectives referring to living things and is more commonly found in the written language. Wherever possible, the ending ان is joined to the word:

friends دوستان = ان + دوست friend دوست

fathers پِدَران = ان + پِدَر father پِدَر

men مَردان = ان + مَرد man مَرد

children کودکان = ان + کودک child کودک

girls, daughters دُختَران = ان + دُختَر girl/daughter دُختَر

Other uses of *ān* ان plural ending

1 In the written language, particularly in a literary text, the plural ending ان *ān* can also be used for some animals:

سَگ *sag* dog → سَگان *sagān* dogs

اَسب *asb* horse → اَسبان *asbān* horses

مُرغ morgh bird → مُرغان morghān birds

شیر shir lion → شیران shirān lions

2 When adjectives such as 'good', 'young', 'great', 'bad', etc., are used in written, literary language to refer to a group of people such as 'the good' or 'the young' the plural ending ان ān is used:

خوب khub good → خوبان khubān the good

جَوان javān young → جوانان javānān the youth

بُزُرگ bozorg great → بُزُرگان bozorgān the great

بَد bad bad → بدان badān the bad

Note: These adjectives in the plural never follow nouns; rather they are used *as nouns.*

In the examples just given, when the adjectives qualifying human beings end in the two long vowels *ā* and *u*, the plural ending becomes a یان *yān*, instead of ان *ān*.

دانا *dānā* wise → دانایان *dānāyān* wise ones, the wise

نابینا *nābinā* blind → نابینایان *nābināyān* blind ones, the blind

سُخَنگو *sokhangu* spokesperson, speaker → سُخَنگویان *sokhanguyān* the speakers

ماجراجو *mājerāju* adventurer → ماجراجویان *mājerājuyān the* adventurers

Similarly, when nouns or adjectives attributable to living things end in the short vowel *e*, indicated by the sign ـه /ه the plural ending changes to گان *gān* and the final vowel sign of ـه /ه is dropped:

بَچه *bache* child, childish → بَچگان *bachegān* children or childish ones.

گُرسنه *gorosne* hungry → گُرسنگان *gorosnegān* the hungry ones

دَرَنده *darande* savage → دَرَندگان *darandegān* the savage ones

سِتاره *setāre* star → سِتارگان *setāregān* the stars

Plural of units of time and place

The plural of units of time and adverbs of place are always made with
ها *hā*.

Time

روز *ruz* day → روزها *ruzhā* days

شَب *shab* night → شَبها *shabhā nights*

هَفته *hafte* week → هَفته ها *haftehā weeks*

ماه *māh* month → ماه ها *māh-hā* months

سال *sāl* year → سالها *sālhā* years

ساعَت *sā'at* hour → ساعَتها *sā'athā* hours

Place

کشوَر *keshvar* country → کشوَرها *keshvarhā* countries

جَنگَل *jangal* forest → جَنگَلها *jangalhā forests*

شَهر *shahr* city, town → شَهرها *shahrhā* cities, towns

Other plurals

In addition to the methods just explained, other ways of forming
the plural exist in Persian that deal almost exclusively with forming
the plurals of Arabic words in Persian. These range from 'feminine
plurals' to 'duals' and the broken plurals.

It is not necessary at this stage in the book to spend time on formation
of these plurals.

Note: In Persian, a quantified noun, i.e. a noun accompanied by a
number, *never* takes the plural. This means that, for example, the

moment you specify *how many* books, apples or tourists you are referring to, you use the *singular noun.* Remember, numbers are always followed by nouns in the singular, not in the plural.

one book یِک کتاب

books کتاب ها

two books دو کتاب lit. two book and *not* دو کتاب ها

thousand books هِزار کتاب

ten boys دِه پِسر

Exercise 3

1 Put the following words into the plural:

خواهَر ماشین پِسَر کِتابخانِه پَنجَرِه روز اُستاد زَن

2 Translate the following plurals into Persian: cities, boys, flowers, cats, women, days, summers, pens, trains, the young, the wise, three sisters, ten birds, two hours.

Things to remember . . .

- Persian numbers are written from left to right, in the opposite direction of the script.
- Combinations of numbers are formed very logically and in pronunciation the numbers are linked by the vowel 'o', short for 'and'. Therefore 451 is ۴۵۱, 'chāhār sad *o* panjāh *o* yek', lit. four-hundred and fifty and one.
- Ordinals are formed by adding '–om' to cardinal numbers but not to number 1 (yek). The ordinal of one (i.e. first) is the Arabic 'avval' but in combined numbers such as 21st 'yekom' can be used (bist o yekom = 21st).

Answer these questions based on material from this unit.

1 Can you count from 1 to 10 in Persian?
2 Write down the number 51 using Persian numerals.

3 Can you name a central Asian capital city with the Persian number two in it?

4 Are combined Persian numbers written from right to left?

5 What is the most common 'counting word' in Persian?

6 How would you say 'four brothers'? Don't forget to use your counting word.

7 What plural endings can you use for the noun 'boy'?

8 How would say 'twelfth' in Persian?

9 Imagine you are in a Persian book shop. Ask for 'these six books, please' in Persian.

10 How would you use the -ān plural with a word such as 'star' in Persian?

3

....

Grammar reference unit

Moving a step further

All the lone words and single phrases of greeting and the names of the days of the week, numbers and plurals should have built up a good store of vocabulary for you. So now it is time to start forming proper sentences, starting with the very simple and gradually working towards understanding and using Persian in a more realistic manner.

Before we can go on, however, we need to look at the most common terminology that is used to describe grammar and rules of forming verbs, tenses and so on. Luckily the rules of Persian grammar are relatively logical and quite simple and, compared with many other languages spoken in the Middle East, can be learnt rather effortlessly. Familiarizing yourself with these technical terms and 'jargon' will therefore make it easier to follow the subsequent units.

Grammatical glossaries and meanings

Syntax and word order

First of all, it is important to note that the simple and normal word order in Persian is:

Subject – object – verb
i.e. I – cat – saw

In English, of course, the word order is:

Subject – verb – object
I saw (the) cat

Gradually, we will be able to introduce other elements into the sentence and will end up with the following:

Subject – adverb of time – adverb of manner – direct object – indirect object – adverb of place – verb.

But, for the time being, let us focus on the fundamental components of the sentence.

Subject

(*I* in the example sentence.) The subject is the doer or the agent or performer of the action in the sentence.

Object

(*cat* in the example sentence.) The object is a noun or equivalent or a string of words forming a clause, towards which the action of the verb is directed or on whom the action is performed.

Verb

(*saw* in the example sentence.) The verb is a word that expresses an action, a state or feeling or what is becoming of, or happening to, someone or something.

I have to tell you that these rules are not always followed in the spoken language and you may often hear native speakers of Persian using the subject–verb–object order in the sentences, which would bring it closer to the English sentence structure.

This word order makes it harder to follow what's going on, because the listener has to wait until the speaker gets to the end of the sentence before he can work out what action is being discussed!

Just remember that in this book the verb in our Persian sentences is the *final component* in the sentence. However, in different situations the word order may be moved around in the sentence. There is not much point in going into detail on all the ways the word order rules can be broken as this is usually done in archaic prose, in the colloquial language or in stylized texts such as film scripts or novels.

For a sentence with the verb 'to be', that is 'am, are, is, were, was', the order is: subject – predicate – 'to be' (known as the *copula*). In such sentences, the subject can be a noun, a phrase or a pronoun, and in more advanced language, the subject of a sentence can be an infinitive for example.

The word order, of course, becomes more complex as we learn more and more about the language. A slightly more advanced sentence will have other components such as question words (interrogatives), adverbs and direct as well as indirect objects and then the sentences can become even more complex as we look at relative clauses and conditional sentences for example. The objective of this book, however, is to teach you the basics of the grammar and, hopefully, you will be able to build on this functional knowledge and take it further.

I have tried to explain the meaning of technical terms or grammatical jargon that I have used in the following units, as it is impossible to avoid them totally. Besides you only ever need to learn these words once and they will always come handy when you try to learn another new language.

Insight

Every Persian verb has an ending known as the 'subject suffix' that tells you who is doing the action. As there are singular and plural second persons in Persian this means that you can have six little endings that tell you who the doer or subject of the verb is. You only need to learn these six endings once (in fact you only need five for simple past tenses) and use them with all the verbs. This would be as if your English verbs would look like, for example, went-I, went-he, went-we or bought-he, bought-I or live-we, live-you, live-they.

Exercise 1

◀) CD 1 TR 4

What form of greeting would you use if you were asked to say:

'good morning', 'good afternoon, Maryam', 'thank you very much, Reza', 'goodbye, Ali, safe journey', 'good night, ladies and gentlemen'?

Aqa Bozorg Mosque and Madrasah Complex, Kashan

4

Where are you from?
What do you do?

In this unit you will learn how to
- *Say where you are from*
- *Ask how someone is*
- *Give basic personal information*
- *Say your nationality and occupation*

Dialogue

◀) CD 1, TR 5

Listen to Maryam (M) and Babak (B) greeting each other and enquiring after each other's health. Maryam then introduces a new friend, Yasaman (Y) to Babak. (Note the use of plural verb endings to show respect and formality.)

مریم جان، سلام!	ب
به! بابک جان، سلام، صبح بخیر. چطوری؟	م
مرسی، قُربانَت، بد نیستم، تو چطوری؟ خوبی؟	ب
خیلی خوبم، مرسی.	م
مریم جان تنها هستی؟	ب
نه، بابک، با دوستم هستم. با دوستم، یاسمَن، یاسمن	م

این بابک است. بابک نَقاش است.

سلام. **ی**

سلام، یاسمن خانم. خوشوقتم. شما ایرانی هستید؟ **ب**

بله من ایرانی هستم ولَی مادرم روس است. شما اَهلِ **ی**
کجا هستید؟

من شیرازی هستم. شما مثلِ مریم دانشجو هستید؟ **ب**

نه، من دانشجو نیستم، من عکاس هستم. **ی**

به! به! چه خوب! مریم، امشب منزل هستی؟ **ب**

بله من و یاسمنِ امشب منزل هستیم. **م**

B	*maryam jān, salām!*
M	*bah! bābak jān, salām, sobh-bekheyr. chetori?*
B	*mersi, qorbānat, bad nistam, to chetori? khubi?*
M	*kheyli khubam, mersi.*
B	*maryam jān tanhā hasti?*
M	*na, bābak, bā dustam hastam. bā dustam, yāsaman. yāsaman in bābak ast. bābak naqqāsh ast.*
Y	*salām.*
B	*salām yāsaman khānom. khoshvaqtam. shomā irāni hastid?*
Y	*bale, man irāni hastam, vali mādaram rus ast. shomā ahl-e kojā hastid?*
B	*man shirāzi hastam. shomā mesl-e maryam dāneshju hastid?*
Y	*na, man dāneshju nistam, man 'akkās hastam.*
B	*bah! bah! che khub! maryam, emshab manzel hasti?*
M	*bale, man o yāsaman emshab manzel hastim.*

B	Hi, (dear) Maryam!
M	Wow! Hi (dear) Babak, good morning. How are you?
B	Thanks, kind of you to ask (lit. I am your sacrifice). (I am) not bad, how are you? Are you well?
M	(I am) very well, thank you.
B	Maryam (dear), are you alone?
M	No, Babak, I am with my friend. With my friend Yasaman. Yasaman, this is Babak. Babak is (a) painter.
Y	Hello.
B	Hello, (miss) Yasaman. Pleased to meet you. Are you (pl.) Iranian?
Y	Yes, I am Iranian, but my mother is Russian. Where are you (pl.) from?

B	I am from Shiraz (lit. I am Shirazi). Are you a student like Maryam?	
Y	No, I am not (a) student, I am (a) photographer.	
B	Wow! Great! Maryam, are you at home tonight?	
M	Yes, Yasaman and I are at home tonight.	

chetor?	*how?*	چِطور؟
i	short, contracted form of *you* (sing.) *are*, i.e. *you're*	ی
tanhā	*alone*	تَنها
dust	*friend*	دوست
-am	[suffix] *my*, دوستَم *my friend*	َم
naqqāsh	*painter*	نَقاش
khoshvaqt	*fortunate, happy*	خوشوَقت
-am	short, contracted form of *I am*, i.e. *I'm*	َم
khoshvaqtam	*I'm happy*	خوشوَقتَم
rus	*Russian*	روس
shomā	*you* (pl.)	شُما
ahl	*native of*, (also *to have a liking for s.t.*)	أهل
kojā	question word *where?*	کُجا
mesl	*like, similar to*	مِثل
dāneshju	*student*	دانِشجو
nistam	negative *of to be*, i.e. *I am not*	نیستَم
'akkās	*photographer*	عکاس
bah! bah!	sign of exclamation meaning *wonderful, lovely*	به! به!
manzel	*home, house*	مَنزِل

Present tense of 'to be'

The dialogue shows you the simple forms of the present tense of the verb 'to be' as in 'I am', 'you are', 'we are', etc.

The Persian verb 'to be' can be expressed in two ways: in the full form or condensed. In English, you can say either 'I am a student' or 'I'm a student'. In other words, there is a full, stand-alone form of the verb, like 'I am' and there is an abbreviated, contracted form like 'I'm'.

The full form of the verb 'to be' in Persian expresses a slightly different state from its English equivalent. It means more 'to exist' or 'there is' than 'to be', while the English variation is really a matter of style: formal or colloquial.

Before we go on any further and look at the Persian form of 'to be' it is important for you to note that the Persian verbs 'to be' and 'to have' are totally irregular. This means that they have rules of their own and do not fit wholly in the more or less regular system of verb conjugation that applies to other Persian verbs. Having said that, they are very easy to learn and getting to grips with them early on will make some future grammatical explanations a lot simpler to follow.

Full forms of 'to be' in the present tense

The six cases of the full present tense of the verb *to be* are shown in the following table.

Singular	Plural
هَستَم *hastam* I am	هَستیم *hastim* we are
هَستی *hasti* you are	هَستید *hastid* you are
هَست *hast* s/he, it, this, that is	هَستَند *hastand* they, these, those are

The use of the full form implies either formality or the sense that one *exists* in the state expressed. For example: من ایرانی هَستَم *man irāni hastam* 'I am Iranian' is used either in a formal setting or means that the speaker wishes to put some stress on the fact that he or she *exists* as an Iranian. Similarly, آنها خسته هستند *ānhā khaste hastand* 'they are tired' means that they are in an exhausted state, putting more stress on the fact that they are tired.

The distinction is not so important in colloquial, spoken Persian.

Insight

The verb 'to be' in Persian behaves very similarly to the English verb 'to be' in the sense that it is irregular and its present, past and conditional forms display hardly any family resemblance. Compare 'I am' to 'I was', 'I would' and 'I will be'. This happens in Persian too.

Attached, contracted forms of 'to be' in the present tense

As already mentioned, the verb 'to be' can also appear as an attached ending, not dissimilar to '*you're* nice' as opposed to '*you are* nice'. The present tense of the verb 'to be', in its attached form, consists simply of six personal endings or suffixes. If you look at the full form, you will see that the short suffixes are just the endings of the full form. These abbreviated suffixes are then fixed onto the preceding word in the sentence. Later on in the book, when we look more closely at forming Persian verbs, these same endings, with one exception, will be used as the compulsory suffixes of all verbs.

The attached forms of 'to be' are found in the following table:

Singular	Plural
م -*am* I am	یم -*im* we are
ی -*i* you are	ید -*id* you are
ست -*ast* he, she, it is	ند -*and* they, these are

The following table illustrates how the endings correspond to the full form of the verb and to the personal pronouns.

Singular	Plural
مَن ↔ I ↔ هَستَم ↔ م ↔ am	ما ↔ we ↔ هَستیم ↔ یم ↔ are
تُو ↔ you (sing.) ↔ هَستی ↔ ی ↔ are	شُما ↔ you (pl.) ↔ هَستید ↔ ید ↔ are
او ↔ he, she, it ↔ هَست ↔ ست ↔ is	ایشان ↔ they ↔ هَستَند ↔ ند ↔ are

The full, complete example of the verb 'to be well', used in the dialogue in this unit, is as follows:

I am well   خوب + م ↔ خوبَم

you are well   خوب + ی ↔ خوبی

he/she/it is well   خوب + ست ↔ خوبَست

we are well   (ما) خوب + یم ↔ ما خوبیم

you (pl.) are well   (شُما) خوب + ید ↔ شُما خوبید

they are well   (آنها-ایشان) خوب + ند ↔ آنها خوبَند

Combination or clash of vowels

As we mentioned earlier in this book, Persian does not allow for a long and a short vowel to come together. This means, for example, that the sound *e* cannot follow the sound *ā* or *u*. This combination of vowels, of course, does not happen in words. However, whenever there is a need to join a short and a long vowel together, as we occasionaly have to do to form verbs, we must insert a *buffer* between the two vowels to ensure that both vowels can be pronounced easily.

There are clear rules for doing this. When short forms of the verb 'to be' are joined to words ending in -*e* (ه ، ـه), such as بچه *bache*, and -*i* (ی), an *alef* is used as a buffer and inserted between the two vowels:

Singular	Plural
I am a child بچه اَم	we are children بچه ایم
you (sing.) are a child بچه ای	you (pl.) are children بچه اید
he, she is a child بچه اَست	they are children بچه اَند

Or using خَسته *khaste*, meaning 'tired' as an example:

Singular	Plural
I am tired خَسته اَم	we are tired خَسته ایم
you (sing.) are tired خَسته ای	you (pl.) are tired خَسته اید
he, she, it is tired خَسته اَست	they are tired خَسته اند

How about a word ending with the long vowel ی *i*, e.g. ایرانی *irāni*, 'Iranian'?:

Singular	Plural
I am Iranian ایرانی اَم / ایرانیَم	we are Iranian ایرانی ایم
you (sing.) are Iranian ایرانی ای	you (pl.) are Iranian ایرانی اید / ایرانیید
he, she, it is Iranian ایرانی‌اَست / ایرانیِست	they are Iranian ایرانی اند / ایرانیَند

And a word ending in long vowel و *u*, like خوشرو *khoshru*, 'cheerful':

Singular	Plural
I am cheerful خوشرویَم	we are cheerful خوشروییم
you (sing.) are cheerful خوشرویی	you (pl.) are cheerful خوشرویید
he, she, it is cheerful خوشروست	they are cheerful خوشرویَند

....

Insight

Persian subject endings or suffixes are culled from the Persian verb 'to be'. In fact they are the truncated, short forms of the verb 'to be'. The verb 'to be' is the only verb that can be shortened. This is not exactly the same but very similar to the verb 'you are' shortened to *you're*. The negative form, however, cannot be shortened in the same way. So there is no *you aren't* in Persian!

Negative form of the present tense of 'to be'

The negative of the present tense of the verb 'to be' is formed by adding the personal subject endings to the verb نیست *nist*. There are *no short forms* for the negative verb of 'to be'.

Singular	*Plural*
I am not نیستَم	we are not نیستیم
you (sing.) are not نیستی	you (pl.) are not نیستید
he, she, it is not نیست	they are not نیستَند

Other examples:

خوبیم we are well

مُعَلِّمَم I am (a) teacher

ایرانیَند/ایرانی اَند they are Iranian

سَردَست it is cold

دانشجوﯾید you are students

دُختَری you sing. are a girl

پِسَرَست he is (a) boy

Since Persian verb forms always tell you who the subject or the 'doer' of the verb is, the additional use of personal pronouns is not always necessary; however, their use emphasizes the person of the subject. For example:

مَن چینی نیستَم، ژاپنی هَستم. I am not Chinese. I am Japanese.

Asking questions in Persian

◀) CD 1, TR 5, 01:23

Persian has the equivalent of all the English question words such
as 'why', 'where', 'who', etc., and some more; however, one of the
easiest ways to form a question is to say something and make
it sound like a question by raising your intonation. This is very
common in spoken Persian, especially in sentences with 'to be'.
Listen to the recording and you'll get a better idea of the change
of tone in question sentences.

They are Iranian. *ān-hā irāni hastand.* .هَستَند ایرانی (آنها)

They are Iranian? (*as opposed to* Are they Iranian?)
ān-hā irāni hastand? ؟هستند ایرانی (آنها)

Tehran is expensive. *tehrān gerān ast.* .است گِران تِهران

Tehran is expensive? (*as opposed to* Is Tehran expensive?)
tehrān gerān ast? ؟است گِران تِهران

Insight

There is a subtle difference between the third person singular
forms 'ast' and 'hast', even if both seemingly mean 'he/she is'.
'ast' corresponds to the English 'is' as in 'this *is* my house' or
'Maryam *is* Shirin's sister'. 'hast', on the other hand, conveys the
English sense of *there is* as in '*there is* a coffee machine on every
floor' or when you call the surgery and ask: '*Is* the doctor in
today?' With the answer: 'Yes, Dr Ahmadi *is* in from 2 to 6 pm.'

Exercise 1

Rewrite the following sentences using the short forms of the verb 'to be', then translate them into English:

۱   این قالیچه گران است.

۲   آن اُتاق خیلی بزرگ نیست ولی تَمیز اَست.

۳   آنها در اُتوبوس هَستَند.

۴   آن دُختَرها خواننده نیستَند.

۵   شُما با مریم دوست هَستید؟

Exercise 2

Translate these sentences into Persian:

1   This peach is delicious.
2   Maryam is a painter.
3   You (pl.) are tired.
4   I am young.
5   We are in Tehran.

> ## Insight
>
> A lot of Persian grammatical functions are performed by adding prefixes or suffixes that themselves are a long or a short vowel, or end or begin with short vowels like 'i' or 'be' or 'na' or 'and'. If two vowels, one as part of the word and the other as part of the suffix or prefix, come together then we have to erect little buffers between these two converging vowels to make sure they each retain their individual pronunciation.

Exercise 3

Give full negative answers to the following questions:

۱   آن پسَرِ اسکاتلندی است؟

۲   شما با ایرَج دوست هَستید؟

۳   من ورزشکار هَستم؟

۴   آنها خیلی خسته اَند؟

۵   شما نَقاشید؟

Exercise 4
Rewrite the dialogue, using the short forms of the verb 'to be'
wherever appropriate.

_____

Something to remember

- As well as using the question words 'what', 'where' and so on,
  Persian speakers use the tone of voice to make questions, while
  in English the word order is changed to make questions. So the
  Persian equivalent of 'Is the library open today?' would still be
  'the library is open today?' but the last word will be uttered in an
  inquisitive more high pitched tone.

Complete the following:

1 In a normal written Persian sentence where would you put the verb?
2 Introduce yourself in Persian, following the pattern: My name
   is _____. I am _____ (place your nationality where the blank is).
3 Ask how someone is using two common Persian models.
4 How do you ask someone you have met for the first time 'What is
   your name?'
5 Put the following in the correct order:
   من- هَست- ایرانی- شوهَرَم- ولی- هَستَم-
6 Say 'they are happy' in Persian using both the full and short forms
   of the verb 'are'.
7 How is the negative of the verb 'to be' in the present tense formed?
   Can you say 'I am not tired' or 'Alex and Isabel are not German'?
8 Do you always need to use a pronoun in Persian sentences? Why?
9 Can you remember three professions or occupations in Persian
   you have seen in the units so far?
10 Correct the following sentence:
   من اهلِ شیراز هستید و در لندن دانِشجو هست.

5

Family, friends and other people

In this unit you will learn how to
- *Give more personal information using pronouns*
- *Describe characteristics using adjectives*
- *Describe family relationships and associations*

Dialogue

🔊 CD 1, TR 6

Listen to the conversation between Maryam and Amir, who have just been introduced by Dariush. Can you work out the relationships?

مریم جان، این دوستِ من اَمیر است. اَمیر، مریم دخترخالهٔ من است.	د
سلام مریم. شما دختر خالهٔ داریوش هستید؟	اَ
بله، من دخترخالهٔ او هستم. شما دوستِ داریوش هستید؟	م
من همکلاسِ داریوش هستم.	اَ
اِسمِ فامیلِ شما چیست؟	م
اِسمِ فامیلِ من اَخوان است .	اَ
اَخوان؟ شما برادرِ سارا نیستید؟	م
چرا، من برادرِ بزرگِ سارا هستم. سارا دوستِ شماست؟	اَ

بله، سارا دوستِ خیلی خوبِ من است و تولدِ من و سارا هم یکروز است.   م

جداً؟ چه جالب! پس تولدِ شما ماه آینده است؟   ا

بله. تولدِ شما کی است؟   م

تولدِ من ماهِ آبان است. مریم خانهٔ تو کجاست؟   ا

خانهٔ من در خیابانِ سعدی است. خانهٔ تو کجاست؟   م

خانهٔ ما در قُلهک است.   ا

D	Maryam (dear), this is my friend Amir. Amir, Maryam is my cousin.
A	Hi, Maryam. Are you Dariush's cousin?
M	Yes, I am his cousin. Are you a friend of his?
A	I am Dariush's classmate.
M	What's your surname?
A	My surname is Akhavan.
M	Akhavan? Are you not Sara's brother?
A	Yes, I am Sara's older brother. Is Sara your friend?
M	Yes, Sara is my very good friend and Sara and my birthdays are on the same day.
A	Really? How interesting! So your birthday is next month?
M	Yes. When is your birthday?
A	My birthday is in the month of Aban. Maryam, where is your house?
M	My house is on Sa'di Avenue. Where is your house?
A	Our house is in Qolhak.

dust	*friend*	دوست
dokhtarkhāle	*cousin, daughter of maternal aunt*	دخترخاله
hamkelās	*classmate*	همکلاس
esm-e fāmil	lit. *family name, surname*	اسم فامیل
tavalod	*birth* (also *birthday*)	تولد
yekruz	lit. *one day*, meaning the *same day too*	یکروز
jeddan	Arabic word structure as adverb meaning *really, seriously*	جداً

QUICK VOCAB

Unit 5   Family, friends and other people   43

che?	*what?* and vocative exclamation as in *how wonderful!*	چه
jāleb	*interesting*	جالِب
pas	*so, in that case, therefore*	پَس
māh	*month; moon*	ماه
āyande	*next, future*	آیَنده
bale	*yes*	بَله
kay	*when?*	کی؟
khāne	*house, home*	خانه
kojā?	*where?*	کُجا؟
dar	*in, at, inside*	دَر
khiyābān	*street, avenue*	خیابان

Steel door panel, Isfahan, 17th century

Personal pronouns

	Singular	Plural
1st	مَن *man* I	ما *mā* we
2nd	تُو *to* you	شُما *shomā* you
3rd	او *u* he, she, it	آنها/ایشان *ānhā* they

44

Persian has an honorific system of pronouns. Something similar happens in French, when you have to choose between 'tu' and 'vous' when addressing a person. In general, all the plural pronouns can be used to indicate formality and respect. For example, in an Iranian primary classroom, children rarely refer to themselves in the first person singular but refer to themselves as 'we' in order to show humility and respect towards the teacher. Similarly, the third person plural 'they' can be used to refer to a singular third party in a formal setting and to show respect. (Incidentally, be warned that the formal pronouns can also be used to show disdain and contempt!) As you can see, there are two second person pronouns:

تو *to*, is used at times of great intimacy to address close friends, loved ones and children

شما *shomā*, as well as its function as the second person plural pronoun, is used to address a singular person to observe formality and to indicate respect between strangers and elders as well as in the peer groups.

Exercise 1
How would you address or refer to the following in Persian? Use the appropriate pronoun.

1 Your new, elderly neighbour.
2 Your closest friend.
3 The bank manager.
4 Your cousin's small child.
5 The immigration officer.

Insight
In a Persian sentence, things that belong together in a clause, such as a noun and its descriptive adjectives, or a noun, its adjectives and its possessor, must be vocally linked by the vowel 'e'. It's almost as if the words in this vocally strung chain end with the vowel 'e' rhyming with the French 'café'.

How to describe something or someone?: linking nouns, adjectives and pronouns

Before being able to use the personal pronouns in even a simple or meaningful construction, such as 'my name', 'your brother' or 'his car', and then giving more information such as 'your elder brother' or 'his blue car', we must learn one of the most fundamental characteristics of the Persian language.

Both in written and in spoken Persian, we must show an agreement and correspondence between nouns, pronouns, adjectives and prepositions. We must be able to demonstrate *possession* or *close association.*

Look at the following English construction: 'my fast, beautiful, expensive, thoroughbred, young horse'. In this example, there is no sign in the script or any indication when spoken, that joins the adjectives ('young, fast, beautiful', etc.) to one another or ultimately to the possessor ('my') and from there onto the noun ('horse').

The native speaker of English knows, and the learner will soon understand, that these adjectives tell us something about the noun ('horse') they describe and that the whole 'package' belongs to a first person speaker, demonstrated by 'my'.

In Persian, however, a noun, the adjectives that describe it and the owner that possesses the whole thing, must be treated as pearls strung together by a thread that runs through them. In other words, a sound or a written sign must hold the whole construction together. This, at times, invisible chord or link, is known as the *ezafe*, literally meaning 'addition'. It sounds like the vowel 'e', as in 'end' or 'ye' as in 'yes'. The complete rules for writing it will be given a little further on in this unit, but first let us see how the adjective works in Persian.

Adjectives

Adjectives in Persian are remarkably similar to adjectives in English with one exception. In Persian, an adjective follows the noun it qualifies or describes, instead of preceding it, as is the case in English. In Persian this combination of a noun and its adjective (or adjectives) is held together by the *ezafe*, a vowel that connects the two.

For example, 'blue pencil' is مداد آبی *medād-e ābi* in Persian, as if you were saying: 'pencil-*e*-blue'.

Here is a trick to help you work out the correct Persian order of nouns and adjectives. Write down your English noun and the adjective that describes it. Write the Persian equivalent of each English word underneath it and then read the Persian words in the natural direction of the language, that is from right to left. This should give you the correct order of nouns and adjectives as spoken or read in Persian. You should be able to see that the adjective is following the noun it describes:

⟶ blue   pencil

آبی   مداد   ⟵

⟵   ⟵

So, adjectives in Persian always *follow* the noun they qualify or describe and are joined to it by the vowel *e* or *ye* ی if the noun ends in a long vowel such as *ā ī* or *u* و.

أبِ گرم – دَرسِ سَخت – هَوای سَرد – شَبهای تاری – موی بُلَند
– صَندَلیِ راحَت

A group, i.e. noun + attributive adjective, may in its turn be qualified by another adjective:

شبِ تاریکِ سرد – پسرِ کوچکِ کَمرو

'shy small boy'   'cold dark night'

When two or more adjectives qualify the same noun in the same way, they are co-ordinated:

شَبِ تاریک و سَرد – تاریخِ سیاسی و اقتِصادی – هَمسایهٔ خوب و مِهربان

Insight

With simple sentences that contain a noun, adjective and possessor, you can write the Persian translation of the English beneath it and then read it from right to left and you will get the correct Persian order. Remember to link the noun and adjective to each other and then to the possessor 'I' with an 'e'. E.g. 'my young friend', read from right to left in Persian, will be 'dust-e javān-e man'. This shows you that in Persian the adjective follows the noun it describes and the possessor, whether just a pronoun or a whole string of words such as 'Ali's classmates', will be last in the chain.

....

Writing rules for the *ezafe* link between noun–adjective, noun–pronoun, noun–noun

There are three ways of 'writing down' this basically vocal 'link' in the script, by adding either an ـ , ی or ء to the word, which is then followed by an adjective or a possessor.

Remember, the first two signs of ـ and ء are only ever used in the script either to help a beginner or to avoid ambiguity.

The following box sets out the rules for the use of the *ezafe* to create a link between the noun, adjective and pronoun or another noun:

---

1 If the word ends in a consonant (e.g. ب،ل، د، ض،گ، چ) always use ـ pronounced *e* as in egg.

2 If the word ends in a short final vowel (e.g. silent *h*, ـه) always use ء pronounced *ye* as in yesterday.

3 If the word ends in the long vowels *u* or *ā* (و، ا) always use ی pronounced *ye* as in yesterday.

The third option must *always* be used if words ending with long vowels ا or و, such as پا *pā* foot, or مو *mu* hair are then linked to an adjective, a pronoun or another noun.

Reminder: The short final vowel is denoted by the *silent h*, in words like خانه *khāne* 'house' or بچه *bache* 'child'.

Use of pronouns 'me', 'you' etc.

◀) CD 1, TR 6

In English, when you identify an object such as a book as yours, you simply say 'my book'. In Persian, the 'book' کتاب *ketāb* and 'my' من *man* must not only be written together, they must also be *linked in speech*, so much so that the final 'b', ب of the کتاب is linked to the initial 'm', م of من, with the help of the *ezafe*, which will either sound like *e* as in 'egg', or a *ye* as in 'yesterday'.

Try reading the following examples, paying full attention to the vocalization, but first listen to the individual words being read out without their being linked:

كتاب *ketāb* book

مَن *man* me, mine, my

كتاب مَن *ketāb-e man* my book (lit. book of me)

سیب *sib* apple

شیرین *shirin* sweet

مَن *man* my

سیب شیرین *sib-e shirin* sweet apple

سیب شیرین مَن *sib-e shirin-e man* my sweet apple

دوست علی *dust-e Ali* Ali's friend

دوست خوب علی *dust-e* khub-e *Ali* Ali's good friend

دوست خوب برادر علی *dust-e khub-e barādar-e Ali* Ali's brother's good friend (lit. good friend of Ali's brother)

خانه *khāne* house

بُزُرگ *bozorg* big, large

تو *to* you (sing.)

خانهٔ تو *khāne-ye to* your (sing.) house

خانهٔ بُزُرگ تو *khāne-ye bozorg-e to* your (sing.) big house

کتاب فارسی *ketāb-e farsi* Persian book

کتاب فارسی من *ketāb-e farsi-ye man* my Persian book

مو *mu* hair

سیاه *siyāh* black

موی سیاه *mu-ye siyāh* black hair

موی سیاه علی *mu-ye siyāh-e Ali* Ali's black hair

Note that 'hair' *mu* ends in a long *u* vowel and therefore the *ezafe* link to the adjective must be a *ye*. Similarly, 'house' *khāne* ends in a short, final vowel (using the letter *h* to represent this vowel) and must be linked to the adjective with a *ye*, indicated by the diacritic ء .

Summary

1 In Persian, unlike in English, adjectives always *follow* the noun: that means you will have to say 'apple sweet', 'book big', 'weather good', 'woman noble'.

2 Similarly, the possessor always comes after the possessed thing, or at the end of the package if the possessed comes with adjectives; that means we have to say 'book my' or 'book Persian my'.

Short cut

Remember that in translating a simple English noun–adjective expression, you can write out the Persian translation of each word directly underneath the corresponding English words and then read the end result from right to left; this should give you the translation of your English phrase:

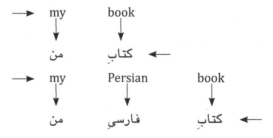

And, of course, the reverse will also work. If you want to translate the Persian into English you can just read the Persian from left to right!

Let's return to the original construction now (earlier in this unit) and see if we can work out how to say 'my fast, beautiful, expensive, thoroughbred, young horse' in Persian:

From left to right:

→ my fast beautiful expensive thoroughbred young horse
Now, write the Persian for each word underneath the English:

Then, choose the appropriate *ezafe* ending for each noun or adjective by looking at the last letter. Is it a consonant, a long or a short vowel?

Now read the linked words from right to left and, bingo!, you should get:

اسبِ جوانِ اصیلِ گرانِ زیبای تندروی من

(This exaggerated construction was made up to illustrate the function of the *ezafe*. In practice very long descriptive constructions such as these are broken into smaller units and linked together with 'and'.)

Insight

If a word that has to be linked to the next ends in a vowel 'ā' or 'u' or short vowel 'e' then your vocal link will sound like 'ye'. After long vowels 'ā' and 'u' this sound **has to be** written in as 'ی'; however, with words ending with the short vowel 'e' all you need is the diacritical marker ء that sits on the vowel-carrying letter and will look like 'ـۀ or ۀ'. This is still pronounced as 'ye'.

Exercise 2

(a) Read the following constructions and then translate them into English:

۶ شبِ تاریکِ سرد

۱ باغِ بزرگ

۷ دانشگاهِ لَندَن

۲ کتابِ فارسیِ مَریَم

۸ خانهٔ قَدیمی

۳ مردِ ایرانی

۹ قوریِ چینیِ خواهرِ مِهرَبانِ بابَک

۴ دخترهای دوستِ مَن

۵ غذایِ خوشمَزه

(b) Translate the following into Persian:

1 Sweet grapes.
2 Maryam's Russian friend.
3 Mr Ahmadi's car.
4 Large, nice room.
5 Handmade, Kashan carpets.

6 Old, historic city.
7 Cold, sunny day.
8 Her neighbour.
9 My green umbrella.
10 Old, kind men.

(c) Translate the following passage into Persian:
My name is Ali. I am Iranian. I am a student in Tehran. This is my sister Maryam. Maryam's birthday is in December. Her friend's brother is my classmate. His name is Mehrdad. Mehrdad's hair is brown. His house is in Afshar Avenue.

(d) Here are some more useful adjectives. Can you join them up with the nouns in the other column?

Adjective	Translation	Noun	Translation
ارزان	cheap	خانه	house
سیاه	black	غذا	food, dish
گرم	warm	میوه	fruit
گران	expensive	صندلی	chair

سَرد	cold	هوا	weather, air	
طلایی	golden	چِشم	eyes	
خوشمَزه	tasty	مو	hair	
بَدمَزه	horrid tasting	گربه	cat	
راحَت	comfortable	تابستان	summer	
ناراحَت	uncomfortable	کَفش	shoe	

Insight

Persian has very clear, intuitive names for the eight sets of cousins on the maternal and paternal sides. The easiest way to deal with these is to learn the four names of aunts and uncles on the maternal and paternal sides and then your cousins will be son, *pesar*, or daughter, *dokhtar* of any of these four.

Talking about yourself and your family

◀) CD 1, TR 6, 03:30

Now that you know how to link words that belong together, you can talk, in very basic terms, about your family. Remember we still haven't got as far as using verbs extensively, so here we will only concentrate on saying things like 'my sister', 'your husband', 'our grandfather' etc.

In order to do this you need to use the relevant personal pronoun chosen from the six given in the table earlier in the unit and link it to the appropriate member of the family. This vocabulary list should help.

mādar	*mother*	مادر
pedar	*father*	پدَر
khāhar	*sister*	خواهَر
barādar	*brother*	بَرادَر

mādar-bozorg	*grandmother*	مادر‌بُزُرگ
pedar-bozorg	*grandfather*	پِدَر‌بُزُرگ
dā'i	*maternal uncle*	دایی
'amu	*paternal uncle*	عَمو
khāle	*maternal aunt*	خاله
'ame	*paternal aunt*	عَمه
zan – hamsar – khānom	*wife*	زَن – (هَمسَر) – خانُم
showhar – hamsar	*husband*	شُوهَر – (هَمسَر)
hamsar	*spouse*	هَمسَر
pesar	*son/boy*	پِسَر
dokhtar	*daughter/girl*	دُختَر

The terms for eight sets of cousins (e.g. son/daughter of maternal aunt):

پِسَر‌خاله / دُختَر خاله.	*pesar-khāle/dokhtar-khāle*
پِسَر دایی / دختر دایی	*pesar-dā'i/dokhtar-dā'i*
پِسَر عمو / دختر عمو	*pesar-'amu/dokhtar-'amu*
پِسَر عَمه / دختر عمه	*pesar-'ame/dokhtar-'ame*

And mother-in-law (two cases) and father-in-law (two cases):

مادَر زن / مادر شوهَر	*mādar-zan/mādar-showhar*
پِدر زن / پدر شوهر	*pedar-zan/pedar-showhar*

So, how would you say 'my brother', 'your (sing.) husband', 'their mother', 'our sister', 'my (daughter of maternal aunt) cousin' and 'his/her uncle's grandmother'?

Here are the answers:

بَرادَرِ مَن	*barādar-e man*
شوهرِ تو	*showhar-e tow*
مادَرِ آنها	*mādar-e ānhā*

خواهرِ ما	*khāhar-e mā*
دُختَر خالهٔ من	*dokhtar-khāle-ye man*
مادربُزرگِ عموی او	*mādar-bozorg-e 'amu-ye u*

Exercise 3

Translate into Persian:

1 My grandmother is 92 years old. (use ساله after number for 'years old')
2 She is my cousin. (daughter of my mother's sister)
3 My uncle (paternal) is your father's friend.
4 Our brother is a doctor.
5 Their sister-in-law (sister of husband) and our sister are in London today.

'Suffixed' or 'attached' possessive endings

◀) **CD 1, TR 6, 04:30**

Listen to the dialogue between Amir and Maryam and see if you can spot a different way of expressing possession, without the use of pronouns:

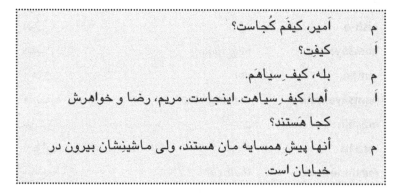

M	Amir, where is my bag?
A	Your bag?
M	Yes, my black bag.
A	Ah, your black bag. It's here. Maryam, where are Reza and his sister?
M	They are at our neighbour's, but their car is outside in the street.

	bag	کیف	
	my	ـَم	
kifam	*my bag*	کیفَم	
kojā	*where?*	کُجا	
-st	short form *is*	ـست	
kojāst	*where is?*	کجاست	
siyāh	*black*	سیاه	
siyāham	*my black . . .*	سیاهَم	
āhā!	*ah!, I see*	آها	
-at	*your*	ـَت	
siyāhat	*your black . . .*	سیاهَت	
dar	*in, at*	در	
khāhar	*sister*	خواهر	
-ash	*his, hers*	ـَش	
khāharash	*his sister*	خواهَرش	
pish-e	*at*	پیشِ	
hamsāye	*neighbour*	هَمسایه	
-emān	*our*	ـمان	
hamsāye-mān	*our neighbour*	هَمسایه	
māshin	*car*	ماشین	
-eshān	*their*	ـشان	
māshineshān	*their car*	ماشینِشان	
birun	*outside*	بیرون	
khiyābān	*street*	خیابان	

In the dialogue, Maryam, looking for her bag, did not say: کیف من *kif-e man* 'my bag' but, instead, said کیفَم *kifam* which is another way of saying exactly the same thing: 'my bag'. Rather than using the pronoun من *man*, Maryam used an attached possessive ending. Similarly, when she identified the colour of her bag she did not say: کیف سیاه من *kif-e siyāh-e man* but کیف سیاهم *kif-e siyāham* meaning 'my black bag'.

No sooner have you got used to the function of the personal pronouns 'I' من , 'you' تو etc. in expressions to show possession, as in 'my friend' or 'your car', then it's time to learn another way of expressing the same thing, this time by using attached pronoun substitutes. This could be a new concept for you as there is no exact equivalent in English. The proper name for the attached pronoun is a 'suffixed possessive pronoun' which means you attach it to the end of the noun.

Writing rules

The attached possessive personal pronouns are shown on the left in the following table, while the full, subject pronouns are listed on the right.

Attached possessive pronouns		Stand-alone subject pronouns		
plural	*singular*	*plural*	*singular*	
1 our مان‌ـ	my مـَ	we ما	من ا	۱
2 your تان‌ـ	your ت‌ـ	you شما	you تو	۲
3 their شان‌ـ	his, hers ش‌ـ	they ایشان/آنها	he, she او	۳

The possessive suffixes are attached directly to words ending in consonants and the long vowel ی:

کِتابَم – پِدَرَش – ماشینِمان – طوطیَش – کیفِشان

However, a buffer needs to be inserted between words ending with the final, short vowel *e*, ـه , ه and the singular attached possessives (م، ت، ش). The buffer is the 'alef' ا:

خانِه اَم – بَچِه اَت – گُربِه اَش

The plural attached pronouns, however, do not need to be separated from the final short vowels by a buffer:

خانه مان – بچه تان – گربه شان

Following آ and و vowels a ی (i.e. *ye*) buffer is inserted between the noun and the attached possessive suffixes:

کتابهایَم – دوستهایِشان – عَمویَت – مویِتان

Exercise 4

Translate the following possessive constructions using both the stand-alone and the attached pronouns:

1 my brother
2 their horse
3 our house
4 your (pl.) black dog
5 their umbrella

6 his friend
7 your (sing.) book
8 my kind (paternal) uncle
9 her grandmother
10 our city

Exercise 5

Translate into English:

۱ مَرد گُرُسنه (hungry)

۲ هَوای (air, weather) خوب

۳ هوای خوبِ آفتابی (sunny)

۴ دُخترِ باهوش (clever)

۵ دانِشجوی (student) جَوان

۶ دانِشجوی جوان ایرلَندی

۷ لیموی (lemon) تُرش (sour)

۸ پنجَرهٔ (window) باز (open)

۹ خانهٔ قدیمی (old)

۱۰ این دو دَرِ باز

۱۱ دَرهای باز

۱۲ این دَرهای باز وَ بُزُرگ

۱۳ آن گُربهٔ (cat) سِفید و قَشَنگ

۱۴ سیبهای سَبزِ تُرش

۱۵ مادَرِ آن دو پِسَر

۱۶ مادَرِ جوانِ (young) آن دو

پسَر کوچکِ (small, young)

۱۷ پدربُزُرگِ مِهَربان (kind)

۱۸ سیبِ شیرینِ شیرازی

۱۹ سیبِ سَبز و پُر تُقالِ شیرین

۲۰ روزِ گرم و شبِ سَرد

۲۱ کِشوَرِ (country) ایران

۲۲ جَزیرهٔ (island) بریتانیا

۲۳ بلیطِ اُتوبوسِ تهران–اصفِهان

۲۴ شهرهای ایران

۲۵ مَغازه‌های پاریس

Exercise 6

Choose your own nouns and adjectives (or groups of adjectives) from the following table to create at least ten noun–adjective + *ezafe* constructions and number them using the Persian numerals.

Adjective	Noun
ارزان	تابستان
سیاه	زِمِستان
گَرم	ماشین
گِران	مو
سَرد	اَنگور
طلایی	بلیط
خوشمزه	صندلی
بَدمزه	چای
راحَت	خانه
ناراحَت	کَفش

....

Insight

A short cut to remember the six attached or suffixed possessive pronouns is to think of some English associations for the singular suffixes first: the 1st person singular 'am' is 'm' for 'mine' or even 'I am'; 'at' sounds related to 'thou- you', and 'ash' sounds like 'she'. Once you learn these, then think of using the '-ān' plural maker that we use for living things which you could add to the singular suffixes and you should get the plural possessive endings 'ān, tān, shān'.

....

Exercise 7

Translate into Persian:

1 My brother.
2 Your small car.

3 Big, expensive house.
4 His comfortable (راحت) room.
5 Cold cup (فنجان) of tea.
6 Our golden pen.
7 Cheap, black shoes.
8 Delicious, sweet apples.
9 Hungry (گرُسنه) young boy.
10 My beautiful country.

Test yourself

1 Do you remember your Persian subject pronouns? How would say 'I', 'he/she' and 'they'?

2 How do Persian speakers demonstrate that an adjective describes a particular noun and, in possessive constructions, that the described item belongs to someone?

3 How would you say 'my books' in Persian? Are there any writing rules that should be observed in this instance?

4 How does the Persian noun–adjective–possessor order differ from that in English?

5 Bābak is my *pesar-khāleh* پسرخاله. What is his exact relationship to me in English?

6 I have two *'amus* عمو (Reza and Cyrus) and one *'ameh* عمه (Maryam), one *khāleh* خاله (Pari) and one *dā'i* دایـی. I have one *dokhtar-'ameh*, one *pesar-khāleh* and one *dokhtar-khāleh* and two *pesar-dā'is*. Draw a diagram to show the exact relation of these aunts and uncles and their children to me and my parents. Can you think of some Persian names to give these cousins?

7 Can you name three colours and three fruits in Persian?

8 Link the following nouns and adjectives in Persian as shown in the English examples: small girl, cold winter, white cat, sweet tangerine:

نارنگی - گرُبه - سَرد - دختر - شیرین - زمِستان - سفید - کوچک

9 Link the correct attached possessive suffixes to their corresponding pronoun in the table below:

مان	من
ش	تو
شان	او
تان	ما
ت	شما
ش	آنها – ایشان

10 How would you link a noun that ends in a short vowel to its adjective or possessor?

6

Is Iran's highest mountain higher than Mt Everest?

In this unit you will learn how to
- *Form and use the comparative*
- *Compare two things*
- *Form and use the superlative*

Bas-relief at Apadana Hall, Persepolis, around 518 BCE

Dialogue
🔊 **CD 1, TR 7**

Listen to Maryam and Amir talk about comparisons:

ا مریم، تهران بزرگتر است یا اِصفهان؟

م تهران بزرگتر است.

ا هوای تهران گرمتر است یا هوای اِصفهان؟

م هوای اصفهان در تابستان گرمتر است. هوای اصفهان از تهران گرمتر است.

ا اُتاقِ من کوچک است.

م اتاقِ من هم خیلی کوچک اَست. ولی اُتاقِ کوچکِ من قَشَنگ است.

ا اُتاقِ تو کوچکتر ولی قَشَنگتَر است.

م اتاقِ تو بزرگتر از اتاقِ من است ولی اتاقِ من از اتاقِ تو قَشَنگتر است.

ا قشنگترین شهرِ ایران کُدام اَست؟

م مَشهَد قشنگ است، شیراز از مشهد قشنگتر است ولی اصفهان قشنگترین شهرِ ایران است.

ا بُلَندترین کوهِ ایران کدام است؟

م دَماوَند بلندترین کوهِ ایران است.

ا دماوند از اورِست بلندتر است؟

م نه. اورِست از دماوند بلندتر است. اورِست بلندترین کوهِ دُنیاست.

A	Maryam, is Tehran bigger or Esfahan?
M	Tehran is bigger.
A	Is the weather warmer in Tehran or in Esfahan?
	(lit. Tehran's weather is warmer or Esfahan's)
M	Esfahan (weather) is warmer in the summer. Esfahan (weather) is warmer than Tehran.
A	My room is small.
M	My room is also very small. However, my small room is nice.
A	Your room is smaller but nicer.
M	Your room is bigger than my room, but my room is nicer than yours.
A	Which is the prettiest city of Iran?
M	Mashhad is pretty, Shiraz is prettier than Mashhad, but Esfahan is the prettiest city in Iran.

Comparative and superlative adjectives

◄) CD 1, TR 7, 01:34

The formation of comparative and superlative adjectives in Persian is quite regular and not dissimilar to how it's done in English.

Comparative adjectives are made by adding a تَر -*tar* to the adjective (similar to adding an '-er' to an English adjective):

$\longrightarrow$ small + er = smaller

كوچَك + تَر = كوچَكتَر ←

kuchaktar

pretty → prettier	زيباتَر ← زيبا *zibā* → *zibātar*
large → larger	بُزرگتَر ← بُزرگ *bozorg* → *bozorgtar*
important → more important	مُهِمتَر ← مُهِم

mohem → *mohemtar*

As you see from the last example, while the formation of the comparative is not always regular in English, you can *always* form the comparative in Persian by adding a تَر -*tar* to the adjective.

The comparative follows the noun in the exact same way as the adjective or pronoun and is linked to the noun with the *ezafe*:

larger house	*khāne-ye bozorgtar*	خانهٔ بُزرگتَر
more important news	*khabar-e mohemtar*	خَبَرِ مُهِمتَر
prettier flowers	*golhā-ye zibātar*	گُلهای زيباتَر

۱ مریم و بهرام یک خانهٔ بزرگتر در شُمالِ تهران خریده اند.

1 Maryam and Bahram have bought a larger house in North Tehran.

64

٢ پِسَر کوچِکترِ من هنوز به مدرسه نمی رَوَد.

2 My younger son doesn't go to school yet.

The superlative is formed by adding a ترین *tarin* to the noun or, if you like, an ین *-in* to the comparative. Again this is similar to adding an '-est' to an English noun to form the superlative:

⟶ small + est = smallest

⟵ کوچِک + تَرین = کوچِکتَرین

kuchaktarin

Or, add an ین to the comparative:

کوچِکتَر + ین = کوچِکتَرین

pretty → prettier → prettiest زیباتَرین ← زیباتَر ← زیبا
zibā → zibātar → zibātarin

large → larger → largest بزرگتَرین ← بزرگتَر ← بُزُرگ
bozorg → bozorgtar → bozorgtarin

important → more important → most important
مُهِمتَرین ← مُهِمتَر ← مُهِم

mohem → mohemtar → mohemtarin

Insight

Forming comparatives and superlatives once again brings home to the learner the closeness of Indo-European languages. But remember that the comparative adjective, formed by addition of '-*tar*', should follow the noun but the superlative, '-*tarin*', must always come before the noun.

Note: Unlike the adjective and the comparative, the superlative *does not* follow the noun but comes before it and there is no *ezafe* link between the superlative and the noun it describes:

large house	*khāne-ye bozorg*	خانهٔ بُزُرگ
larger house	*khāne-ye bozorgtar*	خانهٔ بُزُرگتَر
the biggest house	*bozorgtarin khāneh*	بُزُرگترین خانه

important news	khabar-e mohem	خَبَرِ مُهِم
more important news	khabar-e mohemtar	خَبَرِ مُهِمتَر
the most important news	mohemtarin khabar	مُهِمترین خَبَر
pretty flowers	golhā-ye zibā	گُلهای زیبا
prettier flowers	golhā-ye zibātar	گُلهای زیباتَر
the prettiest flowers	zibātarin golhā	زیباترین گُلها

Tehran is the largest city in Iran. *tehrān bozorgtarin shahr-e irān ast.*

تهران بزرگتَرین شهرِ ایران است.

My brother's best friend lives in an old house. *behtarin dust-e barādaram dar yek khāne-ye qadimi zendegi mi-konad.*

بِهتَرین دوستِ برادرم در یک خانهٔ قدیمی زندگی می کند.

'Yalda' (winter solstice) is the longest night of the year. *shab-e 'yaldā' bolandtarin shab-e sāl ast.*

«شَبِ یَلدا» بُلَندترین شبِ سال است.

Other irregularities

Occasionally, the adjective and its comparative are different words and again there is a parallel for this in English: good → better → best.

The same principle can apply to the adjective خوب *khub* 'good' in Persian too:

khub, behtar, behtarin   خوب ← بِهتَر ← بِهترین

Although you can use خوبتر too but this is less common:

khub, khubtar, khubtarin   خوب ← خوبتر ← خوبتَرین

Showing the degree of comparison

Two nouns in a sentence are compared by the use of comparative adjectives and the preposition از *az*, meaning 'than'. There are two types of word order in Persian to express any comparison. Look at the following simple example: Tehran is colder than Shiraz.

This sentence can be translated in two ways in Persian:

۱ تهران اَز شیراز سردتر است.

۲ تهران سردتر اَز شیراز است.

Both sentences are perfectly correct and commonly used. If you look at them closely the second sentence is perhaps closer to the English word order as the comparative adjective, 'colder', separates the two nouns (cities) that are being compared. Ignoring the verbs shown in parentheses, see how closely the sentences compare:

⟶ Tehran (is) colder than Shiraz.

⟵   تِهران سردتر از شیراز (است).

In the first sentence, however, the preposition از *az* separates the two nouns that are being compared, and the comparative adjective follows the second noun:

First sentence: تهران از شیراز – سردتر – است.

Literally: Tehran *than* Shiraz – colder – is,

In either case, از *az* than always comes *before* the noun or object that is the standard or basis of comparison.

In the second sentence the word order is closer to the English, especially if you were to move the verb to the end of the sentence!

تهران سَردتر از شیراز– است.

Tehran colder than Shiraz – is.

Here are some more examples:

موتورسیکلتِ بابک از ماشینِ اَحمد تُندتَر می رَوَد.

motorsiklet-e bābak as māshin-e ahmad tondtar miravad.
Babak's motorbike goes faster than Ahmad's car.

غَذای هِندی از غَذای تایلَندی تُندتَر است.

ghazā-ye hendi az ghazā-ye tāylandi tondtar ast.

Indian food is hotter than Thai food.
(**Note:** تند *tond* means both 'fast' and 'spicy-hot'.)

گلِ لاله خیلی قَشنگتَر از گلِ میخَک است.

gol-e lāle kheyli qashangta az gol-e mikhak ast.
Tulips are much prettier than carnations.
(**Note:** خیلی 'very', adverb of intensity, can precede a comparative.)

ما خیلی زودتَر از شُما به مهمانی رَسیدیم.

mā kheyli zudtar az shomā be mehmāni rasidim.
We arrived at the party much earlier than you.

زَبانِ فارسی سَختتَر است یا زبانِ عَربی؟

zabān-e farsi sakht-tar ast yā zabān-e 'arabi?
Is Persian (language) more difficult or Arabic?

حَسَن بیشتَر پول دارَد یا بیژَن؟

hasan bishtar pul dārad yā bizhan?
Has Hasan got more money or Bizhan?
(**Note** the use of بیشتَر *bishtar* as 'more'.)

Insight

Persian comparative formation is a lot more regular than English.
You can add '-tar' to any Persian adjective to get its comparative
but you can't add '-er' to all English adjectives. You can have 'nicer'
or 'kinder' but not 'beautifuler' or 'advanceder'.

Exercise 1
Translate the following into Persian.

1 Their house is nearer to the shops.
2 Maryam's brother is much taller than my brother.
3 The tallest girl in the room is Brazilian.
4 His house is much bigger than mine, but my garden is bigger.
5 They work much harder than you.
6 You speak better Persian than Maria.
7 Tonight is warmer than last night.
8 This is the longest night of the year.

9 My best friend lives near the park.
10 This film is very long, longer than 'Dr Zhivago'.

Insight

When translating a sentence where two items are compared just translate each English word into Persian as you read it out, but don't forget to keep your verb to the last. This should give you the Persian version of all simple comparative sentences.

Exercise 2

Translate the following sentences into English:

١ امروز گَرمتر از دیروز است ولی هَنوز خیلی سرد است.

٢ اِسمِ کوچکترین بَچهٔ خواهَرم رویاست.

٣ گوشتِ مُرغ کم چربیتر است یا گوشتِ ماهی؟

٤ شما زودتر از ما به رستوران رسیدید.

٥ امروز حالَش از دیروز بِهتر است.

Exercise 3

◄) CD 1, TR 7, 03:28

Take part in a conversation with Amir, to practise comparing. You may need the following words: 'fog' is مِه, 'sand' is ماسه, 'return' is بازگشت, 'king' is پادشاه, 'like' as in 'similar' is مِثلِ, and 'bend it' as a footballing term is شوت بزن! or شوت کن!.

You	Is Isfahan or Tehran bigger?
Amir	تهران بزرگتر است. آیا لندن از تهران بزرگتر است؟
You	Yes, London is bigger than Tehran. But the weather in Tehran is warmer.
Amir	خانهٔ شما به مرکز شهر نزدیکتر است یا خانهٔ افسانه؟
You	My house is nearer to the city centre but Afsaneh's house is the nearest to the park.
Amir	بهترین فیلم امسال کدامست؟
You	'The House of Sand and Fog' is very good, 'Return of the King' is better, but the best film is 'Bend it Like Beckham'.

Exercise 4

🔊 CD 1, TR 7, 05:42

Maryam wants to know your opinion about her new dress. Translate the English into Persian and see if you can understand what Maryam is saying:

You	Maryam, what a lovely dress!
Maryam	قربانِ تو، مرسی. این لباس خواهرم است.
You	Is your sister older or younger than you?
Maryam	خواهرم چهار سال از من کوچکتر است. او کوچکترین فرزند خانواده است.

Test yourself

1. How do you form the comparative adjective in Persian?
2. Does this rule apply to all adjectives or are there adjectives, as in English, whose comparative cannot be formed in this way?
3. Where does the comparative adjective go in relation to the noun?
4. How do you form Persian superlatives?
5. What is the noun–superlative order in Persian?
6. How do you express 'than' in Persian?
7. Form the Persian comparative of the following: warm, small, pretty, good.
8. What are the superlatives of the above adjectives?
9. How are two things compared in Persian?
10. Rearrange this sentence into its correct Persian comparative order: 'My house is warmer than Ali's (house)'.

7

Where is it? What?
Whose is it? Why?

In this unit you will learn how to
- *Ask questions about time, place and actions*
- *Talk about possession ('mine', 'your', etc.)*
- *Understand different functions of question words*

Dialogue

◀) CD 2, TR 1

At the London Film Festival, Maryam meets someone who studies Persian and has been to Iran. She asks him about his trip, where he has been, for how long, when and how did he get around:

م   شما چه سالی به ایران رَفتید؟

پ   من سالِ ۲۰۰۲ به ایران رَفتَم.

م   چَند ماه در ایران بودید؟

پ   دو ماه و نیم در ایران بودم.

م   در داخِلِ ایران خیلی مسافرت کردید؟

پ   بله. به بیشترِ شهرهای بزرگِ ایران سَفَر کُردَم.

م   مَثَلاً به کُدام شهرها؟

پ   به یَزد، شیران، اِصفَهان، هَمِدان، تَبریز و اَلبَتّه تهران.

M	What year did you travel to Iran?
P	I went to Iran in (the year) 2002.
M	How many months were you in Iran?
P	I was there (in Iran) for two and a half months.
M	Did you travel within Iran?
P	Yes, I travelled to most of the large Iranian cities.
M	For example (to) which cities?
P	To Yazd, Shiraz, Esfahan, Hamedan, Tabriz and, of course, Tehran.
M	How did you get around (lit. travelled by which means)?
P	I travelled mostly by plane, bus and private car.

che?	*what?*	چه؟
che sāli?	*what year?*	چه سالی؟
be	*to*	به
raftid	*did you* (2nd person pl.) *go* [plural used for formality]	رَفتید
sāl-e do-hezār o do	*the year 2002*	سالِ ۲۰۰۲
raftam	*I went*	رَفتَم
chand?	*how many?*	چَند؟
māh	*month*	ماه
budid	*you* (2nd person pl.) *were*	بودید
nim	*half*	نیم
budam	*I was*	بودَم
dar	*in, at*	در
dākhel	*inside, within*	داخل
kheyli	*much, very, many*	خیلی

72

mosāferat kardid	you (2nd person pl.) travelled [plural used for formality]	مُسافِرَت کردید
bale	yes	بَله
bishtar	[followed by an ezafe (e)] most of, many of	بیشتَر
shahr, shahr-hā	city, cities	شهر pl. شهرها
bozorg	large, big, great	بُزُرگ
safar kardam	I travelled	سَفَرکَردَم
masalan	for example, for instance	مَثَلًا
kodām?	which?	کُدام؟
albate	of course	اَلبَتِه
bā	with, by	با
vasile-i	means, tools, (here of transport) ways	وَسیله ای
havāpeymā	aeroplane	هَواپیما
otobus	bus	اُتوبوس
māshin	car	ماشین
shakhsi	personal, private	شَخصی

Interrogative adjectives, adverbs and pronouns

Before you start learning Persian question words it's worth mentioning several general points about them. Persian question words seem, on the whole, to begin with the letters 'k' ک or 'ch' چ, similarly to the English question words, which often begin with the 'wh' sound. Another important point is that while all English question sentences start off with the question words, such as 'where are my glasses?', 'how did you get here?', 'who was that man?', and so on, the Persian question word's place in a sentence is where you expect to find the *answer*. For example if you ask 'who brought these flowers?', then the Persian interrogative 'who', کی will go at the *beginning* of the question sentence, because we are asking who the doer of the action is, i.e. we are enquiring about the identity of the 'subject' of the sentence, which always sits at the beginning of the Persian sentence or immediately after the adverb of time. However, if we ask 'where is your brother?', the Persian interrogative 'where', کجا does not start the sentence, rather it will be somewhere nearer the verb, where we expect to find adverbs of place. So the order would be 'your brother where is? You will soon get used to the fact that unlike English, the Persian interrogatives do not have a fixed opening place in the sentence but their position is where you would expect to find the noun, adjective or adverb answer.

Insight

Unlike English, Persian question words do not always start the sentence but rather they can appear at the beginning, in the middle or way down near the verb in a sentence, where you would expect to find the answer. Therefore, while you will find 'why' at the start of a sentence, you will find the question word 'when' *kojā* near the verb as if you were to say in English: 'Last night with your Iranian friends *where* did you go?' or 'With your savings you want *what* to do?'

Persian interrogatives may be used as pronouns, i.e. replacing nouns or subjects such as 'who', 'what' and 'which one', as adjectives, when they are followed by nouns as in 'which book', 'what country', 'how many days' and 'what kind of . . . ', or, finally, as adverbs, for example 'when', 'where', 'why' and 'how'.

The question words in the dialogue are interrogative adjectives, such as 'what year', چه سالی, 'how many months', چند ماه, 'which cities', کدام شهرها.

Dialogue

🔊 **CD 2, TR 1, 01:22**

Listen to this dialogue between Maryam and Ali, paying special attention to the position of question words in the sentences:

م علی، دیشب کُجا بودی؟

ا دیشب به سینما رَفتم.

م چه فیلمی دیدی؟

ا یک فیلمِ کُمدی عِشقی دیدم.

م اسمِ آن فیلم چی بود؟

ا اِسمِش «یک خَتم و چَهار عَروسی» بود.

م این فیلم چطور بود؟

ا خیلی خوب و خَنده دار بود.

م با کی به سینما رفتی؟

ا با فَرهاد به سینما رفتم.

م چرا با نامزَدت نَرَفتی؟

ا چونکه او خیلی کار داشت.

م کی به خانه برگَشتی؟

ا ساعتِ یازده به خانه برگشتم.

M	Ali, where were you last night?
A	I went to the cinema.
M	What film did you see?
A	I saw a romantic comedy (film).
M	What was it called? (What was its name?)
A	It was called 'Four Weddings and a Funeral'.
M	How was it?
A	It was very good and funny.
M	Who did you go to cinema with? (*lit.* with whom . . .)
A	I went with Farhad.
M	Why didn't you go with your fiancée?
A	Because she was very busy (had a lot to do).
M	What time did you get home? (*lit.* returned)
A	I returned home at 11 o'clock.

dishab	*last night*	دیشَب
kojā?	*where?*	کُجا؟
budi	*you* (sing.) *were*	بودی
cinamā	*cinema*	سینَما
raftam	*I went*	رَفتم
che?	*what?*	چه؟
filmi	*film*	فیلمی
komedi	*comedy*	کُمِدی
'eshqi	*romantic, lovey-dovey*	عِشقی
esm	*name, title*	اِسم
ān	*that*	آن
chi?	*what?*	چی؟
esmash	*its name*	اِسمَش
khatm	*funeral*	خَتم
chahār	*four*	چهار
'arusi	*wedding*	عروسی
in	*this*	این
chetor?	*how?*	چطور؟
khande-dār	*funny,* lit. *with laughter*	خنده دار
bā	*with*	با
ki?	*who, whom?*	کی؟
cherā?	*why?*	چرا؟
nāmzad	*fiancée*	نامزد
nāmzadat	*your fiancée*	نامزَدَت
narafti	*you did not go*	نَرَفتی

chonke	because	چونکه
kār dāsht	was busy (lit. had work)	کار داشت
key?	when?	کی؟
khāne	house	خانه
bargashti	you (sing.) returned	بَرگَشتی
sā'at	here means o'clock, hour of	ساعَت
yāzdah	eleven	یازده
bargashtam	I returned	برگشتَم

Grouping of question words

Interrogative pronouns
The following are the main interrogative pronouns:

(a) که or کی (ki) 'who', pronoun:

کی بود؟ Who was it?

آنها کی هَستند؟ Who are they?

(b) چه or چی 'what' as a pronoun ('what things') and as adjective 'which' ('which book' or 'what a nice man')

برای من چی آوردی؟ What have you brought for me?

مَریم به تو چی (چه) گفت؟ What did Maryam tell you?

(c) کُدام 'which one', pronoun (note it is not 'which book' or 'which teachers'; that would make it an interrogative adjective):

از این دو کتاب کُدام را می خواهَند؟ Which one of these two books do they want?

Interrogative adverbs
The following are some common adverbial question words or interrogative adverbs:

(a) کُجا 'where', adverb of place.

دیروز کُجا بودی؟ Where were you yesterday?

(b) کی 'when', also چه وَقت, چه موقَع .

(c) چرا 'why', also برای چی or برای چه .

(d) چطور 'how', also چگونه .

(e) چِقَدر 'how much', چَند تا 'how many'.

Use of māl مال, 'property' to show ownership

To express possession in Persian and to distinguish between 'this is my book' and 'this book is mine', you place the noun مال *māl*, lit. 'property' after the possessed and before the possessor. Note that the word مال is linked by an *ezafe* to the possessor but is not vocally linked to the possessed:

آن خانه مالِ من است. That house is mine. (lit. my property)

این کتابها مالِ آنهاست. These books are mine.

آن دو صَندَلی مالِ این اُتاق است ولی این میزِ چوبی مالِ آن اتاق است.

Those two chairs belong to this room but this wooden table belongs to that room.

Note: You can introduce a question without using any of the interrogative words but instead using the particle آیا (*ā yā*). This is usually done in written Persian:

آیا این کتاب مالِ شماست؟ *āyā in ketāb māl-e shomāst?*

Is this book yours?

آیا آن پالتو گِران اَست؟ *āyā ān pālto gerān ast?*

Is that coat expensive?'

In spoken Persian, questions that do not contain an interrogative word are usually indicated by a rising intonation at the end of the sentence, rather than the use of آیا.

Answers to questions

Both چرا *cherā* and بله *bale* mean 'yes', but the difference between them is that *bale* is the positive answer to a positive (affirmative) question. For example, if the answer to 'Is your brother here?' is positive then we *must* use بله *bale* as the answer:

آیا بَرادَرَت اینجاست؟ بله، اینجاست.

But if the question is negative and the answer is positive then چرا *cherā* must be used:

Is your brother not here? بَرادَرَت اینجا نیست؟

Yes, he is here. چرا، اینجاست.

Exercise 1
Translate the following dialogue into English:

م این عِینک مالِ کیست؟

د کُدام عِینک؟

م این عِینک آفتابی. مالِ توست داریوش؟

د نه، این عِینک مالِ من نیست، مالِ اَمیر است. این کتابها و این کلید مالِ کیست؟

م کتابها مالِ برادرم است و کلید مالِ من است.

◀ CD 2, TR 1, 02:14

Exercise 2

Give your own answers to the following questions in Persian:

۶ شما کُجا به دنیا آمدید؟	۱ اسم شما چیست؟
۷ شما روزها چکار می کنید؟	۲ اسمِ فامیلِ شما چیست؟
۸ آیا دانشجو هَستید؟	۳ خانهٔ شما کجاست؟
۹ آیا خواهر یا برادر دارید؟	۴ اسمِ مادر و پدرِ شما چیست؟
۱۰ ساعَتِ الآن چند است؟	۵ تَولُدِ شما کی اَست؟

There is no exact equivalent of 'mine' or 'yours' in Persian so, for example, to say 'this book is mine' you have to say 'this book belongs to me' using the word *māl*.

Reply to the following question:

1 What are the two most common letters found in almost all Persian question words?
2 Can you think of three Persian interrogatives (that is question words)?
3 Do Persian question words always start the sentence?
4 Does Persian have a mechanism for expressing the notion of possession such as 'mine', 'yours'?
5 When do we use 'Āyā' in Persian?
6 What would be the positive answer to a negative question?

8

Likes and dislikes

In this unit you will learn how to
- *Use the verb 'to have' (past and present)*
- *Say some more about yourself*
- *Talk about your likes and dislikes*

Dialogue

◀) CD 2, TR 2

Listen to Maryam and Dariush tell us more about themselves and talk to each other about some likes and dislikes:

م   من یک خواهر و یک برادر دارم. برادرِ من کوچکتر و
خواهرم بزرگتر است. اسم برادرِ کوچکترِ من رضاست. اسمِ
خواهرم نسرین است. من در بچگی یک گربهٔ سفید داشتَم و
برادرم یک خرگوشِ سیاه دارد. خواهرم، نسرین، حیوان در
خانه دوست ندارد. پدرم دَندانساز است و مادرم نقاش
است. ما یک خانهٔ قشنگ در مرکزِ شهر داریم. پدر و مادرم
خیلی دوست و آشنا دارند. داریوش تو چند تا خواهر و
برادر داری؟

د   من خواهر ندارَم و فَقَط یک برادر دارم. نامِ برادرِ من
اردشیر است. من دوست خیلی زیاد دارم. خانهٔ من بیرون

از شهر است. من و برادرم یک اَسب داریم. اسمِ اَسبِ ما رَخش است. در هفته من خیلی کار دارم و برای سواری وقت ندارم. من در مَدرَسه چند تا دوستِ خارجی داشتم: دو پسرِ فرانسوی، یک آمریکایی و یک دخترِ مِصری. من و آن دخترِ مصری و پسرِ آمریکایی دوچرخه داشتیم ولی آن دو پسرِ فرانسوی دوچرخه نداشتند.

م   داریوش تو غذای فرانسوی دوست داری؟

د   بله، من غذای فرانسوی دوست دارم، ولی غذای ایرانی و لبنانی بیشتر دوست دارم. تو چطور؟

م   من هم غذای ایرانی خیلی دوست دارم. ولی خواهرم غذای ژاپنی دوست دارد. تو موسیقی، فیلم و ورزش دوست داری؟

د   من موسیقی جاز، پاپ و کلاسیک دوست دارم. برادرم فوتبال و بَسکتبال دوست دارد و من خیلی تنیس دوست دارم. ما، هر دو، فیلم پلیسی خیلی دوست داریم.

Design on large metal dish, 12th–13th century

M   I have a brother and a sister. My brother is younger and my sister is older. My younger brother's name is Reza. My sister's name is Nasrin. I had a white cat in childhood and my brother has a black rabbit.

My sister, Nasrin, does not like animals in the house. My father is a dentist and my mother is a painter. We have a nice house in the centre of the city. My mother and father have many friends and acquaintances. Dariush, how many brothers and sisters do you have?

D   I don't have sisters and only have a brother. My brother's name is Ardeshir. I have very many friends. My house is outside the city. My brother and I have a horse. The name of our horse is 'Rakhsh'. I am very busy during the week and have no time for riding. I had several foreign friends at school: two French boys, one American and an Egyptian girl. The Egyptian girl, the American boy and myself had bicycles, but the two French boys did not have a bike.

M   Dariush, do you like French food?

D   Yes, I like French food, but I like Persian and Lebanese food more. How about you?

M   I also very much like Persian food. However, my sister likes Japanese food. Do you like music, films and sports?

D   I like jazz, pop and classical music. My brother likes football and basketball and I really like tennis. We both really like detective films.

khāhar	sister	خواهر
barādar	brother	برادَر
kuchaktar	smaller, younger	کوچَکتَر
bozorg-tar	bigger, older	بُزُرگتَر
Rezā	boy's name	رِضا
Nasrin	girl's name	نَسرین
bachegi	childhood	بَچِگی
gorbe	cat	گربه
sefid	white	سفید
dāshtam	I had	داشتَم
khargush	rabbit	خَرگوش
siyāh	black	سیاه

QUICK VOCAB

dārad	*he, she has*	دارَد
khāharam	*my sister*	خواهرَم
heyvān	*animal*	حیوان
dar	*in*	در
khāne	*house, home*	خانه
dust	usually *friend,* here, *liking*	دوست
-na	negative marker	نه
na-dārad	*does not have*	نَدارَد
dandānsāz	*dentist*	دَندانساز
naqqāsh	*painter*	نقّاش
markaz	*centre*	مرکَز
shahr	*city*	شهر
dārim	*we have*	داریم
kheyli	*very, much*	خیلی
dust	*friend*	دوست
va	*and*	و
āshnā	*acquaintance*	آشنا
dārand	*they have*	دارَند
chand tā	(as question) *how many?*	چَند تا
dāri	*you have*	داری
na-dāram	*I don't have*	نَدارَم
faqat	*only*	فَقَط
Ardeshir	boy's name	اَردِشیر
kheyli ziyād	*very much*	خِیلی زیاد
khāne-ye man	*my house* (lit. *house of mine*)	خانۀ مَن

birun	*outside*	بیرون
az	*of*	اَز
asb	*horse*	اَسب
mā	*us*	ما
Rakhsh	name of legendary horse	رخش
hafte	*week*	هَفته
kār	*jobs, work, things that keep one busy*	کار
kār drram	*I am busy*	کار دارَم
barāy-e	*for*	برای
savāri	*riding*	سواری
vaqt	*time*	وَقت
vaqt nadāram	*I don't have time*	وَقت نَدارم
madrese	*school*	مَدرسه
chand tā	*several*	چَند تا
khāreji	*foreign*	خارجی
dāshtam	*I had*	داشتَم

To have

The verb 'to have' داشتَن *dāshtan* is an irregular verb, more irregular than our standard irregular Persian verbs such as 'to come' آمدن *āmadan*, which we will look at in detail shortly, but not as irregular as the verb 'to be', discussed earlier.

The various forms of the verb 'to have' can be conjugated regularly but this verb does not take on any verbal prefixes such as the continuous prefix -*mi* می or the subjunctive prefix -*be* بِ that we will cover in later units.

This irregularity does not affect the formation of the simple past tense but, as with all other irregular Persian verbs, we need to know the present stem before we proceed to work out the various present tense forms of the verb. The present stem of the verb داشتن can be found in the list of irregular stems provided in the appendix.

Insight

After the verb 'to be' the next verb that sometimes defies the straightforward rules of conjugation is the Persian verb 'to have'. In its present tense it should not take the prefix -*mi* می. Nor should it take the -*mi* می with the habitual past tense. Having said that, some educated native speakers adopt this wrong use of the -*mi* prefix with the verb 'to have' making its erroneous use more common.

Present tense of داشتن 'to have'

The present stem of داشتن is دار *dār*. However, the standard present tense formation formula (shown in full in Unit 13) cannot be applied to this verb in its entirety.

The irregular nature of 'to have' in Persian dictates that this verb does not take any prefixes in its present tense forms. Therefore the general formula which is: present tense = subject endings + present stem + می -*mi* has to be modified for the verb 'to have'.

The modified formula is: present tense of داشتن = subject endings + دار *dār*.

The six forms of the present indicative of 'to have' are:

Singular	Plural
1 دارَم *dāram* I have	داریم *dārim* we have
2 داری *dāri* you have	دارید *dārid* you (pl.) have
3 دارَد *dārad* he, she, it has	دارَند *dārand* they have

The negative present tenses of 'to have' are:

	Singular	Plural
1	نَدارَم *nadāram* I do not have	نَداریم *nadārim* we do not have
2	نَداری *nadāri* you do not have	نَدارید *nadārid* you (pl.) do not have
3	نَدارَد *nadārad* he, she, it does not have	نَدارَند *nadārand* they do not have

Exercise 1

Translate into Persian:

1 Maryam and Amir have a very nice, small house.
2 I don't like Japanese food, but like Lebanese food.
3 They have a lot of work tomorrow.
4 Do you have any friends in Paris?
5 My brother's wife has six uncles (maternal).

Exercise 2

Translate into English:

من یک کُلبهٔ کوچک در کوهِستان نزدیکِ دریاچهٔ مازَندران دارم.
این کلبه نه بَرق دارد نه تِلفن ولی مَنظرهٔ آن خیلی قشنگ است.
نزدیکِ کلبه یک چِشمهٔ آب است. این کلبه دو تا سه تا صِندَلی، یک
میزِ چوبی، یک تَختِخواب بزرگ، یک آشپزخانهٔ کوچک و یک
بُخاری دیواری دارد. این کلبه دور از شهر بهترین جا برای
اِستِراحَت است.

Past tense of داشتَن

For the simple past we follow the standard formula that helps us form all past tense verbs: past tense = subject ending + past stem.

Subject endings are the same as the endings of all Persian verbs that tell you who the doer of the verb is. Their use is compulsory and without them the verb will be incomplete. They tell us exactly who the subject of any action is and therefore, unlike English, we do not need to use a subject pronoun in a Persian sentence. The subject pronouns were discussed in detail earlier in the book but the following table lists the verb ending for use in this unit.

Singular	Plural
1st م ا -am	we یم -im
2nd you ی -i	you ید -id
3rd s/he د * no suffix for past tenses	they ند -and

*د -ad is never used with the past tense verbs: this means that the third person singular of Persian past tense verbs does not have an attached subject marker or suffix.

The past stem of داشتن is formed by dropping the ن -an ending which leaves us with داشت dāsht.

The six forms of 'to have' in the simple past can be seen in the following table.

Singular	Plural
1 داشتم dāshtam I had	داشتیم dāshtim we had
2 داشتی dāshti you had	داشتید dāshtid you (pl.) had
3 داشت dāsht he, she, it had	داشتند dāshtand they had

The six negative forms are shown in the following table.

Singular	Plural
1 نداشتم nadāshtam I did not have	نداشتیم nadāshtim we did not have
2 نداشتی nadāshti you did not have	نداشتید nadāshtid you (pl.) did not have
3 نداشت nadāsht he, she, it did not have	نداشتند nadāshtand they did not have

Remember that there is no subject suffix (or ending) for the third person singular in *any* of the past tense verbs.

Exercise 3

Translate the following sentences into Persian:

1 We had two cars in Iran.
2 She had a horse, two cats, chickens and rabbits in her house in Turkey.
3 They had several friends in Tehran.
4 How much money did you have yesterday?
5 I did not have a television but had an old radio.

Exercise 4

Fill the gaps with an appropriate past tense form of the verb to have or the correct subject pronoun:

۱ من در ایران چند دوستِ ایتالیایی ـــــــــ.

۲ ـــــــــ در أن شهر خیلی دوست و أشنا داشتید؟

۳ ـــــــــ روزِ سه شَنبه خیلی کار داشت.

۴ ما سه روز برای کار در لندن بودیم ولی برای گردِش وَقت نَـــــــــ

۵ أنها چقدر پولِ یورو» ـــــــــ؟

Advanced use of present and past forms of 'to have'

In more advanced use of language, the verb 'to have', in both present and past tenses, is also used as an auxiliary verb, expressing the sense of progression of an action, i.e. that an action is taking place right now or will take place imminently, or that it was taking place when it was superseded or interrupted by another action.

In the present tense

For example, someone is telling you to 'Hurry up and get going'. The response might be:

دارَم می آیَم.   I am coming!

Or someone asks, 'What is Ali doing just now?' The reply:

علی دارد کتاب می خوانَد.   Ali is reading his book (right now).

In the past tense

'What were you doing when I called last night?':

داشتم تلویزیون تَماشا می کَردَم.   I was watching television.

داشتم از در بیرون می رَفتَم که تلفن زنگ زد.   I was about to leave when the phone rang. (*lit.* leaving through the door)

The indefinite: 'a' or 'one' added to nouns, 'some'

The status of a noun in Persian is not exactly the same as it is in English and the ideas of 'definite' or 'indefinite' do not correspond exactly to what we understand by these terms in English.

The Persian noun appears instead in two ways, the 'absolute' and the 'non-specific'. What do we mean by these terms? The noun in its *absolute* state is a noun with no attachments, no suffix or any other 'bits' joined on to it. It is the word as found in a dictionary. Such a noun can indicate both a very specific singular word and the generic. In English, the generic, which is the general term for something or a group of things, is usually rendered by the plural. For example, گل *gol* flower means both 'the flower', about which we know something already, and 'flowers' in general, as in 'I like to have flowers in the house'.

How do you render the sense of 'a house', 'a book' or 'a car' in Persian, that is, how do you form the *non-specific* also known as the *indefinite* in Persian?

Broadly speaking, a noun becomes *indefinite*, or *non-specific*, in Persian through the addition of the suffix (or attachment) ی *i* to its pure form as found in a dictionary.

indefinite = ی + noun

This is, of course, not at all dissimilar to the way in which a non-specific English noun is formed, except the 'a' is not attached the English word; the ی is joined onto the Persian word if possible: 'a book', simply means any old book, as in 'I found a book on the shelf' not a particular, specific book:

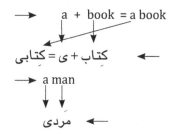

The indefinite is expressed in three ways in Persian:

1 by adding an ی to the end of the noun as just demonstrated
2 by putting the word 'one'/ 'a', یک yek, before the definite noun
3 by using both یک and ی (the most common spoken form).

Look at these examples:

a book ketābi کتابی = ی + (book) کتاب

a/one book yek ketāb یک کتاب = کتاب + (one) یک

a book yek ketābi یک کتابی = ی + کتاب + یک

If two or more nouns are joined by the 'co-ordinate' و va and are all non-specific (indefinite), the indefinite marker ی i is added to the final one only, the group being regarded as a whole:

کتاب و مداد (pencil) و قَلَم (pen) و خُودکاری (biro)

The ی i is only added to the last word in the group, which is خُودکار khodkār biro.

Writing rules

That's all there is to the formation of non-specific words in Persian! Before we move on, however, we must look at how to add an ی i to the end of a word that already ends with a vowel; words such as آقا āqā 'gentleman'; بو bu 'smell'; سینی sini 'tray'; and خانه khāne 'house'.

If the noun ends with a final, short vowel or the 'silent' he, the indefinite ی is spelt with an alef + ی i.e. (ای), that is still pronounced as i:

a house khāne-i خانه ای = ی (ا) + خانه

Care must be taken to distinguish between the final, silent he, which is simply an indicator of the presence of a final short e vowel, and the real letter he, which is a true consonant and therefore the indefinite article ی can join onto it directly:

خانه ای a house khāne-i

بچه ای bache-i a child

میوه ای a (piece of) fruit mive-i

As opposed to words that end in the letter ه/ـه h:

کوهی a mountain kuhi

ماهی a moon māhi

راهی a path or road rāhi

Similarly, if a word ends in the long vowel ی i, e.g. صندلی sandali 'chair' or طوطی tuti 'parrot', the indefinite ending will be ای i:

a chair sandali-i صندلی ای = ی (ا) + chair sandali صندلی

Other vowel endings
If the word ends in either an ا ā such as آقا āqā 'gentleman' or و u as in مو mu 'hair', the ی of the indefinite marker is simply doubled to compensate for two vowels coming together:

a gentleman āqā-i آقایی = i (a, one) یی + gentleman āqā آقا

a hair mu-i مویی = i (a, one) یی + hair mu مو

An alternative to doubling the ی of the indefinite marker is inserting a hamze over a bearer (ئ) between the final long vowels ا ā and و u and the indefinite article ی:

a foot pā-i پائی or پایی ← پا

a hair mu-i موئی or مویی ← مو

92

Writing rules at a glance

Example	Indefinite ending	Example	Vowel ending word
صَندَلی ای	ای	صَندَلی ای	ی
خانه ای – میوه ای	ای	خانه – میوه	ه – ـه
مویی	یی	مو	و
آقایی	یی	آقا	ا

The indefinite marker ی *i* can accompany a plural as well as a singular word and the plural, non-specific noun will be translated as 'some' instead of 'a' or 'one':

کتابهایی *ketābhā-i* some books

شهرهایی *shahrhā-i* some cities

If the most common form of Persian plural, i.e. ها *hā*, is used then the plural of all nouns formed in this way will inevitably end with the long vowel ا *ā* and the indefinite of all plurals made this way will always be هایی or هائی, that is the ی will be doubled. For example:

some books کتابهائی or کتابهایی

some girls دُخترهایی

some flower pots or vases گُلدانهائی or گُلدانهایی

Exercise 5

Form the indefinite of the following:

پَرَنده	شَب	کِشوَر
اُستاد	صُبح	میز
مَرد	هَفته	کوه
همسایه	آقا	کِتاب
خوابگاه	پا	دوستان

شَهر	راه	صَندَلی
اَسبها	ماهی	دَر
خانه	سِتاره	روز

Exercise 6

Translate the following into Persian:

a man	a house	some boys
a cat	a star	a flower
some cities	some fruits	a child

9

Grammar reference unit

Time for another pause to look at some more grammatical terminology before we start learning proper verbs and all the different tenses that we need.

Verbs

Verbs are words or phrases that express what someone or something is doing or feeling, or the state somebody or something is in or is becoming. In many Indo-European languages, verbs can be grouped together according to the way they behave or conjugate. In some languages, and English is an example, verb conjugation is very simple. For example, the verb 'to cost' possesses only three forms: 'cost', 'costs' and 'costing'. (Similarly the verb 'to cut'.)

Persian verbs are not as simple to conjugate as English verbs but compared with German or French, for example, they are still a lot easier to learn.

Persian has developed a very logical system for verb conjugation. There are very simple formulas that the learner can quickly grasp in order to arrive at the correct form of verbs for any sentence. However, like most other languages, Persian verbs are either regular or irregular. The irregularity of a Persian verb affects it only in the present tenses (as in 'I travel', 'you are going' or 'they want to sell'). Otherwise the formulas for conjugation of verbs are very straightforward.

Before we start on the verbs it is important to get used to certain terminology.

In many languages a verb consists of the following parts.

Infinitive

This is the form by which the verb is usually listed in dictionaries or is referred to. In English there is only one pattern for infinitives. It is always 'to read', 'to speak', 'to dance'. In Persian, as we shall see very soon, infinitives fall into three distinct patterns.

Root

This is the most basic form of the verb to which other prefixes or suffixes are added to form other parts. 'Do' is the root of 'to do' and '-ing' or '-es' can be added to create other forms of the same verb.

The Persian verb has two roots or *stems* as it is also sometimes called. I find it easier to think of the infinitive of the verb as an egg with the egg white and the egg yolk as its two roots or stems. Each can be separated from the whole and, by adding different ingredients to the roots, other forms of the verb can be made, in exactly the same way that mayonnaise or meringues can be made, starting with the base material of either an egg yolk or an egg white.

Mood

This is, if you like, how a verb expresses itself to tell us whether it is indicative, subjunctive, conditional or imperative (as in giving commands). For a culinary equivalent think of milk chocolate, plain chocolate, white chocolate and cooking chocolate as different moods of the same verb.

Indicative mood states a real action such as 'I arrived yesterday' or 'I am writing a letter'.

Subjunctive is the mood for expression of the desired, the anticipated, the feared, the possible, obligatory, doubtful, implied or conditional action, e.g. 'I hope to go to Iran in the summer', 'He may find a cheaper ticket' or 'They don't want to leave London, but he has to find a new job'.

In other words, in opposition to the indicative, which is the mood of real action, the subjunctive is used in situations where the realization of the action is not considered as certain.

Tense

This is the form of the verb indicating the time of the action, as in past or present or future etc.: 'I went to Canada last summer', 'They are sitting in the car', 'We will be in Europe next July'.

....

Insight

Don't forget the very important endings that tell you who is doing the action! Without them you won't know who is doing what. These endings are the short forms of the verb 'to be' in the present tense.

....

10

What are you learning?

In this unit you will learn how to
- *Use simple verbs*
- *Form the simple past tense*
- *Use different verbs for situations in the past*

Dialogue

◄» CD 2, TR 3

Listen to the informal chat between two people finding out about what the other does. Listen closely to the verbs appearing at the end of each sentence:

● شما اینجا دانشگاه می رَوید؟

■ بله، من دانشجو هستم.

● چه می خوانید؟

■ زبان می خوانَم.

● چه زبانی می خوانید؟

■ زبانِ فارسی می خوانَم. شما چه می خوانید؟

● من هم زَبان می خوانم.

■ شما چه زبانی می خوانید؟

● من فرانسه می خوانم.

شما کُجا فارسی یاد گِرفتید؟ ■

در تهران فارسی یاد گرفتَم. ●

چند سال در تهران بودید؟ ■

سه سال آنجا بودم. ●

کِی به تهران رفتید؟ ■

هفت سالِ پیش به تهران رفتم. ●

کِی برگَشتید؟ ■

چهار سالِ پیش برگشتم. ●

در تهران چه می کردید؟ دانشجو بودید؟ ■

نَخیر، دانشجو نَبودم. کار می کردم. ●

کجا کار می کردید؟ ■

در سفارتِ اسپانیا کار می کردم. ●

تهران چطور بود؟ ■

تهران خیلی خوب بود وَلی اصفهان بِهتَر بود. تهران خیلی ●
شُلوغ است و به قشنگی اصفهان هم نیست.

●	Do you attend university here?
■	Yes, I am a student.
●	What do you study (*lit.* read)?
■	I study languages.
●	What language do you study?
■	I study Persian. What do you read/study?
●	I study languages too.
■	What language do you study?
●	I study French.
■	Where did you learn Persian?
●	I learnt Persian in Tehran.
■	How many years were you in Tehran?
●	I was there (for) three years.
■	When did you go to Tehran?
●	I went to Tehran seven years ago.

■ When did you return?
● I came back four years ago.
■ What did you do in Tehran? Were you (a) student?
● No, I was not (a) student. I was working.
■ Where did you work?
● I worked in the Spanish Embassy.
■ How was Tehran?
● Tehran was very good (nice), but Esfahan was better. Tehran is very busy and is not as beautiful as Esfahan.

dāneshgāh	university	دانِشگاه
miravid	you go	می رَوید
dāneshju	student	دانِشجو
hastam	I am	هَستَم
che?	what?	چِه؟
mikhānid	you read	می خوانید
zabān	language	زَبان
zabāni	a language	زبانی
mikhānam	I read	می خوانم
ham	also	هَم
farānce	French	فرانسِه
kojā?	where?	کَجا؟
yād gereftid	you learnt	یاد گِرِفتید
yād gereftam	I learnt	یاد گِرِفتَم
chand?	how many?	چَند؟
sāl	year	سال
budid	you were	بودید
budam	I was	بودَم

100

key?	*when?*	کِی؟
be	*to*	بِه
raftid	*you went*	رَفتید
sāl-e pish	*year(s) ago*	سالِ پیش
haft	*seven*	هَفت
raftam	*I went*	رَفتَم
bargashtid	*you returned*	بَرگَشتید
bargashtam	*I returned*	بَرگَشتَم
dar	*in, at*	دَر
che mikardid?	*what did you do?*	چِه می کَردید؟
nakheyr	polite *no*	نَخیر
nabudam	*I was not*	نبودَم
kār	*work, job*	کار
kār mikardam	*I worked*	کارمی کَردم
kār mikardid	*you worked*	کارمی کردید
sefārat	*embassy*	سفارت
espāniā	*Spain*	اِسپانیا
chetor?	*how*	چطور؟
chetor bud?	*how was it?*	چطور بود؟
kheyli khub	*very good*	خیلی خوب
vali	*but, however*	وَلی
behtar	*better*	بِهتَر
sholugh	*busy, crowded*	شُلوغ
ast	*is*	اَست
be qashanigi	*as pretty as*	به قَشَنگی
nist	*is not*	نیست

The infinitive

All Persian verbs are derived from the infinitive root. In Persian dictionaries the verbs are listed in their infinitive form.

All Persian infinitives end in ن ‎-*an* (as all German infinitives end in -*en*, e.g. *spielen*). For example:

رَفتَن *raftan* to go   آمَدَن *āmadan* to come

خَریدَن *kharidan* to buy   نِشستَن *neshastan* to sit

بُردَن *bordan* to win   پَریدَن *paridan* to jump

پُختَن *pokhtan* to cook   دادَن *dādan* to give

دَویدَن *davidan* to run

If you look more closely, however, you will see that Persian infinitives actually have three distinct endings which are: تَن‎– ‎-*tan*, دَن‎– ‎-*dan* and یدَن‎– ‎-*idan*.

Insight

Delete all the '-an' endings of Persian infinitives and what you are left with is your past stem. Plug this information into the various formulas for making past tenses and you get the verbal form you need.

Verb formation

Simple past

Stage I

By far the easiest Persian verbs to form are the past tense verbs, that is verbs referring to actions that happened in the past. The main component that will enable you to form Persian past tense verbs is the past stem. The past stem, also known as the short infinitive, is made by simply dropping the ن ‎-*an* ending of the infinitive.

For example, the past stem (or short infinitive) of the preceding examples, after dropping the ن‎ -an, will be:

Infinitive		Past stem (short infinitive)	
رفتَن	→	رَفت	raft
نِشَستَن	→	نِشَست	neshast
پُختَن	→	پُخت	pokht
آمَدَن	→	آمَد	āmad
بُردَن	→	بُرد	bord
دادَن	→	داد	dād
خَریدَن	→	خَرید	kharid
پَریدَن	→	پَرید	parid
گُفتَن	→	گُفت	goft

Look closely at these short infinitives. Can you work out their common features? Look even closer. What are the endings of the past stems given here as examples in the right-hand column? It should be fairly obvious that all Persian past stems end in either ت‎ *t* or د‎ *d*.

The past stem in Persian has another special feature. It is identical to the third person singular past tense of that verb, i.e. the same as an action done by the doer in the simple past. So just by using the past stem on its own you can convey a very simple, but perfectly accurate, idea in Persian, such as 'Maryam went', 'he jumped', 'Darius said' and 'she arrived'. Bearing in mind that, in Persian word order, the verb always comes at the end of the sentence, and that there is no gender ('he' or 'she' is always او‎) these four short sentences can be translated as:

Maryam went.	مریم رَفت.
He jumped.	او پَرید.
Darius said.	داریوش گُفت.
She arrived.	او آمَد.

How about using the following combinations as subjects (that is the agents or doers) of the verb to form your own sentences using those same verbs: 'my mother', 'his younger brother', 'our guest' and 'her Iranian friend'? These are all third person, singular subjects. Your sentences should look like these:

My mother went.	مادَرم رَفت.
His younger brother jumped.	بَرادَر کوچَکَش پَرید.
Our guest said . . .	مهمانِ ما گُفت...
Her Iranian friend arrived.	دوستِ ایرانیَش آمَد.

As you can see, even before learning to form the Persian verbs in full you can easily create short sentences.

Insight

If you look up a verb in a Persian dictionary you'll find it in its infinitive form. Unlike English infinitives that appear in the uniform pattern of 'to go', to eat' or 'to buy', for example, the Persian infinitives have three distinct endings of '-tan', '-dan' or '-idan'; basically they all end in '-an', a little like the German infinitive that all end in '-en'.

Stage II

Apart from the past stem, which is the main component of past tense verbs, we need another ingredient before we construct a Persian verb referring to an action done in the past. This crucial ingredient is the subject verb ending, which is an essential part of the Persian verb. The English verb, on its own, does not tell us who the agent is. We say: 'I went', 'you went', 'we went', 'they went', 'she went' and so on. It is therefore crucial that a proper name or a pronoun or noun is used in the English sentence to indicate who the doer of the action is. In Persian however, the doer of the verb must be clearly represented in the structure of the verb, which means a suffix is attached as a verb ending. This will show us who the subject is.

The good news is that you will only have to learn these endings once. Incidentally, once we reach the unit on present tense verbs you will see that, with one small exception, the same endings are used for present tenses too.

The following table shows you the subject of the verb in the endings or suffixes in Persian and demonstrates to which pronoun or person they correspond:

Singular	Plural
1st م ا *-am*	we یم *-im*
2nd you ی *-i*	you ید *-id*
3rd s/he *no suffix*	they ند *-and*

Conjugation, or verb formation, in Persian is so regular that you can actually use a simple formula to construct almost all the verbs of your choice.

The formula for simple past tense in Persian is: simple past = past stem + personal endings.

Let us start with one of the simplest examples and work our way through. How would you say 'I went' in Persian?

To begin with, let us find what the *infinitive* of the verb 'to go' is in Persian. The vocabulary at the back of the book or any good dictionary should tell you that 'to go' in Persian is: رفتن *raftan*. Remember, though, that in the dictionary you look up 'go' and not 'to go'.

Can you extract the past stem from the infinitive رفتن? All you have to do is drop the ن *-n* from the ending: رفتن → رفت *raft*.

Next, look for the verb ending that corresponds to 'I', which the table should give you as: م *-am*. Now put these ingredients in our simple past formula: 'I went' = رفت + م = رفتم *raftam*.

How about 'you went'? Again as in the above example, find the corresponding subject ending for 'you' singular which is ی *-i*, therefore: 'you went' = رفت + ی = رفتی *rafti*.

Now try 'she went' in Persian. What is the subject ending for third person singular that corresponds to 'he' or 'she'? The table will show you that there is no ending for the third person singular subject. So our formula will look like this: 'she went' = رفت + _ = رفت *raft*.

Reminder: The third person singular of any Persian verb referring to the simple past is exactly the same as the past stem of that verb.

Note: As Persian verbs always contain an ending which tells us who the subject is, there is rarely any need to use a subject pronoun in the sentence. For example, to translate the sentence 'we arrived', it is enough to say آمدیم *āmadim*, and it is not necessary to translate the 'we' as well, since the ending یم *im*, already indicates who is the agent of the verb 'to arrive'. However, subject pronouns are used for extra emphasis, for example, if we want to stress the fact that it was *we* who arrived and not another group then the sentence can be translated as ما آمدیم *mā āmadim.*

Exercise 1

Complete the following sentences using the appropriate subject verb endings.

۱ شما به خانهٔ علی رفت...

۲ آنها، صبح به بازار رفت...

۳ ما دیروز در یک چلوکبابی ناهار خورد...

۴ تو کی به لندن آمد...؟

۵ دیشب برادرِ تو را در سینما دید...

۶ مریم و بابک در کتابخانه بود...

۷ من دیروز در خانه ماند...

۸ من و برادرم یک گربهٔ سفید داشت...

۹ دیشب هوا سرد بود...

۱۰ شما چند روز پیش به تهران رسید ...؟

Insight

Remember that there is no subject ending for an action done by he/she or it, in the simple and habitual past. The 3rd person singular doer of a verb is conspicuous by the absence of a subject indicator. He/she or it are not represented by a suffix stuck to the end of the verb in these two types of past tense verbs.

···

Exercise 2
🔊 **CD 2, TR 3, 01:20**

Translate the following sentences into Persian:

1 She came to our house last night.
2 I was in Shiraz for three years.
3 We arrived in London two days ago.
4 Maryam and Ali saw a very good film on Saturday.
5 Did you (sing.) buy anything in the market this morning?

Abu Reyhan Biruni, 11th-century
mathematician, Lalleh Park, Tehran

Things to remember

- Persian verbs have three distinct endings, 'tan', '-dan' and '-idan', from which you can extract two vital bits of information to form your various verbs such as 'I went' or 'she goes' or 'they used to buy'. These two vital ingredients are your past stems and present stems.
- The simplest Persian verb form is the simple past tense such as '**we went** to a museum in Tehran' or '**I bought** a nice rug yesterday'. This is made by using the formula (going from right to left): subject ending + past stem (that is the infinitive without -an).

←——————

- The subject endings are:

‫یم‬ -im	‫م‬ -am
‫ید‬ -id	‫ی‬ -i
‫ند‬ -and	**no suffix

Reply to the following questions.

1 What information can a Persian infinitive give the learner?
2 What are the common Persian infinitive endings?
3 What is the simplest Persian verb form to make?
4 How do we know who is the subject (the doer) of the Persian verb?
5 The short infinitive or the past stem is identical to what?

11

How did you get here
so quickly?

In this unit you will learn how to
- *Describe how things happened or were done*
- *Describe where things happened or were done*
- *Describe in what manner things happened or were done*

Adverbs

What are adverbs? Adverbs are words that affect the meaning of a verb, an adjective or another adverb and are mainly used to nuance the action of verbs, for example, in the sentences 'she ran quickly' or 'you spoke beautifully', the words 'quickly' and 'beautifully' are adverbs, giving more information about the verbs 'ran' and 'spoke' respectively.

An adverb can also affect an adjective as in: 'I saw a very pretty bird'. Here the adverb 'very' intensifies the meaning of the adjective 'pretty'.

And finally, an adverb can add more emphasis to another adverb, as in 'he walks very quickly'. Here 'very' emphasizes the sense of 'quickly', itself an adverb describing the state of the verb 'walk'.

Before we look at some examples of common Persian adverbs I must remind you that in Persian, adverbs and adjectives often look the same. For example the word 'pretty' can mean both 'beautiful' or 'beautifully' depending on what part of the sentence it is used to describe:

نامهٔ قَشَنگ شما رِسید. Your beautiful letter arrived.

شما قَشَنگ می نویسید. You write beautifully.

In the first sentence, the word قَشَنگ *qashang* means 'pretty' and is an *adjective* for 'letter', but, in the second sentence, قَشَنگ means 'beautifully' and is an *adverb* for the verb 'you write'.

However, some adverbs, such as 'never' هَرگِز, 'now' – الآن اَکنون, 'still' هَنوز, 'suddenly' نا گهان, 'usually' معمولاً, 'very' خیلی and so on, only ever act as adverbs and cannot be used as adjectives.

Adverbs of time

Some common adverbs of time are:

today	اِمروز
tonight	اِمشب
tomorrow	فَردا
yesterday	دیروز
last night	دیشب
this year	اِمسال
now	اَکنون
never	هَرگِز
always	هَمیشه
sometimes	گاهی
often	اَغلَب
later	بَعداً

Adverbs of place

Any word that tells us *where* an action is taking place but here are some general adverbs of place:

there	آنجا
here	اینجا

up	بـالا
down	پـایین
front	جِلو
back	عقب
outside	بیرون–خـارج
inside	دَرون – داخل

Adverbs of manner

For sequence

first, second, fourth, tenth, etc.	اَوَل، دُوم، چَهـارم، دَهم
then	سِپَس
time to time	دَمـادم
then	پَس
one after the other	پُشتِ سرِ هم
continuously	پیاپی
one by one	یکی یکی

For quantity

little	کم
much, very	زیـاد
many, much, very	بسیار
much, very	خیلی
little, a bit	اند
a bit, just a little, a touch	کُرده

Many adjectives such as 'fast', 'slow', 'pretty', 'ugly', 'good', 'bad' and so on can be used as adverbs. These phrases can be used similarly (and some can double as adjectives):

friendly	دوستانه
luckily, fortunately	خوشبختانه
unfortunately	بَدبختانه
gradually, 'slowly, slowly', 'calmly, calmly'	آرام آرام
fast, quick (as adj.), fast, quickly (as adv.)	تُند
with enmity, angrily	خَصمانه
smilingly, cheerfully	خَندان
in tears, tearfully	گِریان
with difficulty	به دُشواری
by force, forcibly, grudgingly	به زور – به زَحمَت
on foot	پیاده
with hesitation, reluctantly	با تَردید

Tools, equipment, modes of transport, etc., can also be used as adverbs. These are often used in conjunction with the preposition با meaning 'by' or 'with':

by air, by aeroplane	با هواپیما
with the hammer	با چَکُش
with a biro, pen	با خودکار
by ship	با کَشتی

Exercise 1

1 We ate our food very quickly.
2 They often wrote nice thank you letters.
3 Luckily, she was a very friendly neighbour.
4 I always saw Maryam in the mornings.
5 He usually lived in that big house with his family.
6 We went to Shiraz last month but unfortunately the weather was not good.

7 Maria dances beautifully.
8 They spoke slowly and we understood well.
9 Did you call them immediately?
10 Fortunately, I had an umbrella.

Exercise 2

Identify the adverbs in the sentences that follow and then translate
the sentences into English:

١ ناگَهان ساعتِ سه صُبح بیدار شدم و أهسته از اتاق بیرون أمدم.

٢ او خیلی نِگران بود.

٣ خوشبَختانه زود به فرودگاه رسیدَند.

۴ او هنوز در لندن است.

۵ ما دیشبِ خیلی دیر به خانه آمدیم.

۶ شما فقط ده دلار دارید؟

٧ من غذای ایرانی دوست دارم، مَخصوصاً باقالی پلو.

٨ آنوقتِ شَب همۀ رستوران ها بسته بودند.

٩ نامۀ تو اقلاً سه روزِ پیش رسید.

١٠ خانۀ ما به پارک نزدیک است.

12

Have you seen Mina's new house?

In this unit you will learn how to
- *Recognize and form other verb forms*
- *Use 'but'*
- *Use 'other' with negative verbs*

Dialogue

🔊 CD 2, TR 4

Listen to Maryam and Amir talking about their friends' living arrangements.

م	اميرِ خانهٔ جديدِ مينا را ديده ای؟
ا	نه، خانهٔ جديدِ او را نديده ام. مگر او با ياسَمَن و پَری زندگی نمی کرد؟
م	نه مينا ديگر در آن خانه نيست. ياسمن برای يکسال به آلمان رفته است و پَری پيشِ خانواده اش برگشته است.
ا	پس مينا حالا کجاست؟
م	او يک اُتاق در يک خانهٔ نو پيدا کرده است.
ا	اين خانه مالِ کيست؟

م خانه مالِ خالهٔ یکی از دوستانِ میناست. ولی صاحبخانه و شوهرَش در انگلستان زندگی می کنُند و خانه را اجاره داده اَند.

أ تو این خانه را دیده ای؟

م وقتی بچه بودم و به مدرسه می رفتَم، هرروز از جلوی این خانه می گُذَشتم، چون این خانه و مدرسه ام هر دو در یک خیابان بود. داریوش و خواهرش چند هفته پیش با مینا به یک مهمانی در آن خانه رفته بودند.

أ این خانه کجاست و چند تا اتاق دارد؟

م در خیابانِ فردوسی است.

أ کُجای خیابانِ فردوسی؟ عموی من هم تا پارسال در خیابانِ فردوسی زندگی می کرد.

م نزدیکِ سینما شَهرفرنگ، دُرُست یک کوچه بالاتر از پیتزا پاتوق. پلاک ۱۹۸ خیابانِ فردوسی.

أ این خانه باغ هم دارد؟

م یک باغچهٔ کوچولو دارد، ولی خیلی تمیز و جا دار است. سه تا اُتاق خوابِ بُزُرگ، دو تا حَمام، یک سالن و آشپَز خانهٔ بزرگ و مُجَهَز.

أ به! به! پس اُمیدوارم که مینا هرچه زودتر یک مهمانی منزِل مُبارکی بِدَهَد و ما را هم دَعوت بِکُنَد!

M	Amir, have you seen Mina's new house?
A	No, I haven't seen her new house. Did she not use to live with Yasaman and Pari?
M	No, she is no longer in that house. Yasaman has gone to Germany for a year and Pari has returned to her family.
A	So where is Mina now?
M	She has found a room in a new house.

A	Whose house is this?
M	The house belongs to the (maternal) aunt of one of Mina's friends. However, the owner and her husband live in the UK and has rented out the house.
A	Have you seen this house?
M	When I was little and used to go to school, I would pass by this house every day, because this house and my school were in the same street. A few weeks ago, Dariush and his sister went to a party in that house with Mina.
A	Where is this house and how many rooms does it have?
M	It is in Ferdosi Avenue.
A	Whereabouts in Ferdosi Avenue? My (paternal) uncle used to live in Ferdosi Avenue until last year.
M	Near Shahr-e farang (*lit.* kaleidoscope) Cinema, exactly one side street up from Pizza Patoq (*lit.* pizza hang-out). Number 198 Ferdosi Avenue.
A	Does this house have a garden too?
M	It has a small flower garden/patio, but it's very clean and spacious: three large bedrooms, two bathrooms, one drawing room and a large, well-equipped kitchen.
A	Wow! I hope Mina gives a house-warming party very soon and invites us too!

new	جَدید	*school*	مدرسه
have you seen	دیده ای	*I used to go*	می رَفتم
I have not seen	نَدیده اَم	*in front of, by*	جلوی
but . . .	مَگَر	*I used to pass*	می گُذشتَم
used not to live	زِندگی نمی کَرد	*because*	چون
		my school	مدرسه اَم
with negative verb no longer, no more	دیگَر	*both of us*	هر دو
		a few weeks ago	چَند هَفته پیش
one year	یک سال	*party*	مِهمانی
Germany	آلمان	*they had gone*	رَفته بودَند
has gone	رَفته اَست	*where is it?*	کُجاست؟

116

to (used for people)	پیشِ
her family	خانِواده اَش
has returned	بَرگَشتِه اَست
now	حالا
room	اُتاق
she has found	پیداکرده اَست
owner, landlord/ lady	صاحِبخانه
husband	شوهَر
her husband	شوهَرش
they are living	زِندگی می کُنند
they have rented out	اِجارِه دادِه اَند
have you seen?	دیده ای؟
when, at the time that	وقتی
I was a child	بَچِه بودم
garden	باغ
small garden	باغچِه
tiny, very small	کوچولو
clean	تَمیز
spacious	جادار
bedroom	اُتاق خواب
bath, bathroom	حَمام
lit. *salon, hall, big room*	سالُن
kitchen	آشپزخانه
how many?	چَند تا
where in?	کُجای؟
paternal uncle	عمو
until, up to	تا
last year	پارسال
used to live	زندگی می کرد
near to	نَزدیکِ
exactly	دُرُست
side street	کوچِه
further up	بالاتر
lit. *favourite meeting place where people hang out;* here, a name	پاتوق
plaque, door number	پِلاک
198	۱۹۸
well equipped	مجهز
how lovely!	به! به!
I hope	اُمیدوار
as soon as possible	هرچه زودتر
house warming	منزِل مبارکی
(subj.) *that she gives*	بِدهد
us too	ما را هم
(subj.) *that she invites*	دَعوَت بِکُنَد

QUICK VOCAB

Many of the verbs used in the dialogue are not the simple past tense verbs that we have seen in the previous units. The verbs refer to actions that had, for example, happened at some point in the past and their effects are either still relevant (such as 'she has found a room') or no longer relevant (such as 'went to a party'). These verbs are discussed in detail later in this unit.

But before we look at the variation on the past tense verbs, let us look at two other important and useful points.

Use of 'but' مگَر , a conjunction question word

When the questioner uses the question word *magar* مگَر with a negative sentence, he or she expects the answer 'yes' and if مگَر is used in a positive sentence it indicates that he or she expects the answer 'no'.

For example مگَر in a negative question: مگَر شما علی را نمی شناسید؟ 'But don't you know Ali?' means that the questioner really expects the addressee to know Ali and to answer 'yes'. The 'yes' answer to these questions is not بلِه *bale*, but چِرا *cherā*.

A positive sentence with مگَر would be like this: مگَر او خیلی پول دارد؟ 'but does he have a lot of money?' The answer to this is expected to be 'no'. 'No, he doesn't have much money'.

Use of دیگر with negative words

دیگر *digar* 'other' acts as an adjective when it qualifies a noun and means 'other' or sometimes 'more' if it is used with a positive verb, such as 'I want the other book' آن کتاب دیگر را می خواهم or 'the other day' روز دیگر. However, if دیگر is used as an *adverb* with a *negative verb* it means 'no longer' or 'no more'.

دیگر به لَندَن نَرَفتند. They no longer went to London.

دیگر پول نداریم. We have no more money. We no longer have money.

Forming the past continuous

In order to form the other past tense verbs in Persian you simply need to expand on the 'formula' that we used for the simple past tense which is: simple past = subject ending + past stem.

The next tense formed from the past stem is the *imperfect* or the *past continuous*. This refers to habitual actions in the past, such as 'I used to live near a lake', as well as actions that continued over a period of time or were in progress at some moment in the past such as 'I was walking along the road'.

Imperfect or *past continuous* (also known as *habitual past* in some books) is formed by adding the suffix می *mi* to the simple past: past continuous/imperfect = simple past + می.

Compare the two tenses given in the following example:

Simple past	Imperfect
I came آمَدَم *āmadam*	می آمَدَم *mi āmadam* I used to come, was coming
you came آمَدی *āmadi*	می آمَدی *mi āmadi* you used to come, were coming
he, she, it came آمَد *āmad*	می آمَد *mi āmad* he, she, it used to come, was coming
we came آمَدیم *āmadim*	می آمَدیم *mi āmadim* we used to come, were coming
you (pl.) came آمَدید *āmadid*	می آمَدید *mi-āmadid* you (pl.) used to come, were coming
they came آمَدَند *āmadand*	می آمَدَند *mi āmadand* they used to come, were coming

Here are some examples in use:

مریم هر سه شنبه به کلاسِ نَقاشی می رَفت.

maryam har seshambe be kelās-e naqqāshi miraft.
Maryam used to go to painting class every Tuesday.

من تا سال ۱۳۷۲ در ایران زندگی می کردم. *man tā sāl-e hezār o sisado haftādo do dar irān zendegi mikardam.* I used to live in Iran until 1372.

وقتیکه جوان بودید تعطیلات کجا می رفتید؟

vaqtike javān budand ta'tilāt kojā miraftid?
Where did you use to go on holiday when you were young?

Note that the verbs 'to be' and 'to have' *do not* take the می *mi* prefix in the past continuous tense.

> ### Insight
> Adding a *mi* می to the simple past creates the imperfect or the English equivalent of *used to* ... e.g. 'I was going' or 'I used to go' is *mi-raftam* می رفتم.

Forming the perfect and pluperfect

The next group of verbs are compound forms that are made using the *past participle*, such as 'I have bought a very pretty hat' or 'I had seen that carpet in a shop in Kerman'. The first sentence refers to an action that was completed in the past while it maintains a link to the present time, i.e. the hat was purchased in the past tense but the sentence hints that the result of the purchase, i.e. the hat, is still very much around and part of the present time. The tense of the verb of this sentence is known as the *perfect tense*.

The second sentence, however, refers to an action that was achieved at a point in the remote past and maintained some relevance for a time but it no longer has any bearing on the present time. This tense is known as the *pluperfect*. It could be said that the pluperfect is the past tense of the perfect tense.

Formation of both of these compound tenses requires what is referred to as the *past participle.* The past participle is then placed in the appropriate formulas for the construction of the perfect and pluperfect tenses.

The past participle is very easily formed. All we need to do is add a final ـه/ه *h* to the past stem, e.g. the verb 'to buy' is خریدن. The past stem of the verb, which if you recall is the same as the short infinitive, is formed by dropping the final ن *an*. Therefore the past stem of خریدن is خرید *kharid*. The past participle is then formed by adding a ـه/ه *h* to this:

خَرید + ه = خَریده *kharide* bought

رَفتَن ← رَفت + ـه = رَفته *rafte* gone

دیدن ← دید + ه = دیده *dide* seen

پیشرَفتَن ← پیشرَفت + ـه = پیشرَفته *pishrafte* advanced, modern

Forming the perfect tense

The perfect (or *past narrative* tense as it is sometimes known) is formed by adding the short forms of the present tense of the verb 'to be' (those that are used after nouns ending in vowels) to the *past participle*: perfect tense = short forms of the verb 'to be' + past participle.

The short forms of the verb 'to be' will act as the subject endings of the verb, telling us who is the agent of the action. Do you remember what these short forms of 'to be' are?

Singular	Plural
اَم *am* I am	ایم *im* we are
ای *i* you are	اید *id* you (pl.) are
اَست *ast* he, she, it is	اَند *and* they are

Using the formula we can work out what the Persian for 'I have gone' is:

'to go' = رَفتَن → past stem = رَفت

past participle = رَفته = رَفت + ه

rafte-am رَفته اَم = رَفته + اَم

The six cases of the perfect tense of 'to go' are shown in the following table:

Singular	Plural
رَفته اَم I have gone	رَفته ا یم we have gone
رَفته ا ی you have gone	رَفته ا ید you (pl.) have gone
رَفته اَست he, she, it has gone	رَفته اَند they have gone

The negative of this tense is formed by prefixing *na* نـ to the participle: 'you (pl.) have not gone' = نَرفته ا ید, 'I've not eaten' = نَخورده اَم, 'you've not said' = نَگفته ا ی

Uses of the perfect

The perfect tense expresses the present result of an action completed in the past:

مَریم آمده است. Maryam has come. (i.e. she arrived, she is here)

آنها از مَنچستر آمده اند و امشب اینجا می مانَند. They have arrived from Manchester and are spending the night here.

It can also indicate an action accomplished in an era considered as closed, for example talking about historical facts that are still relevant to today or speaking of long ago. In English, however, the simple past is the more commonly used tense for these instances:

کورُوش پادشاه دادگری بوده است. Kurosh was a just king.

(lit. has been a just king)

Forming the pluperfect

The pluperfect, also known as the *remote past*, is formed with the past participle followed by the simple past tense of the verb 'to be': pluperfect tense = simple past of 'to be' + past participle.

The six cases of the pluperfect of 'to buy' are shown in the following table:

Singular	Plural
خریده بودم I had bought	خریده بودیم we had bought
خریده بودی you had bought	خریده بودید you (pl.) had bought
خریده بود he, she, it had bought	خریده بودند they had bought

Uses of the pluperfect

The following examples demonstrate the use of the pluperfect in Persian:

وقتی رسیدَم همهٔ دوستانم رفته بودند. When I arrived all of my friends had gone.

این کتاب را سه سال پیش نوشته بود. She had written this book three years ago.

تا امروز او را ندیده بودیم. We had not seen him until today.

Note that in English the simple past may sometimes be used instead of the pluperfect.

Exercise 1

Translate the following into Persian:

1 Maryam is asleep in that room. (**Note:** Persian uses 'has slept' for the English present.)
2 We have never been (gone) to Iran.
3 You have lived in Africa before.
4 Their friends have arrived from Paris.
5 I have stayed in this small hotel.

Exercise 2

Translate into English:

۱ از دیروز تا حالا به اداره نیآمده است.

۱ از صبح تا حالا در پارک بوده ام.

۳ برای شام خوراک مرغ و سبزیجات پُخته ایم.

۴ چند سال در ایران زندگی کرده اید؟

۵ آنها سه بار به اصفهان رفته اند.

Insight

Pluperfect tenses (as in: 'we had seen') are used more frequently in Persian compared to English. In English a simple past tense is used while Persian tends to use the pluperfect.

Exercise 3

◀ CD 2, TR 4, 02:22

You have rung Ali at home to see if he is back from work as you wish to talk to him. Ali's wife, Nasrin, answers the phone. Can you follow the dialogue and provide the Persian translation of the English lines?

You	Hello. Mr Afshar's residence?
Nasrin	بله، بفرمایید.
You	Are you Miss Nasrin? I'm Pedram.
Nasrin	سلام پدرام خان، بله، نسرینم. حالتون چطوره؟ خوب هستید؟ خانم حالشان چطوره؟
You	I am very well, thank you. My wife is well too. She is in France at the moment. She is at her mother's.
Nasrin	برای چه مدت به فرانسه رفته اند؟
You	She has gone for a week. She hasn't seen her mother for four months. Her brother has also come over from the States too. The whole family are there now.
Nasrin	چه عالی. جای بقیهٔ فامیل خالی.
You	Excuse me, is Ali at home?
Nasrin	بله، علی تازه از اداره آمده است. پس از من خداحافظ. سلام برسانید.
You	Bye for now, Miss Nasrin. Hope to see you soon.

Test yourself

1 What is the positive answer to a negative question sentence starting with 'magar' دیگَر ?
2 What does 'digar' دیگر mean when used with a negative verb?
3 Does Persian have double negatives?
4 How can you express the habitual action 'I used to . . .' in Persian?
5 How is a Persian past participle formed?
6 Are the verb subject endings for present perfect the same as other past tense endings?
7 What are the endings for past or pluperfect tenses in Persian?
8 When is pluperfect used in Persian?
9 How do you form the negative of perfect tenses?
10 Conjugate the present and pluperfect of 'to find' پیدا کردن.

13

....

An invitation to supper

In this unit you will learn how to
- *Recognize and apply more verbs*
- *Form and use compound verbs*

_____

Dialogue

◀) CD 2, TR 5

Amir and Maryam talk about an invitation to supper at his house. Listen to the dialogue and pay special attention to the verbs:

م   اَمیر، دیروز کُجا بودی؟

ا   دیروز صبح در مَغازه کار می کردم. بعد ساعتِ چهار به
      کتابخانه رفتم و تا ساعت شش و نیم آنجا درس خواندم.

م   من، دیروز بعداز ظُهر به منزلت تلفن زدم و با مادرت
      حَرف زَدَم. مادرت، من و خانواده ام را به شام دعوت کرد.

ا   چه خوب. کی برای شام پیشِ ما می آیید؟

م   سه شنبهٔ آینده می آییم. امیر مادرت چه گُلی دو ست دارد؟

ا   مادرم گلِ سرخ و لاله خیلی دوست دارد. وقتی در شیراز
      زندگی می کردیم باغِ ما پر از گلِ بود.

م   بسیار خوب، پس من چند شاخه گلِ سرخ و یک جعبه
      شیرینی برای او می آوَرَم.

M	Amir, where were you yesterday?
A	I was working in the shop yesterday morning. Then, at four o'clock I went to the library and studied there till 6.30.
M	I called your house yesterday afternoon and spoke to your mother. Your mother invited me and my family to supper.
A	How wonderful. When are you (pl.) coming to us for supper?
M	We are coming next Tuesday. Amir, what flowers does your mother like?
A	My mother likes red roses and tulips. When we lived in Shiraz our house was full of flowers.
M	OK, in that case I will bring her several stems of roses and a box of chocolates.

QUICK VOCAB

yesterday	دیروز
morning	صبح
shop	مغازه
I was working	کار می کَردَم
then, next	بعد
four o'clock	ساعَتِ چهار
library	کتابخانه
until, up to	تا
6.30	شِش و نیم
I studied	درس خواندَم
afternoon	بعدازظهر
your house	منزلَت
I telephoned	تلفن زدم
your mother	مادَرت
I spoke	حرف زَدَم
my family	خانواده اَم
direct object marker	را

to	بِه
supper, dinner	شام
she invited	دَعوَت کرد
when?	کِی؟
for	برایِ
you (pl.) come	می آیید
Tuesday	سِه شَنبه
future, next	آینده
we will come	می آییم
flower (arch. roses)	گُل
a flower	گُلی
she likes	دوست دارَد
red, crimson	سُرخ
tulips	لاله
when, at the time that	وَقتی
we lived	زِندِگی می کَردیم
garden	باغ
full of	پُراز
then, in that	پَس
several	چَند
branch, stem	شاخه
box	جَعبه
confectionery	شیرینی
for her (or him)	برایِ او
I will bring	می آوَرَم

Compound verbs

The verbs کار کردم, 'I worked', درس خواندم 'I studied', حَرف زَدَم, 'I spoke or talked to', دَعوَت کرد, 'she invited', دوست دارد 'she likes' and زندگی کَردیم, 'we lived', used in the dialogue, are known as *compound verbs*. As you can see they contain a noun as well as the verb element. Compound verbs don't behave any differently from ordinary, single verbs. When we form the different tenses and persons of these verbs, we still only conjugate the verbal element and the noun component does not get changed in any way whatsoever. The infinitive of a compound verb can consist of a noun + verb or a preposition + verb as in the following examples:

زَندَگی کَردَن (زندگی + کردن)	*zendegi kardan*	to live
زِندِگی	*zendegi*	life
کَردَن	*kardan*	to do
دَرس خواندَن (درس + خواندن)	*dars khāndan*	to study
دَرس	*dars*	lesson
خواندَن	*khāndan*	to read
بَر گَشتَن (بر + گَشتَن)	*bar gashtan*	to return, to turn back
بَر	*bar*	over, on, top
گَشتَن	*gashtan*	to go round, to search
(دَر + آوَردَن) دَر آوَردَن	*dar āvardan*	to get out, take out, earn (lit. fetch out from the inside)
دَر	*dar*	in, at, inside
آوَردَن	*āvardan*	to bring, to fetch

QUICK VOCAB

Single versus compound

Let us look at the formation of different tenses of a compound verb in comparison to a single verb. Let's take the verbs 'to live' and 'to go' and look at different forms of these verbs in the past tense.

Single verb 'to go'	Compound verb 'to live'
رفتَم *raftam* I went	زندگی کردم *zendegi kardam* I lived
رفتی *rafti* you went	زندگی کردی *zendegi kardi* you lived
رفت *raft* he, she, it went	زندگی کرد *zendegi kard* he, she, it lived
رفتیم *raftim* we went	زندگی کردیم *zendegi kardim* we lived
رفتید *raftid* you (pl.) went	زندگی کردید *zendegi kardid* you (pl.) lived
رفتَند *raftand* they went	زندگی کردند *zendegi kardand* they lived

The noun or the preposition complement of a compound verb simply tags along as the appropriate tenses of the verb are formed. All particles, such as the negative نـ *na-* or the continuous prefix می *mi-*, are only ever attached to the verbal part of a compound verb and never on to the noun or preposition part. Therefore, the past continuous or habitual 'I used to live' will be زندگی می کَردم *zendegi mi-kardam*. Similarly, 'they did not live there' will be آنجا زندگی نکَردند آنها *ānhā ānjā zendegi na-kardand*.

> ## Insight
>
> Compound verbs are made up of a verbal element combined with a preceding noun (e.g. 'to live', lit. *to do life*), a preposition (e.g. 'to pick up') or in some cases the short infinitive of another verb. In advanced or idiomatic Persian a compound verb could be made up of a preposition and noun plus the verb element (e.g. 'to be born').

Exercise 1
Translate the following sentences into Persian:

1 She lived in our house in Shiraz.
2 I used to study in the morning and work in the afternoon.

3 You (sing.) don't like our food, but you like our tea.
4 We listened to the radio this morning.
5 They thought today was Monday.
6 You were surprised when you saw Maryam.
7 He made a difficult decision.
8 Have you repaired the car?
9 I have not worked since Tuesday.
10 Amir and Maryam sang at Pari's wedding.

Some useful compound verbs

to listen	گوش کردن or گوش دادَن
to think	فکر کردَن
to be surprised	تَعَجُب کردن
to decide (lit. take decisions)	تَصمیم گرِفتَن
to repair, mend	دُرست کردن
to work	کار کردن
to sing	آواز خواندن

Insight

Only ever conjugate the verbal element of a compound verb and not the noun or preposition.

Exercise 2

Translate the following passage into English, paying attention to the compound verbs:

ما سه سالِ پیش در شهر «بوردو» در فرانسه زندگی می کردیم.
پدرم در یک بانکِ تجاری کارمی کرد و مادرم در مدرسهٔ محلی
پیانو درس می داد. من در مدرسه با چند پسر و دختر ایرانی آشنا
شدم. ما آخرِهرِ هَفته یا در کوچه ها دوچرخه سواری می کردیم یا
در اِستَخر شِنا میکردیم. مادرِ یکی از پسرهای ایرانی هر یکشنبه

برای ما شام درست می کرد. من غذای ایرانی خیلی دوست دارم. اما کارِ پدرم در فرانسه تمام شد و ما اِمسال تابستان به لندن برگشتیم.

Insight

The negative marker or the prefix -mi are only ever attached to the verbal part and not the noun or preposition of compound verbs.

Exercise 3
◆ CD 2, TR 5, 01:13

Use the Persian compound verbs 'to live', 'to work', 'to play', 'to speak' and 'to return' in this dialogue about your weekend:

	شما آخرِ هفته چکار کردید؟ در لندن بودید؟
You	No, I worked all Saturday morning, then in the evening I went to my cousin's house by the lake.
	آنجا چکار کردید؟ حتماً شب دیر رسیدید؟
You	No, I got there at about 9:30. We had supper and talked a little and then went to bed.
	یکشنبه چکار کردید؟
You	On Sunday morning we went to a local market and then played golf. I came back home at about 6pm.
	پسرعموی شما تمام هفته آنجا زندگی میکند یا فقط روزهای شنبه و یکشنبه؟
You	My cousin lives there the whole time.

Test yourself

1 Are most Persian verbs single or compound?
2 Do compound verbs behave differently from single verbs?
3 What do compound verbs consist of?

4 How are the negatives of compound verbs formed?

5 Where do you place the mi-prefix in a compound present tense?

6 What is the most common verbal element in compound verbs?

7 Form the correct compound verbs by linking the noun, preposition and verbal components below:

	درس
	تلفن
زدن	دست

خواندن	پیانو
کردن	شنا
داشتن	درست
انداختن	زندگی
دادن	دور
	حرف
	مسواک

8 How are the subjunctives of compound verbs formed?

9 What are the passives of compound verbs with 'kardan' کـردن?

10 Can compound verbs consist of prepositions and adjectives and a verbal element?

14

He saw me in the library; the man was seen

In this unit you will learn how to
- *Identify the direct object of verbs*
- *Recognize and form transitive and intransitive verbs*

Dialogue

◄) CD 2, TR 6

Mona, a visiting student in Tehran, posts a letter for the first time and tells Parvin about it. (Can you pick out the word *rā* را used only in some of the sentences?)

پ   دیروز صُبح کُجا بودی؟

م   به پُستخانه رفتم و یک بسته و دو نامه را به لَندَن فرستادم.

پ   با پستِ زمینی یا هوایی؟

م   دو نامه را با پستِ هوایی و بسته را با پستِ سِفارشی فرستادم.

پ   بسته خیلی سَنگین بود؟

م   بله، آنرا روی ترازو گُذاشتَم. تَقریباً یک کیلو و دویست گِرَم بود. و این دو فرم را هم پرکردم.

134

پ   حَتماً گران شُد. به اندازهٔ کافی پول داشتی؟

م   خوشبختانه پول نَقد داشتم. کارمند پُستخانه به من کمک کرد و تمبرِ درست را روی نامه ها چَسباند. من دو تا کارت پستال هم خریدم. یکی را برای مادرم فرستادم ولی آن یکی دیگر را هنوز برای کسی نَفرِستاده ام.

Mountain village of Masouleh

P	Where were you yesterday?
M	I went to the post office and sent a parcel and two letters to London.
P	By surface mail or airmail?
M	I sent the two letters airmail and the parcel by special (registered) mail.
P	Was the parcel very heavy?
M	Yes. I put it on the scales. It was about one kilogram and 200 grams. And I also filled in these two forms.
P	It must have been expensive. Did you have enough money?
M	Luckily, I had cash. The post office cashier helped me and stuck the correct stamps on the letters. I bought two postcards too. I sent one to my mother but I haven't sent the other one to anybody yet.

post office	پُستخانه	became, was	شُد
parcel	بَسته	size, amount	أندازه
letter	نامه	sufficient	کافی
direct object marker	را	luckily	خوشبختانه
I sent	فِرستادم	cash	نَقد
surface, land	زمینی	employee, here cashier	کارَمند
air	هَوایی		

QUICK VOCAB

special, registered	سِفارشی	helped	کُمَک کرد
heavy	سَنگین	stamp	تَمبرِ
scales	ترازو	correct, right, exact	دُرُست
I placed	گُذاشتَم	stuck down	چَسباند
approximately, nearly	تَقریباً	postcard	کارت پِستال
form	فُرم	the other one	آن یِکی دیگر
I filled	پُرکَردَم	still, as yet	هَنوز
for	برای	someone, no one with negative verb	کَسی

Use of the direct object market *rā* را

So far we have described the word order in a Persian sentence as *subject, object, verb*. We can now expand on this and add that the object of a sentence in Persian, as in English, can be either *direct* (specific) or *indirect* (non-specific). What do these terms mean?

Look at the following two sets of sentences:

> We saw **him**.
> She heard **the news**.
> Did you buy **those new shoes** yesterday?

> I went by <u>bus</u>.
> He slept well in <u>his bed</u>.
> They came to <u>London</u> three years ago.

The *objects* in the first group of sentences (in bold) are specific persons or items *directly* referred to, while the *objects* of the second group of sentences (underlined) are unspecific. Also, the direct objects follow the English verbs in the first set of sentences but a preposition such as 'by', or 'in' or 'to' separates the indirect objects of the second set of sentences from the verb.

A *specific* or *direct object* is that part of the sentence which is the immediate objective or purpose of the verb or the action in the sentence, while an *indirect object* means that there is enough information in a verb already to illustrate an action, and the *object,* usually with the aid of a preposition, gives further information about the action referred to and how it is related to the verb.

Insight

Verbs that are used in conjunction with a preposition in English will also be used with a preposition in Persian (e.g. 'to go to', 'to live in'). These verbs will not take *rā* را.

Writing rules

In Persian, when a definite noun, i.e. a noun as it appears in the dictionary, is the immediate and direct object of the verb, it has to be 'marked'. The marker is a suffix or *postposition* that comes immediately after the *direct object*. The direct object marker is را *rā* in Persian. The direct object can be simply one word, a string of words or it can be a whole sub-clause. را *rā* always comes at the end of the entire group of words that make up the object of the verb.

Learning how and where to use را *rā* is one of the more difficult aspects of Persian grammar, especially for speakers of modern European languages, where the equivalent of *rā* does not exist.

While you will have no problems translating a Persian sentence containing a *direct object* into English, because the marker را *rā* is there to be seen, you must make extra sure to remember to put a *rā* in, if necessary, when translating from English into Persian.

Types of verb: transitive or intransitive?

How will you know when a sentence requires را *rā*? The *direct object* of a sentence usually needs to be marked by the suffix را *rā* if the verb of the sentence is transitive. Therefore, before starting on the examples of را in Persian, we should perhaps learn how to identify a *transitive* verb. Fortunately, transitive and intransitive verbs are the same in Persian and English.

It is safe to say that a verb is either *transitive* or *intransitive*, although there are a very few verbs that can be described as *both* transitive and intransitive. A *transitive* verb is one that can take a *direct object*: e.g. the verbs 'to buy', 'to see', 'to bring', 'to read' and 'to deliver'. The main object of these types of verb has to be followed by را. Transitive verbs can be directly linked to their main objects as in 'I saw the photographs and heard the music', where *the photographs* is the *direct object* of the verb *saw* and *the music* is the *direct object* of *heard*.

An *intransitive* verb, on the other hand, is a verb that *never* takes a direct object. Verbs such as 'to go', 'to sit', 'to sleep', 'to live', and 'to be' are examples of intransitive verbs. These verbs never need را; however, they often need a preposition, such as 'to go *to* the cinema', 'to sit *on* a bench' so that the *purpose* of the action is further clarified. The intransitive verb is not linked directly to its objects, but the preposition that comes in between may relate it to the object, i.e. you cannot 'go the cinema', 'sleep the train' or 'sit the comfortable chair'.

You can assume that unless the sentence has a transitive verb in it you don't need to worry about putting a را *rā* in after its *object* when you translate it into Persian. But how can you tell if a verb is transitive or intransitive?

Here is a simple way of working this out. If you turn around and say to someone: 'I *saw*' and leave it at that, the question they are most likely to ask you to find out more is: 'You saw *what*?' or '*Whom* did you see?' Similarly, if you say: 'Maryam *bought*', without elaborating further, the listener is likely to ask: '*What* did Maryam buy?' However, if you say 'we *sat*', or 'they *went*', the question words that the listener will use to get more information won't be 'what' or 'whom', but he or she may ask: '*Where* did you sit'; '*Why* did you sit' or '*When* did they go' and

'*How* did they go'? No one ever asks, '*What* did you sit?' or '*Who* did they go?' unless they then add a preposition and turn the questions into: '*What* did you sit *on*?', or '*Whom* did they go *with*?'. Without adding the prepositions 'on' and 'with' to the last two questions the sentences 'What did you sit?' or 'Who did they go?' make no sense.

Only verbs that can be sensibly used with interrogatives (question words) 'what' and 'who/whom' are *transitive* verbs and their objects, in Persian, are almost always followed by را *rā*. The verbs that cannot fit into a 'what' or 'who/whom' question sentence without the need for a preposition such as 'by', 'to', 'on', 'from' etc., are *intransitive* and as a rule do not take the را *rā* in modern Persian.

Example

Let us work this out by way of an example. Look at the following two sentences:

(a) Ali saw his brother.
(b) Maryam went to the park.

Now make question sentences using only the 'what' or 'who/whom' question words:

(a) *What* or *whom* did Ali see?
(b) *What* or *whom* did Maryam go?

As you see, question sentence **(a)** makes sense but question **(b)** is nonsensical. The verb 'to see' is *transitive* and therefore responds to a 'who/whom' or 'what' question, while the verb 'to go' is *intransitive* and does not work with these question words.

Having established the nature of the verb, we will next try to find out what the specific *direct object* of the verb 'to see' is in sentence **(a)**. The direct object is always the answer to the question we form, i.e. 'his brother' (*Whom* did Ali see? Ali saw *his brother* برادرش).

The specific direct object of the sentence is then followed by را in Persian.

علی برادرش را دید.

Very soon you will build up a vocabulary list of both *transitive* and *intransitive* verbs in Persian and will automatically work out if your Persian sentence containing these *transitive* verbs needs a را *rā* or not.

When to use *rā* را with transitive verbs

Here are more guidelines for when to use را *rā* in Persian.

Always use *rā* را

(i) After all proper nouns, such as Maryam or London:

مَریَم را دیدید؟ *Maryam rā didid?* Did you see Maryam?

لَندن را دوست دارَند. *Landan rā dust-dārand.* They like London.

(ii) After all personal and demonstrative pronouns, such as 'I', 'you', 'he', 'they' or 'this', 'that' and 'it':

من را در کتابخانه دید – مرا در کتابخانه دید. *man rā dar ketābkhāne did.* She (or he) saw me in the library.

تو را نمی شناسَم – تُرا نمی شناسم. *to rā nemishenāsam.* I don't know you.

بابَک آن را به من داد. *Bābak ān rā be man dād.* Babak gave it (lit. that) to me.

(iii) After all nouns described by demonstrative adjectives or by the possessive *ezafe*:

آن خانه را دیدم. *ān khāne rā didam.* I saw *that* house.

خانهٔ او را دیدم. *khāneh-ye u rā didam.* I saw *his* or *her* house.

کتابهای شما را خواندَم. *ketāb-hā-ye shomā rā khāndam.* I read *your* books.

آن خَبَر را نَشنیدم. *ān khabar rā nashenidam.* I have not heard *that* news.

(iv) When personal suffixes refer to individuals and thus specific persons:

کتابَم را بُرد. *ketābam rā bord.* S/he took (away) *my* book.

اسمَش را نَشنیدم. *esmash rā nashenidam.* I did not hear *her/his* name.

Summary

Direct objects of transitive verbs are always followed by را.
Intransitive verbs, however, do not take a specific direct object,
and therefore never come with را. The bridge between the object
of the sentence and the verb is usually a preposition. Look at these
examples:

کتاب فارسی را به کلاس آوردَم. I brought the Persian book to the class.

دوستِ مریم را در مهمانی دیدم. I saw Maryam's friend at the party.

حَسَن دیشب به سینما رفت. Hasan went to the cinema last night.

امروز عَصر، دو ساعت در پارک راه رَفتَم. This afternoon I walked in the
park for two hours.

Once you get used to the idea of an object marker in Persian, you
will be able to make the final leap in this chapter and learn that
there are instances when the object or purpose of *transitive verbs*
is not followed by a را *rā*. Don't be deceived into thinking that
because the sentence has a transitive verb ('to buy' or 'to hear')
then there must be a را in there somewhere! You must always
think about the *meaning* of the sentence and also look for the
other giveaway clues listed in points **(i)** to **(iv)** earlier.

Look at the following sentences:

1 سوسَن کتاب را خَرید. Sussan bought *the book*.

2 سوسَن کتاب خرید. Sussan bought *books*.

Although the verb 'to buy' is a transitive verb and therefore capable
of having a specific direct object, it is only so in sentence 1. Here, 'the
book' is a definite noun and the immediate object of the verb is the
purchase of a specific book.

In sentence 2, however, the emphasis is on the *action* and on the
activities of the agent, Sussan, who is the doer of the verb, and *not*
on the verb's object. The message of this sentence is that Sussan
bought books *in general* as opposed to, for example, 'sat in a café
while she was at a conference in Tehran' or 'bought decorative tiles
on a visit there'.

You will also notice that none of the earlier guidelines **(i)** to **(iv)** applies to sentence 2.

If a noun is followed by a modifier, the postposition را is placed after the entire group, even if it is long:

حَسَن را دیدَم. I saw Hasan.

خانهٔ حَسَن را دیدَم. I saw Hasan's house.

خانهٔ دوستِ حسن را دیدم. I saw Hasan's friend's house.

خانهٔ دوستِ آلمانیِ حَسَن را دیدم. I saw Hasan's German friend's house.

آن کتابِ خیلی گران را خرید. He bought that very expensive book.

شُماره تلفُنِ مغازهٔ دُخترخالهٔ مریم را داری؟ Do you (sing.) have the telephone number of Maryam's cousin's shop?

When two or more nouns are objects of the same verb, the particle را appears only once – at the end of the entire group:

خانه و باغِ حسن را دیدم. I saw Hasan's house and garden,

آن کتابِ گران و این گُلدان را خریدم. I bought that expensive book and this vase.

Insight

If any of the following comes immediately after the English verb, you must use *rā* را in the Persian translation: a proper noun, any pronoun (e.g. 'I, you, they'), any possessive (e.g. *'my, his, our'*), *'the, that, these'* or similar demonstratives.

Exercise 1

Translate the following sentences into Persian:

1 I heard his voice.
2 My friend bought these books from the shop.
3 They brought the parcel to our house.
4 She gave these flowers to her.

5 I didn't see Maryam's mother yesterday.
6 We ate all those apples.
7 I took some food for him.
8 She gave it to her brother.
9 I saw you in the bakery yesterday. What did you buy?
10 Didn't you want this book?
11 Have you seen my friend?
12 I don't know them.
13 Have you heard the news?
14 I want the other car.
15 Who brought these flowers?
16 I gave your address to the students.
17 I ate well yesterday.
18 I ate at your sister's yesterday.
19 I ate the chocolate in the fridge.
20 Did you like the film?

Exercise 2

◄» CD 2, TR 6, 02:05

Listen to the following text being read. Now translate it into English:

سه سالِ پیش در یک مهمانی در لَندن با یک دُخترِ ایرانی آشنا
شُدم. نامِ او مَریم است. مریم عکاس است و روزهای سه شنبه و
چهارشنبه در یک استودیوی عکاسی کار می کند. مریم خیلی سفر
می کند و اورا زیاد نمی بینَم.

دیروز، پس از مُدّتها او را در یک مهمانی، در خانهُ دوستم دیدم. پس
از احوالپرسی و خوش و بِشِ معمول گفت که خانه اش را عوض
کرده و حالا در غَربِ لندن زندگی می کند. او گفت آپارتمانِ جدیدش
را خیلی دوست دارد. مریم آدرس و شماره تلفن جدیدش را به من
داد. این آپارتمان را مریم و دوستش اُمید، با هم پیدا کردند. اُتاق ها
را رَنگ زدند، موکت آن را عَوَض کردند، آشپَزخانه را تَمیزکردند و

در باغچهٔ کوچکِ آن گل کاشتند. پَنجرهٔ حَمام شکسته بود و آنرا هم دُرُست کردند. بَعد، اسباب های مریم را به این آپارتمان آوردند. اُمید هم در مهمانی بود و مریم او را به من مُعَرِفی کرد. مریم و اُمید ماشینشان را نیاورده بودند و بعد از شام من آنها را به منزل رِساندم.

Exercise 3

CD 2, TR 6, 03:55

Last week you bought a book for a friend but she already has it, so you must go back to the bookshop to return it. The English part of the dialogue is your cue. Can you say these sentences in Persian and work out what is being said in Persian?

You	Good morning, madam. I bought this book last Thursday. It was for a friend but she already has this book.
Assistant	کتاب را از این کتابفروشی خریدید؟
You	Yes, I bought it from here.
Assistant	متاسفانه ما نمیتوانیم پول کتاب را پس بدهیم ولی میتوانید آنرا عوض کنید و یک کتاب دیگر بخرید.
You	OK. In that case I'll exchange it with these two books, and I also want this book on Iran. How much is it?

Test yourself

1 What verbs are used with prepositions in Persian?
2 Is there a correlation between verbs that are used with prepositions in English and Persian?
3 How do we identify Persian verbs as transitive or intransitive?
4 How do we mark the specific direct object of a verb in Persian?

144

5 What is the simplest rule of thumb for knowing whether to use a 'rā' را or not when translating English sentences into Persian?

6 Does the object of a transitive verb followed by a number or 'a', 'an' or 'some' in an English sentence take 'rā' را in Persian?

7 Do intransitive verbs such as 'to live', 'to sit' or 'to go' ever take 'rā' را in Persian?

8 Must transitive verbs such as 'to buy', 'to see' or 'to like' always have a 'rā' را in Persian?

9 How many rā' را can any one sentence take?

10 Give four instances when rā' را must be used in Persian.

15

Going for a quick snack

In this unit you will learn how to
- *Form the present tense*
- *Talk about what is happening now*

Dialogue

◀) CD 2, TR 7

In this dialogue Shahriar is tempted to take a break:

●   شهریار، خیلی کار داری؟

ش   نه خیلی کار نَدارَم، چطور مگر؟

●   یک کافهٔ خیلی قشنگ نزدیکِ اینجا می شناسم. من، گاهی، به آنجا می رَوَم و چیزی می خورم. برویم آنجا و چیزی بخوریم؟

ش   بد فکری نیست. من دو سه ساعت بیکارم وگُرسنه هم هَستم. با تو یک قهوه ای می خورم.

●   قهوهٔ این کافه در تمامِ لندن معروف است. کیک و شیرینیهایش هم، خانگیست و خیلی خوشمزه است. آب میوه های خیلی تازه هم دارد.

146

ش   خوب، پس من به جای قهوه آب میوه می خورم. چه جور آب میوه هایی دارد؟

●   هر جور میوه ای که در بازار هست. تمام میوه ها را می گُذارند توی یک سبدِ بزرگ. تو میوه را انتخاب می کنی و آنها همانجا برای تو آب می گیرند.

ش   تو چه میخوری؟

●   من یا شیرکاکائو با کیک می خورم یا بستنی.

ش   این کافه ساندویچ هم دارد؟

●   بــله. همه جور ساندویچ دارد. ساندویچ مرغ، پنیر، ماهی تُن، کالباس، تُخم مُرغ.

ش   پس من یک ساندویچ مرغ و سالاد با یک لیوان آبِ انار می خورم.

●	Shahriar, are you very busy?
S	No, not much to do (am not very busy), why are you asking (lit. but how come?)
●	I know a very nice café near here. I sometimes go there and eat something. Shall we go there and eat something?
S	It's not a bad idea. I am free (lit. without job) for two or three hours and am also hungry. I'll have a coffee with you.
●	The coffee in this café is famous throughout London. Its cakes and pastries are also home-made and very delicious. It has very fresh fruit juices too.
S	OK, I'll have (lit. eat) fruit juice instead of coffee. What sort of juices does it have?
●	Any fruit that is in the market. They put all the fruit in a large basket. You choose the fruit and they 'juice it' for you there and then.
S	What will you have (lit. eat)?
●	I'll either have hot chocolate with cake or an ice cream.
S	Does this café do sandwiches?

QUICK VOCAB

you are busy	کارداری
to be busy, have things to do	کار داشتن
idiomatic why? why do you ask?	چطور مَگر
I know	می شِناسَم
sometimes	گاهی
I go	می رَوَم
something	چیزی
I eat	می خورَم
let us go	بَرَویم
let us eat	بِخوریم
thought, idea	فِکر
fruit juice	آب میوه
fresh	تازه
instead of	به جایِ
what kind?, sort?	چِه جور؟
all sorts, kinds	هَر جور
that	کِه
they place, put	می گُذارَند
a thought, an idea	فِکری
a bad idea or thought	بَد فِکری
two or three hours	دو سِه ساعَت
I am free (lit. without job, preoccupation)	بیکارَم (بیکار هَستَم)
hungry	گُرُسنه
(spoken) a coffee	یک قَهوه ای
all of the . . .	تَمامِ
famous	مَعروف
home-made	خانِگی
delicious, tasty	خوشمَزه
they extract the juice	آب می گیرَند
will you eat?	می خوری؟
either . . . or	یا... یا
ice cream	بَستَنی
bird, hen, chicken	مُرغ
cheese	پَنیر
tuna fish	ماهی تُن
garlic sausage	کالباس

inside, into	توى	eggs	تُخم مُرغ
basket	سَبَد	glass, tumbler	لیوان
you choose	اِنتِخاب می کُنی	pomegranate juice	آب ِ اَنار
there (and then)	هَمانجا		

Forming the present tense

Persian verbs fall into two categories: regular and irregular. This should not come as too much of a surprise for speakers of English as many common English verbs are also irregular. Just look at these examples:

eat	eaten	win	won
meet	met	do	done
drink	drunk	fly	flown
buy	bought	have	had

The irregularity of a Persian verb does not affect its formation in past tenses and, as we have seen, you can easily extract the 'past stem' of any Persian verb from its infinitive by dropping the ending نَ -an. The irregularity of some Persian verbs, however, means that extracting the 'present stem' is a little more difficult.

With regular verbs, all you have to do is to drop the complete ending of the infinitive, i.e. drop either the تَن -tan, دَن -dan or یدن -idan and what you are left with is the present stem. But how can you tell a regular Persian verb from an irregular one when you have just started learning the language? Well, I'm afraid, you can't. I can tell you that almost all infinitives that end in یدن -idan are regular and almost all infinitives ending in تَن -tan are irregular. Infinitives ending in دَن -dan are sometimes regular and sometimes irregular. What you can also do is to use the table of common irregular verbs (in Unit 16). If your infinitive is not listed in this table, it means that the verb you are looking for is regular and you simply drop the full ending of the infinitive to arrive at the required present stem. You will be surprised how quickly you will come to learn a lot of the common, irregular present stems by heart and you will need to use the table less and less.

Once you have extracted the present stem, all you need to do is to use a simple formula to form your present indicative tense, i.e. the simple present tense. This simple formula is: present indicative = subject (personal) verb endings + present stem + می.

> **Insight**
> Drop the complete ending of the infinitive (that is drop the -*dan*, -*tan* or -*idan*) to get the present stem.

Let's work out the various components in this formula:

* می -*mi*, known also as the continuous marker, giving the sense of an ongoing or prevalent action; is the non-removable part of all present tense verbs in Persian with the exception of 'to be' and 'to have'. (I hope you still remember that 'to be' and 'to have' are irregular and do not always follow rules that apply to other verbs!)

* The present stem can be found either by looking up in the table or by dropping the full ending.

* Appropriate subject endings for present tense verbs include the five endings which we have been using for the past tense verbs plus one extra ending for the third person singular, i.e. for 'he', 'she', 'it', 'this' and 'that'.

These subject endings, which tell you who the agent or the doer of the verb is, are shown in the following table:

Singular	Plural
م ... -*am* I	یم ... -*im* we
ی... -*i* you	ید ... -*id* you
د ... -*ad* he, she, it	ند ... -*and* they

Note that the only difference between subject endings for past and present tenses is the extra ending for third person singular in present tense formation, shown in bold in the table.

Example 1: the present tense of 'to buy' kharidan خَریدَن

The verb 'to buy' is a regular verb in Persian and therefore its present stem is formed by dropping the full ending of the infinitive, which means deleting یدن -idan. This leaves خر khar, as the 'present stem'.

Inputting the information in the formula: present tense = subject endings + خَر + می:

you (pl.) buy می خَرید = ید + خَر + می

Singular	Plural
می خَرَم mikharam I buy	می خَریم mikharim we buy
می خَری mikhari you buy	می خَرید mikharid you buy
می خَرَد mikharad he, she, it buys	می خَرَند mikharand they buy

Example 2: the present tense of 'to go' raftan رَفتَن

'To go' is an irregular verb in Persian. Therefore we can refer to our table of irregular verbs and we will see that the irregular stem of this verb is رَو rav.

Using the present tense formula: present tense = subject endings + رو + می:

I go می رَوَم = م + رَو + می

Singular	Plural
می رَوَم miravam I go	می رَویم miravim we go
می رَوی miravi you go	می رَوید miravid you go
می رَوَد miravad he, she, it goes	می رَوَند miravand they go

Insight

There are six subject verb endings for the present tenses. These are: -am, -i, -ad, -im, -id and -and. Remember that unlike the simple past tenses there is a third person singular verb ending for *he/she* or *it*.

Uses of the present tense

This is the tense of action happening in the present time, e.g. 'I am writing letters' or 'they are working':

نامه نویسَم می   I am writing letters.

کار می کُنَند.   They are working.

It also refers to habitual actions, e.g. 'He buys a newspaper every day', 'We never eat breakfast':

(او) هَر روز یِک روزنامه می خَرَد.   He buys a newspaper everyday.

ما هیچوَقت صُبحانه نِمی خوریم.   We never eat breakfast.

Similarly, the present tense is used when describing an action that was started in the past but continues in the present time:

بیست سال است رُکسانا را می شناسَم.   I have known Roxana for 20 years. (Lit. It is 20 years that I know Roxana.)

اَز وُرودِ من به ایران پَنج ماه می گُذَرَد.   I have been in Iran for five months. (Lit. Five months pass since my arrival in Iran.)

Persian also allows you to use the present tense to refer to an action happening in the future. This is particularly so in spoken Persian:

فَردا عَصر به شیراز می رَوَند.   Tomorrow afternoon, they are going to Shiraz.

سالِ دیگر یِک ماشینِ نو می خَریم.   Next year we will buy a new car.

> ## Insight
> Always use the *mi* می prefix with present tense verbs except with 'to be' and 'to have'. You don't say *mi-hastim* or *mi-hastand* and you shouldn't use it with *dāshtan* either so no *mi-dārid* or *mi-dāram*. Having said that some educated native speakers use it erroneously so you can be forgiven if you lapse and use it too!

Exercise 1
Translate into Persian. Remember that some verbs may have a specific direct object.

1 I go to my mother's house every Saturday and take her to the supermarket.
2 She lives in a nice, large flat with two cats.
3 Every morning we see your cousin on the bus.
4 Are you (sing.) writing a letter to Maryam?
5 They are coming to our party on Wednesday.

Exercise 2

From the following table match the present tense and past tense verbs that have the same infinitive.

Present tense	Past tense
می گویم	خریدیم
می روید	أمدند
می نشینیم	ماندی
می گیرم	گفتم
می خوری	رفت
می أیند	نوشتند
می مانند	گرفتید
می خرد	نشست
می أوری	خوردیم
می نویسند	دیدم
می بینم	أوردی

Test yourself

1 What are the essential ingredients for forming the present tense?
2 Do subject endings for the present and past tense differ?
3 What are the present tense verb subject endings?
4 How do we extract the present stem of Persian verbs?
5 What happens if the verbs are irregular?
6 Do the verbs 'to be' and 'to have' follow the same rule in forming their present tense?
7 How are the negatives of Persian present tenses formed?
8 How do we express an on-going, progressive present tense action in Persian?
9 When can we use the Persian present tense?
10 How is the Persian present tense formed?

16

Grammar reference unit

Table of present stems of irregular verbs

Translation	Present stem	Verb	Verb
to arrange, adorn, decorate	آرا	ārāstan	آراستن
to offend, vex, molest, torment	آزار	āzordan	آزُردن
to test, examine, experience	آزمـا	āzmudan	آزمودن
to rest, repose, find peace of mind	آسـا	āsudan	آسودن
to fall, happen, be omitted	اُفت	oftādan	اُفتادن
to create	آفَرین	āfaridan	آفَریدن
to increase, add	افزا	afzudan	اَفزودن
to pollute, taint, contaminate	آلا	āludan	آلودن
to come, arrive	آ	āmadan	آمدن
to learn	آموز	āmukhtan	آموختن
to hoard, to store	انبـار	anbāshtan	انبـاشتن
to drop, throw	اَنداز	andākhtan	اَنداختن
to save, amass, accumulate	اندوز	andukhtan	اَندوختن
to assume, suppose	انگار	engāshtan	انگاشتن
to bring, fetch	آر or آور	āvardan	آوردن

to stand up, stop	ایست idtādan	ایستادن
to bestow, give	بخشا or بخش bakhshudan	بخشودن
to take, carry away	بر bordan	بردن
to tie up, close	بند bastan	بستن
to be	باش budan	بودن
to cook, to bake	پز pokhtan	پختن
to accept, agree	پذیر paziroftan	پذیرفتن
to pay, devote time	پرداز pardākhtan	پرداختن
to suppose, imagine	پندار pendāshtan	پنداشتن
to join, connect	پیوند peyvastan	پیوستن
to be able to, can	توان tavānestan	توانستن
to search, seek, look for	جو jostan	جستن
to cut, pick, display, lay out	چین chidan	چیدن
to stand, get up	خیز khāstan	خاستن
to want, desire, wish, need, be about to do sth	خواه khāstan	خواستن
to give, pay, offer	ده dādan	دادن
to have, possess, hold	دار dāshtan	داشتن
to know, understand	دان dānestan	دانستن
to sew, stitch	دوز dukhtan	دوختن
to see, realize, visit, view	بین didan	دیدن
to steal, rob, hijack, snatch	ربا robudan	ربودن
to go, leave, move	رو raftan	رفتن
to hit, strike, play (instrument)	زن zadan	زدن
to make, manufacture, build	ساز sākhtan	ساختن
to entrust, deposit, leave	سپار sepordan	سپردن
to compose	سرا sorudan	سرودن

English	Present stem	Transliteration	Infinitive
to burn (int.), suffer, grieve, pity	سوز	sukhtan	سوختن
to become, get	شو	shodan	شُدن
to wash, rinse	شوی or شو	shostan	شُستن
to break, shatter	شکن	shekastan	شکستن
to count, include, reckon	شُمار	shomordan	شُمردن
to recognize, know someone	شناس	shenākhtan	شناختن
to hear, listen to	شنو	shenidan	شنیدن
to send, despatch, transmit	فرِست	ferestādan	فرِستادن
to order, command, say (formal)	فرما	farmudan	فرمودن
to sell	فُروش	forukhtan	فروختن
to squeeze, apply pressure	فِشار	feshordan	فِشردن
to sow, cultivate, plant	کار	kāshtan	کاشتن
to do, complete	کُن	kardan	کردن
to place, put; allow, let	گذار	gozāshtan	گذاشتن
to pass, cross; forgive; give up	گُذَر	gozashatan	گُذشتن
to take, grab; seize; block	گیر	raftan	گرفتن
to flee, escape, run away	گُریز	rikhtan	گریختن
to weep, cry	گِری	geristan	گریستن
to turn; walk about; seek	گرد	gashtan	گشتن
to open (door, exhibition, etc.)	گُشا	goshudan	گُشودن
to say, utter, tell, speak	گو	goftan	گفتن
to die, pass away, perish	میر	mordan	مُردن
to sit, land, perch, reside	نِشین	neshastan	نِشستن
to play (instrument)	نَوا	navākhtan	نواختن
to write, jot down	نویس	neveshtan	نوِشتن
to place	نِه	nahādan	نِهادن
to find, locate	یاب	yāftan	یافتن

17

In a huff, through the door

In this unit you will learn how to
- *Use prepositions ('at', 'to', 'from', 'by', etc.)*
- *Put prepositions into idiomatic use*

Persian has only a small number of proper prepositions and this can cause some confusion for someone who speaks English, for example, which offers more choice of prepositions. This also explains why Iranian learners of English 'arrive *with* bus' or 'leave something behind *in* granny's': the prepositions 'by' and 'with' are the same in Persian, as are 'in' and 'at'.

Persian prepositions are divided into two groups: those that are followed by the *ezafe* and those which are not. There are only eight prepositions in the first group: جُز، بَر، تا، بی، اَز، دَر، به، با. The six most used of these, تا، بی، اَز، با، دَر، به, are explained in detail here, with examples of their use.

Prepositions that don't take the *ezafe*

به *be* 'to', 'in', 'into', 'at', 'on', 'with'

This is used in a variety of contexts but predominantly with verbs that are concerned with direction or location and would normally take a 'to', 'at' or 'in' preposition in English. It covers motion towards in a figurative sense. It is also used with adverbs of manner and in oaths.

(Note the necessity of use of prepositions in Persian and its occasional absence in the English translation.)

دیشب به سینما رفتیم. *dishab **be** cinemā raftim.* Last night we went *to* the cinema.

این کتاب را به مریم داد. *in ketāb rā **be** maryam dād.* He/she gave this book *to* Maryam.

به دَر زد و وارد شُد. *be dar zad va vāred shod.* He knocked (lit. *on* the door) and came in.

مریَم و برادَرش به آنها کُمَک کَردَند. *maryam va barādarash **be** ānhā komak kardand.* Maryam and her brother helped them.

آیا فَردا به خانهٔ ما می‌آیی؟ *āyā fardā **be** khāneh-ye mā mi'āyi?* Will you come *to* our house tomorrow?

امروز به همکارَم تِلفُن می کُنَم. *emruz **be** hamkāram telefon mi-konam.* I will call my colleague today. (Lit. I will make a telephone call *to* my colleague today.)

در اصفَهان خیلی به ما خوش گُذَشت. *dar esfahān kheyli **be** mā khosh gozasht.* We very much enjoyed ourselves in Esfahan. (lit. A good time was had *by* us in Esfahan.)

آن قالیچه را به ما نمی فُروشَند. *ān qāliche rā **be** mā nemi-forushand.* They won't sell that (small) carpet *to* us.

این مُشکِل به من مَربوط نیست. *in moshkel **be** man marbut nist.* This problem does not concern me. (It's none of my business or of no concern *to* me.)

خواهش می‌کُنَم به فارسی بنویسید. *khāhesh mi-konam **be** fārsi benevisid.* Please, write it (pl.) *in* Persian.

تاریک بود ولی هُتل را به راحتی پیدا کردیم. *tārik bud vali hotel rā **be** rāhti peydā kardim.* It was dark but we found the hotel easily (lit. *in* comfort, *with* ease).

بَهرام به دست و دلبازی مَعروف است. *Bahrām **be** dast o del-bāzi ma'ruf ast.* Bahram is known for (his) generosity (*lit.* for his open hand and heart).

دَر **dar** 'in', 'at', 'into', 'by', 'of'

This preposition is used to describe an area:

خواهرِ مَریَم دَر لندَن زِندگی می کُنَد. *khāhar-e maryam* **dar** *landan zendegi mi-konad.* Maryam's sister lives *in* London.

دَر تابِستان **dar** *tābestān in* the summer

اِمروز صُبح، دَر فِکرِ تو بودَم. *emruz sobh* **dar** *fekr-e to budam.* I was thinking *of* you this morning.

(Note: You can use the preposition بِه here too and say: امروز صبح به فکرِ تو بودم.)

رومی، شاعرِ ایرانی، دَر اروپا و آمریکا خِیلی طَرَفدار دارد.
rumi, shā'er-e irāni, **dar** *orupā va āmrikā kheyli tarafdār dārad.*
Rumi, the Iranian poet, has a big (lit. very) following *in* Europe and *in* America.

آشپَزخانۀ این آپارتمان شِش مِتر دَر چهار اَست. *āshpazkhāneh-ye in āpārtemān shesh metr* **dar** *chahār ast.* The kitchen in this flat is six metres *by* four.

اَز **az** 'from', 'by', 'through', 'of', 'than', 'among', 'by way of', 'out of', 'about'

اَز is used to express comparison, to denote direction or commencement of time and journey, to give an idea of distance, material make-up of something, causes or partition:

اَز این کوچه به بَعد پارکینگ مَجانی اَست. **az** *in kuche be ba'd pārking majāni ast.* Parking is free *beyond* (lit. from this street onwards) this street.

اَز صبح ساعت هَشت مُنتظرِ شما بوده ام. **az** *sobh, sā'at-e hasht, montazer-e shomā bude-am.* I have been waiting for you *since* 8 o'clock this morning.

دَرسِ ما اَز فَردا شُروع می شَوَد. *dars-e mā* **az** *fardā shoru' mishavad.* Our lessons will start *from* tomorrow.

این خانه اَز آجُر ساخته شده اَست. *in khāne* **az** *ājor sākhte shode ast.* This house is made (lit. built) *of* brick.

آن مُجَسَمه از مَرمَر است یا از بُرُنز؟ *ān mojassame **az** marmar ast yā boronz?* Is that statute (made) *of* marble or bronze?

بابک در خانه اش یک سگِ بزرگ دارد و من از ترسِ آن سگ هیچوقت به خانهٔ او نمی روم. *bābak dar khāneh-ash yek sag-e bozorg dārad va man az tars-e ān sag hichvaqt be khāne-ye u nemiravam.* Babak has a large dog in his house and I never go to his house because *of* the fear of that dog (because I am so fearful of that dog).

او از غصه بیمار شده است. *u **az** ghosse bimār shode ast.* He has become sick *because of* sorrow.

همسایهٔ ما خیلی از فیلمِ جدیدِ جیمز باند تعریف می کرد. *hamsāye-ye mā kheyli az film-e jadid-e jaims bānd ta'rif mikard.* Our neighbour was full of praise *of* (lit. was very complimentary *about*) the new James Bond film.

مادرِ مریم از همکارِ من خوشش نمی آید. *mādar-e maryam **az** hamkār-e man khoshash nemi-āyad.* Maryam's mother does not like (lit. draws no liking *from*) my colleague.

ما دیشب دیروقت از کرمان رسیدیم. *mā dishab dir-vaqt **az** kermān rasidim.* We got back late *from* Kerman last night.

خانواده من از کاشان می آیند. *khānevāde-ye man **az** kāshān mi-āyand.* My family come *from* Kashan.

او از خانوادهٔ بزرگی اَست. *u **az** khānevāde-ye bozorgi ast.* He comes (lit. is) *from* a large family.

آن نقاشی از کمال الملک است. *ān naqqāshi **az** kamāl ol-molk ast.* That painting is *by* Kamal ol-Molk.

آن داستان از یک نویسندهٔ جوان است. *ān dāstān **az** yek nevisande-ye javān ast.* That story is *by* a young writer.

از شهرهای ایران کدام را بیشتر دوست دارید؟ **az** *shahr-hā-ye irān kodām rā bishtar dust dārid?* Which one *of* the Iranian cities (lit. *among* Iranian cities or *of* all Iranian cities . . .) do you like most?

Different word order for this example can be:

کُدامیک از شهرهای ایران را بیشتر دوست دارید؟

از خواهرهای علی کدام در تهران به دانشگاه رفته اند؟

***az** khāhar-hā-ye ali kodām dar tehrān be dāneshgāh rafte-and?*
Which one *of* Ali's sisters has gone to university in Tehran?

این جاروبرقی خراب شده است، از آن استفاده نکنید. *in* **jāru** *barqi*
kharāb shode ast, **az** *ān estefāde nakonid.* This (electric) vacuum
cleaner is broken down, do not use it (lit. make no use *of* it).

چند ماه است که از برادرم خبر ندارم. *chand* **māh** *ast* *ke* **az**
barādaram khabar nadāram. It's a few months since I had any
news *of* my brother. (Lit. it is a few months *that* I have no news of
my brother.)

تند نرو! از مغازهٔ گلفروشی رد شدیم. *tond naro!* **az** *maghāze-ye gol-*
forushi rad shodim. Don't go fast! We passed the flower shop.

این حرف را از عَصبانیت زدم. *in harf rā* **az** *'asabāniyat zadam.*
I said this *out of* anger.

دوستم از من بهتر فارسی حرف می زند. *dustam* **az** *man behtar farsi*
harf mizanad. My friend speaks better Persian *than* me.

جلوگیری از زلزله ممکن نیست. *jelogiri* **az** *zelzele momken nist.*
It's impossible to prevent earthquakes (lit. prevention *of* is
impossible).

Note: The following are compounds made with از.

پیش از or قبل از 'before', 'prior to'
These are usually synonymous and interchangeable in use.

پیش از ناهار یک ساعت پیاده روی کردم. ***pish-az** nahār yek sā'at*
piyade ravi kardam. I went for an hour-long walk *before* lunch.

قبل از اینکه به ایران بروم کمی فارسی یادگرفتم. ***qabl-az-inke** be*
irān beravam kami fārsi yād gereftam. I learnt some Persian *before*
going to Iran.

بعَد از or پس از 'after', 'afterwards'

پس از سه روز در شیراز به بندرعباس رفتیم. pas-az se ruz dar shirāz be bandar-abbās raftim. *After* three days in Shiraz we went to Bandar Abbas.

اِمشب، بعد از شام به منزلِ شما می آییم. emshab, ba'd-az shām be manzel-e shomā mi-āyim. We are coming to your house *after* supper tonight.

جُز از or غیر از 'apart from', 'other than'

غیر از پروین، دو پسرِ دیگر هم در این آپارتمان زندگی می کنند.

gheyr-az parviz, do pesar-e digar ham dar in āpārtemān zendegi mikonand. *Apart from* Parviz two other boys also live in this apartment.

خارج از or بیرون از 'outside'

قیمت زمین خارج از شهر ارزانتر است. qeymat-e zamin **khārej-az** shahr arzāntar ast. Land prices are cheaper *outside* the city.

شما نمی توانید این لباس را بیرون از منزل بپوشید. shomā nemitavānid in lebās rā **birun-az** manzel bepushid. You cannot wear this dress (or clothes) *outside* the house.

با bā 'with', 'by', 'despite', 'because', 'in', 'to'

سارا دیگر با من حرف نمی زَند. sārā digar **bā** man harf nemizanad. Sara no longer speaks *to* (lit. *with*) me.

با من مَشوَرَت کرد و با پولَش یک ماشین خرید. **bā** man mashvarat kard va **bā** pulash yek māshin kharid. He consulted me and bought a car *with* his money.

نرگس با اتوبوس به تبریز رفت. narges **bā** otobus be tabriz raft. Narges went to Tabriz *by* bus.

این فرم را لطفاً با خودکار یا قلم پُر کنید. in form rā lotfan **bā** khodkār yā qalam por konid. Please fill in this form *in* biro or pen.

احمد با خواهر شیرین ازدواج کرده است. *ahmad **bā** khāhar-e shirin ezdevāj karde ast.* Ahmad has married (lit. got married *to/with*) Shirin's sister.

دوست رویا با برادرش در سوئد زندگی می کند. *dust-e royā **bā** barādarash dar su'ed zendegi mikonad.* Roya's friend lives *with* her brother in Sweden.

با شنیدن این خبر خیالم راحت شد. ***bā** shanidan-e in khabar khiyālam rāhat shod.* My mind was comforted (rested) *after* hearing this news.

بهتر است با غذا آب نخورید. *behtar ast **bā** ghazā āb nakhorid.* It is better if you don't drink water *with* food.

مریم با سوسن میانهٔ خوبی ندارد. *maryam **bā** susan miyāne-ye khubi nadārad.* Maryam doesn't get on well *with* Sussan.

با ادب و احترام بسیار از او خواهش کردیم که سالن را ترک کند. ***bā** adab o ehterām besiār az u khāhesh kardim ke sālon rā tark konad.* We asked him politely and with respect (lit. we asked *of* him) to leave the hall.

آنها همیشه با یکدیگر دعوا می‌کنند. *ānhā hamishe **bā** yekdigar da'vā mikonand.* They always fight *with* each other.

بی *bi* 'without'

بی can also be added to nouns and adjectives to form the opposite or convey the sense of 'without', 'un-', or '-less'.

بی خود این پول را به الهه دادی. ***bi**-khod in pul rā be elāhe dādi.* You shouldn't have given the money to Elahe. (Lit. You gave her the money with *no* good reason.)

بی تعارف می گویم، هر وقت دوست دارید به خانهٔ ما بیایید. ***bi**-ta'ārof miguyam, har vaqt dust dārid be khāne-ye mā biyāid.* I am saying it *without* ceremony (i.e. without just trying to be nice), come to our house whenever you like.

می گویند گربه حیوانِ بیو فاییست. *miguyand gorbe heyvān-e **bi-vafāyist**.* They say that a cat is a faith*less* (*un*faithful) creature (animal).

Similarly:

بی + کار = بیکار   unemployed, jobless

بی + ادب = بی ادب   impolite, rude (lit. without culture)

بی + تردید = بیتردید   undoubtedly, without a doubt

بی + چاره = بیچاره   helpless, wretched, hopeless

تا *tā* 'until', 'as soon as', 'by' (showing the extent or limit of things), 'as far as', 'in order to'

محسن از لندن به استانبول پرواز کرد و از آنجا تا تهران با اتوبوس رفت.
*mohsen az landan be estānbol parvāz kard va az ān jā **tā** tehrān bā otobus raft.* Mohsen flew from London to Istanbul and from there took the bus *to* Tehran (*as far as* Tehran).

این کتاب را تا فردا تمام می کنم. *in ketāb rā **tā** fardā tamām mikonam.* I'll finish this book *by* tomorrow (lit. till tomorrow).

کلاس فارسیِ او تا ماه آینده تمام می شود. *kelās-e fārsi-ye u **tā** māh-e āyande tamām mishavad.* His Persian classes will come to an end *by* next month.

تا مرا دید از اتاق بیرون رفت. *tā marā did az otāq birun raft.* He left the room *as soon as* he saw me.

من به ایران آمده ام تا خانوادهٔ شوهرم را ببینم. *man be irān āmade-am **tā** khānevāde-ye shoharm rā bebinam.* I have come to Iran *to* see (lit. in order to see) my husband's family.

Here تا acts as a co-ordinate linking two clauses rather than as a preposition.

سالار هر شب از ساعت هشت و نیم تا نه و نیم به کلاس پیانو می رود.
*sālār har shab az sā'at-e hasht o nim **tā** sā'at-e noh o nim be kelās-e piyāno miravad.* Salar goes to piano classes every night from 8.30 *to* 9.30 p.m.

دو روز است که از صبح تا شب دُنبالِ این کتاب می گردم. ‎*do ruz ast ke az sobh **tā** shab donbāl-e in ketāb migardam.* I have been searching for (looking for) this book for two days, from dawn *till* night.

حیف که تا آخرین روز اقامتَش در یونان باران آمد. ‎*heyf ke **tā** ākharin ruz-e eqāmatash dar yunān bārān āmad.* Pity that it rained *until* (or *to*) the last day of his stay in Greece.

در این مغازه به جهانگردان تا ده درصد تخفیف می دهند. ‎*dar in maghāze be jahāngardān **tā** dah dar sad takhfif midahand.* In this shop they give tourists *up to* 10% reduction.

Prepositions that take the *ezafe*

There are great many prepositions that are linked to the noun following them by the *ezafe*. They are rather too numerous to list here, but the following are some of the most commonly used prepositions of this category: پَهلویِ، کنارِ، نزدیکِ، بدونِ، دُنبالِ، دَم، سَرِ، لَب، دربارهٔ، پیش ‎، برای، بالایِ، زیرِ، رویِ، پایینِ، جلویِ، پشتِ.

Note that if the preposition ends with a vowel then the *ezafe* will take the form of the ی *ye* or the hamze sign ء. For example بالا 'up', ends with the long vowel ‎ا *ā*, therefore the preposition 'above' will be بالای *bālā-ye*.

Here are some examples of usage:

برای 'for'

لُطفاً یک چای برای من بیاورید. Please bring me a (cup of) tea.

این کتاب را برای تو خریدم. I bought this book *for* you.

بالای 'above', 'top', 'on'

طَبَقهٔ بالای این ساختمان مال یک پزشک است. The *top* floor of this building belongs to a physician.

لیوان آب میوه را بالای تلویزیون نَگُذار! Don't put the glass of fruit juice *on top of* the television!

پایین 'below', 'beneath'

پایین تَپه یک دریاچهٔ خیلی قشنگ است. *Below* (at the foot of) the hill there is a very pretty lake.

زیر 'underneath', 'under'

در پیاده روهای لندن زیر پایت را همیشه نگاه کن! Always look '*under* your feet' on the pavements of London.

مُواظب باش زیر ماشین نرویی! Be careful not to get run over by a car (don't go *under* a car)!

گَردَنبَند ژاله را زیر میز آشپزخانه پیدا کردیم. We found Zhale's necklace *under* the kitchen table.

روی 'above', 'on top of'

کلید شما روی میز راهرو است. Your keys are *on* the hall table.

اگر چیز داغ روی کامپیوتر بگذارید خراب می شود. If you place a hot thing *on top of* the computer it will get damaged.

جلوی 'in front of'

شَبها فقط جلوی تلویزیون می نشینند. At night they just sit *in front of* the TV.

باید به هر قیمت جلوی جنگ را بگیرند. They must stop (lit. prevent, stand *in front of*) the war at any price.

پشت 'behind'

چرا پُشتِ سرِ او حرف می زنید؟ Why are you talking *behind* his back?

خانهٔ ما پُشتِ سینما است. Our house is *behind* the cinema.

پَهلوی   'beside', 'by the side of', 'next to'

در سینما یک آقای پرحرف نشسته بودم.   In the cinema I was sitting *next to* a chatterbox (man).

کنار   'next to', 'by'

در هواپیما و اتوبوس دوست دارم کنارِ پنجره بنشینم.   On the plane and on the bus I like to sit *next to* the window.

آنها خانهٔ قشنگی کنارِ دریا دارند.   They have a nice house *by* the sea.

نزدیک   'close to', 'near'

مدرسهٔ بچه های من نزدیک یک پارک بزرگ است.   My children's school is *near* a big park.

صدای آنها را خیلی خوب شنیدیم چون نزدیک صَحنه بودیم.
We heard their voices very well because we were *close* to the stage.

بدون   'without'

ایرانیان نمی توانند بدونِ ویزا به اروپا سفر کنند.   Iranians may not travel to Europe *without* a visa.

دُنبال   'after', 'for'

(in the sense of 'to go after something', 'to look for something', 'to go and pick up someone')

چکار می کنی؟ دُنبالِ عینکَم می گردم.   What are you doing? I am looking *for* my glasses.

آیا می توانید روزِ شنبه در فرودگاه به دُنبالِ ما بیایید؟ Can you come and pick us up (lit. come *for* us) from the airport on Saturday?

دَم   'next to', 'by', 'close to'

دَم درِ نانوایی مُنتظرِ شما خواهم بود.   I'll be waiting for you *by* the entrance (lit. door) of the bakery.

سَر many meanings

(prefixed to a noun 'at the head of', 'at the end of', 'at the table', 'in the', 'during')

سر کوچهٔ ما یک بقالیست. There is a grocer's *at the top of* our street.

سر کار با مَرجان آشنا شدم. I met Marjan *at* work.

سر شام خیلی ساکت بود. He was very quiet *during* supper.

نباید سر کلاس حرف بزنید. You must not talk *in* the class.

لَب 'edge of'

اگر این گلدان را لب میز بگذارید می افتَد. If you put the vase on the *edge of* the table it will fall.

دربارهٔ 'about', 'on the subject of', 'concerning'

این کتاب دربارهٔ چست؟ What is this book *about*?

با دوستم دربارهٔ جَشنوارهٔ فیلمهای ایرانی حرف می زدم. I was talking to my friend *about* the Iranian Film Festival.

پیش 'in the presence of', 'in front of' 'before', 'with', 'to'

کتاب من پیش شماست. My book is *with* you. (You have got my book.)

حالش خوب نبود و او را پیش دکتر بردند. He wasn't well and they took him *to* the doctor.

چرا پیش ما نمی آیید؟ Why don't you come *to* us?

پیش اُستاد عُمومی موسیقی ایرانی یادمی گیرند. They are learning Persian music *with* Master Omumi.

فردا شب پیش خواهرم می روم. I will go *to* my sister's tomorrow night.

Note: There is a very clear distinction between the uses of به 'to', and پیش 'to'. The preposition به is used for indicating the direction of movement *towards* something, as in 'going to a city' or 'into a house'.

However, the English idiomatic saying 'going to someone's', even though direction is indicated, must be translated using the Persian preposition پیش. به really means towards or into, so to say 'I am going to Yazd, to my friend's' would be: به یزد، پیش دوستم می روم.

Exercise 1

🔊 **CD 2, TR 8**

Listen to the recording demonstrating the use of prepositions. Then translate the text into English:

مَغازهٔ پِدِرزنِ سیروس

پدرزنِ سیروس یک مغازهٔ سبزی (vegetables, herbs) و میوه فروشی دارد. مغازه اش در خیابانِ فردوسی است. جلوی مغازه یک پیاده روی (pavement) باریک (narrow) و جوی آب است. چند درختِ بلُند و یک دکهٔ روزنامه فروشی هم جلوی مغازه هست. در طرف راست مغازه یک شیرینی فروشی و در طرفِ چپِ آن یک کَفاشیست. روبروی مغازه، آنطرفِ خیابان، یک آرایشگاه (hairdresser, beauty salon) یک بانک و یک آموزشگاه زبان های خارجی است. روی مغازه، مطب (surgery) یک دکتر است و پشتِ مغازه، یک پمپ بنزین است. پدرزنِ سیروس از صبحِ زود تا شب در این مغازه کار می کند ولی گاهی برای ناهار به چلوکبابی نزدیکِ سینما می رود.

خیابان فردوسی همیشه شلُوغ است. فقط صبح های زود کمی خَلوَت (quiet) می شَوَد. در این خیابان همه جور مغازه هست: کتاب فروشی، عکاسی، خیاطی، نجاری، بوتیک لباس، جواهرفروشی، نانوایی، قصابی، داروخانه و مغازه های دیگر. پدرزنِ سیروس همه نوع سبزی و میوه در مغازه اش می فروشد: جَعفَری، نَعناع، اِسفِناج،

170

سیر، کَدو، پیاز، بادنجان، گوجه فرنگی، سیب زمینی، پرتقال، موز، انگور، انار، سیب، هُلو، گُلابی و خربزه و غیره.

Exercise 2

Translate the following sentences into Persian:

1 Maryam came to our house last night.
2 We went to Ali's house by bus.
3 She put the vase on the table.
4 His shoes are under the bed.
5 I want to go to my grandmother's this weekend.
6 There is some food in the fridge.
7 Don't fill in the form in pencil.
8 Where are you going for your holidays?

Design on pottery, 12th century

18

Suggesting a visit to a friend

In this unit you will learn how to
- *Ask for things*
- *Ask someone else to do something for you*
- *Express wishes, hopes and plans*

Dialogue

◀) CD 2, TR 9

In the dialogue, Maryam suggests a visit to a friend's house. (Listen carefully to the verbs.)

م   میخواهی امشب پیش هوشنگ برویم؟

ا   نه مرسی. من امشب نمیتوانم هیچ جایی بروم.

م   چرا نمیتوانی؟

ا   امشب باید حتماً به کتابخانه بروم.

م   چرا؟

ا   چون فردا امتحان دارم و باید درس بخوانم.

م   چه اِمتحانی داری؟

ا   امتحانِ جغرافی دارم.

م   امتحانت ساعت چند شروع میشوَد؟

أ   ساعت دو بعدازظهر شروع می‌شَوَد.

م   کی تَمام می شَوَد؟

أ   ساعت چهارتَمام می شَوَد. می توانیم فردا شب پس از امتحانم پیشِ هوشنگ برویم.

م   بسیار خوب، به او تلفن می کنم تا بگویم تا فردا شب می آییم.

M	Do you want (us) to go to Hushang's tonight?
A	No, thanks. I can't go anywhere tonight.
M	Why can't you?
A	I have got to (definitely) go the library tonight.
M	Why?
A	Because I have got an exam tomorrow and must study.
M	What exam have you got?
A	I have got a geography exam.
M	What time does your exam start?
A	It starts at two o'clock (*lit*. hour of two) in the afternoon.
M	What time (when) does it end?
A	(It) ends at four o'clock (*lit*. hour of four). We can go to Hushang tomorrow night, after my exam.
M	Very well, I will call him to say that we will come tomorrow night.

mi-khāhi?	*do you* (pl.) *want?*	میخواهی (خواستَن)
beravim	(subjunctive) *(for us) to go*	بِرَویم (رفتن)
nemitavānam	*I cannot*	نمیتوانَم (توانِستَن)
hich jā-i	*to nowhere – to anywhere*	هیچ جایی
beravam	(subjunctive) *(that) I go*	بِرَوَم
bāyad	*must*	باید
hatman	*definitely*	حَتماً
chon	*because*	چون
emtehān	*examination*	اِمتِحان

QUICK VOCAB

| **dars bekhānam** | (subjunctive) *(that)* I *study* | درس بِخوانَم (درس خواندن) |
| **joghrāfi** | *geography* | جُغرافی |

> ## Insight
>
> The present subjunctive is quite similar to the present indicative in formation but instead of the *mi* می prefix you must use the *be* بِ prefix. There must always be another element in the sentence too that will make it a subjunctive sentence.

Forming the present subjunctive

When we use the present indicative mood, that is the simple present tense, we imply that an action has either actually happened once and continues habitually (e.g. 'I live in Iran', 'I work in an office') or will happen or is happening right now. The subjunctive mood, by way of contrast, implies that an action is possible, or suggested, i.e. it may, should or could happen.

In other words, while the indicative mood describes a *real* action, the subjunctive mood is used in sentences where the action is not definitely going to happen. The subjunctive verb is used when we make a wish, express a fear, anxiety or desire, point out a possibility or doubt or set a condition.

Therefore the formation of the present subjunctive is similar to that of the ordinary present tense with one small difference. The present subjunctive is formed from the present stem of the verb plus the addition of the personal endings and, here is the difference, the prefix بِ *be* is used instead of the prefix می *mi*, which is used for the ordinary present tense.

First, we need to work out the present stem in exactly the same way as we did in Unit 15 to form the simple present tense: infinitive → present stem. We can then use the formula: present subjunctive = personal endings + present stem + بِ.

For example, the present subjunctive of the verb خوابیدن 'to sleep' is formed by working out the present stem first: خوابیدن ← خواب. Then, following the formula we get the following:

Plural		Singular				
بخوابیم	بخوابَم		یم	مَ		
بخوابید	بخوابی	=	ید	ی	ی + خواب + بِ	
بخوابند	بخوابَد		ند	دَ		

These give you the present subjunctive of the verb 'to sleep'. However, these verbs are only occasionally used on their own in a sentence. A subjunctive sentence normally needs its main subjunctive verb and also another word or verb to point out the sense of 'possibility', 'wishfulness', 'fear', 'obligation' or 'desire' and so on. For example, in English, we usually say "I <u>want</u> to buy an umbrella', 'She very much <u>hopes</u> to go to Iran this summer', 'We <u>may</u> come to your house', 'I <u>must</u> see that film' and 'They <u>can't</u> go to the party'. The underlined verbs in these examples, known as 'modals' ('can', 'want', 'must') *modify the main verb* by indicating the possible, wishful or obligatory sense of the action. They will look like this:

I *want* to buy an umbrella.   می خواهَم یک چَتر بِخَرَم.

She very much *hopes* to go to Iran this summer.

او خیلی اُمیدوار است (کِه) اِمسال تابستان به ایران بِرَوَد.

We *may* come to your house.   ما شاید به خانهٔ شما بیاییم.

(ما مُمکِن است به خانهٔ شما بیاییم.) is also possible.)

I *must* see that film.   باید آن فیلم را بِبینَم.

They *can't go* to the party.   (آنها) نمی توانند به مهمانی بِرَوَند.

The subjunctive form stays the same whether the modal is in the present or the past. The present subjunctive is indicated by the stressed prefix بِ in the positive and by نَ in the negative. In many cases, the subjunctive, and thus the prefix بِ is the equivalent of an English infinitive, e.g. 'want *to go*', 'able *to stay*', 'hopes to *travel*', 'have got *to run*', etc.

Insight

Unlike other verbs the negative of the present subjunctive is not formed by adding a *ne* نـ to the verb but rather you must drop the *be* بـ prefix and just add the *ne* نـ.

Other examples using modals

I can (am able to) see Reza. می توانم رضا را ببینم.

They could (were able to) come by bus.

می توانستند با اتوبوس بیایند.

You must (have to) work. (تو) باید کار بکنی.

A variety of adjectives may be used for the notion of 'must', e.g.:

I am forced to/must work. مجبورم کار بکنم.

I have no choice but to work. ناچارم کار بکنم.

It is better that you go/leave. بهتر است بروی.

Subjunctive elsewhere

There are many expressions besides the modals which also modify an action as hope, possibility, desire, intent, etc., e.g.:

I hope he phones today. اُمیدوارم (که) امروز تلفن بکند.

I feel like/inclined to sleep. میل دارم بخوابم.

It is possible that he may go/leave today.

ممکن است که امروز برود.

We wish to travel to China next year.

آرزو میکنیم که سال دیگر/آینده به چین سفر بکنیم.
(کاش سال دیگر به چین سفر بکنیم.) is also possible.)

The subjunctive is also used for suggested action, e.g. 'shall we . . .', 'let' (بگذارید), 'before' (قبل از اینکه / پیش از اینکه), 'please' (لطفاً/میکنم), 'instead of' (بجای اینکه), 'they decided' (تصمیم گرفتند), 'apart from' (جز اینکه/بغیر از اینکه), etc. خواهش

176

Insight
The present subjectives of 'to be' and 'to have' are irregular
and have their own unique formation.

Exercise 1

🔊 CD 2, TR 9, 01:04

Read the story about Mr Halu, an absent-minded husband, and follow
it on the recording. Then translate it into English:

آقای کم حافِظه:

وقتیکه آقای کم حافِظه، صبح ،از خانه اش بیرون می آمد، زنش
ي   نامه به او داد و گفت: این نامه را حتماً امروز پست کن.
نامه   خیلی مهمی است. فراموش نکن.«

ولی آقای کم حافِظه حرفِ زنش را فراموش کرد و نامه را به
صندوقِ پست نیانداخت. وقتی از اتوبوس پیاده شد و دوان دوان به
طرف اداره اش می رفت ناگهان ي   آقایی آهسته به شانه اش زد و
گفت: نامه یادتان نرود!«

آقای کم حافِظه خیلی تعجب کرد و نامه را به صندوق انداخت و به
طرفِ اداره اش راه افتاد. در راه ناگهان خانم خوشگلی به او گفت:
آقا، نامه تان را فراموش نکنید.«

ایندفعه آقای کم حافِظه ایستاد و با تعجبِ زیاد گفت: خدایا! این
مردم از کجا می دانند که من باید نامه ای را پست کنم؟ من از چند
دقیقه پیش أنرا پست کردم!«

در جواب خانم خندید و گفت: پس لطفاً این یادداشت را از پشتتان
بردارید.«

روی یادداشت نوشته بود: خواهش می کنم به شوهرم بگویید نامه
را فراموش نکند.«

Exercise 2

Translate the following sentences into Persian:

1 They want to see you tomorrow night.
2 I can't go to my Persian class this evening.
3 We hope to buy a bigger house next summer.
4 She wanted to travel to Shiraz too.
5 Please call before going to his house.

Insight

The third person singular of the present subjunctive 'to be', باشد
is used in spoken Persian to mean 'OK' or 'all right'.

Test yourself

1 When do we use the subjunctive in Persian?
2 How similar is the formation of the present subjunctive to that of the simple present indicative?
3 Can the present subjunctive be used entirely on its own or does the sentence require any other element that necessitates the use of subjunctive?
4 What are the verb subject endings for the present subjunctive in Persian?
5 How are the negatives of the present subjunctive formed?
6 Can there be more than one subjunctive verb in a sentence?
7 How are possibilities, wishes and hopes expressed in Persian?
8 Are the present subjunctives of the verb 'to be' formed the same way as those for all other verbs?
9 What are the present subjunctives of the verb 'to be' in Persian?
10 What does it mean if the third person singular of the present subjunctive 'to be', i.e. 'bāshad' باشد, is used in spoken Persian?

19

Planning a summer trip

In this unit you will learn how to
- *Use the proper future tense*
- *Talk about holidays and holiday destinations*

Dialogue

🔊 CD 2, TR 10

د امسال تابستان چکار میکنی؟

م چند هَفته کار می کنم ولی بعد به ایران خواهم رفت. اُمیدوارم هر چه زودتر ویزایم را بگیریم.

د چه خوب. در ایران چه کارها خواهی کرد و کجاها خواهی رفت؟

م من با یک دوستم به ایران میروم. ما چند روز در تهران خواهیم ماند و بعد به چندین شهر سفر خواهیم کرد.

د در ایران دوست و آشنا دارید؟

م آره، تنها نخواهیم بود. در ماه ژوئیه چندنفر دیگر از همکلاسی هایم هم به ایران خواهند آمد.

د مطمئنم خیلی به شما خوش خواهد گذشت.

D	What are you doing this summer?
M	I shall work for a few weeks and will then go to Iran. I hope to get my visa as soon as possible.
D	How wonderful. What sorts of things will you be doing in Iran and where (lit. which places) will you go to?
M	I am going to Iran with a friend of mine. We will spend a few days in Tehran and will then travel to a few cities.
D	Do you have friends and acquaintances in Iran?
M	Yup, we won't be alone. A few of my classmates will also come to Iran in July.
D	I am sure you will have a very good time.

Forming the proper future tense

It is quite normal to use the present tense for the future. However, there is a proper future tense in Persian and it is generally used for rather emphatic statements with reference to the future.

The formation of the future tense requires the help of the present tense of the auxilary verb 'to want' خواستن *khāstan* (present stem: خواه) and the past stem of the main verb. Remember that the می -*mi* prefix that is mandatory for present tenses is omitted from the formation of the future tense (see table).

Singular	Plural
خواهَم رفت I shall go	خواهیم رفت we shall go
خواهی رفت you shall go	خواهید رفت you (pl.) shall go
خواهَد رفت he, she, it shall go	خواهَند رفت they shall go

Compound verbs are formed in exactly the same way: the verb element is conjugated and the *noun* or *preposition* component tags along. For example, زندگی کردن 'to live' is shown in the following table.

180

Insight

Present tense verbs can be used for future actions. However, the proper future tense is used in simple predictive or expected future as in the English: 'I will go to Iran next summer' تابستان آینده به ایران خواهم رفت or 'they will be arriving soon' به زودی خواهد رسید.

Singular	Plural
زندگی خواهم کرد I shall live	زندگی خواهیم کرد we shall live
زندگی خواهی کرد you shall live	زندگی خواهید کرد you (pl.) shall live
زندگی خواهد کرد he, she, it shall live	زندگی خواهَند کرد they shall live

An example of preposition + verb compound verb, درآوردن 'to take out, to get out' is shown in the following table.

Singular	Plural
در خواهم آورد I shall bring it out	در خواهیم آورد we shall bring it out
در خواهی آورد you shall bring it out	در خواهید آورد you (pl.) shall bring it out
در خواهد آورد he, she, it shall bring it out	در خواهَند آورد they shall bring it out

Exercise 1

Translate the following sentences into Persian, using the proper future tense:

1 I will see you tomorrow evening.
2 Will they travel by bus or by train?
3 She will write this letter next week and give it to me.
4 They will call us when they get back from Paris.
5 We will buy a much bigger house soon.

Exercise 2

Translate into English:

۱ هفتهٔ آینده به ایران می روم و سه ماه در تهران خواهم ماند.

۲ حتماً امروز عصر این نامه را خواهند نوشت.

۳ کی به خانهٔ خواهرتان خواهید رفت؟

۴ پیام شما را ما به بابک خواهیم داد.

۵ چند ساعتِ دیگر کارتان با کامپیوتر تمام خواهد شد؟

Exercise 3

◄€ CD 2, TR 10, 00:57

In the dialogue below you hope to finish a letter in Persian in time to send it off to Iran with your friend's husband. Put the English sentences into Persian and translate the Persian parts too.

Friend	شما این نامه را کی تمام خواهید کرد؟
You	I'll try to finish it tomorrow evening, but I can't promise. Will you be at home?
Friend	بله، امیدوارم که بعداز ساعت هفت خانه باشم. من میتوانم به شما کمک کنم که نامه‌را به فارسی بنویسید.
You	That would be very helpful. I will come to your house after dinner at about 9:30.
Friend	شما شام بیایید پیش ما. بعداز شام نامه را مینویسیم ومن آنرا به شوهرم میدهم که روز بعد با خودش به ایران ببرد.

Test yourself

1 Is it absolutely imperative to use the proper future tense in Persian?
2 How else can we express future action in Persian?
3 Which auxiliary (helper) verb is used in the formation of future tense?
4 How are the subjects, that is the doers, of the future tense in Persian represented in the verb?
5 Is the component of the main verb in the Persian future tense extracted from the present or the past stem?
6 How are negative future tenses formed?
7 How would you say 'I will go to Iran next year'?
8 How would you say 'We will not stay at this hotel again'?
9 How would you say 'She will be in her office till 6 pm'?
10 What are the two way to say: 'Will you (pl.) come to the cinema with us?'

20

....

How are you feeling?

In this unit you will learn how to
- *Use idiomatic impersonal verbs*
- *Express likes and dislikes*
- *Describe the various stages of going to sleep*
- *Say you are tired*
- *Say you are having a good time*

Dialogue

◄» CD 2, TR 11

● مریم جان، چطوری؟ خوبی؟ اِنگار خیلی خسته ای؟

■ نه، چیزیم نیست. فقط خوابم می آید.

● چرا؟ مگر دیشب خوب نخوابیدی؟

■ چرا، خوب خوابیدم ولی دیر خوابیدم. دیشب به یِ مهمانی رفته بودیم و خیلی دیر به منزل برگشتیم.

● مهمانی چطور بود؟ خوش گذشت؟

■ جای شما خالی، خیلی مهمانیِ خوبی بود و جداً به ما خوش گذشت. غذای خوشمزه، موسیقیِ عالی، بیشتر دوستان و فامیل هم بودند و تا دیروقت رقصیدیم.

● غذا را کی پخته بود؟

● How are you, dear Maryam? Are you well? You seem very tired.
■ No, there is nothing wrong with me. I am just sleepy (lit. my sleep is coming).
● Why? Did you not sleep well last night?
■ Yes, I did sleep well but I went to bed late (lit. slept late). We went to a party last night and returned home very late.
● How was the party? Did you have a good time (lit. did the time pass pleasantly)?
■ Wish you were there (lit. your place was empty – you were conspicuous by your absence); it was a very good party and we had a truly good time (lit. the time passed seriously, pleasantly): delicious food, fantastic music, most of our friends and family were there too and we danced till late.
● Who had cooked the food?
■ They had brought the food from an Iranian restaurant. I can't remember the name of the restaurant (lit. the name of the restaurant is not [in] my memory) but all the guests liked the food (lit. their pleasure came from the food).

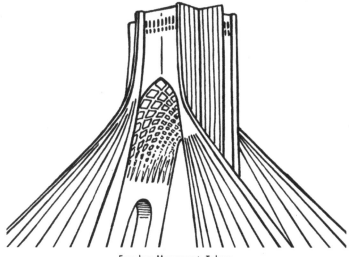

Freedom Monument, Tehran

When we first discussed the formation of Persian verbs we emphasized that the ending of every verb lets you know who the subject is, that is the agent of the action undertaken by the verb, so when we see or hear the verb رفتیم *raftim*, by looking at the ending یم *-im* we know immediately that the action of 'going' was done by 'us', as in 'we went'. However, there are a small group of Persian verbs that do not follow this pattern. These verbs are normally known as impersonal verbs and their formation requires a slightly more advanced knowledge of grammar. As these verbs refer to some of the most basic everyday actions and, furthermore, are very frequently used by native speakers of Persian it is important you should know something about their use and formation. In addition, for some actions, such as 'to fall asleep', there are no verbs other than these impersonal constructions.

Impersonal verbs usually refer to actions that are perceived as involuntary. Sometimes this is clear to see, as in the example in the dialogue for instance. 'To fall asleep', for example, is usually outside our control and it happens while the subject, or the doer of the action, has very little say or control on the outcome. Other examples are 'suddenly to forget something' or 'suddenly to remember'. The impersonal nature of these verbs is more or less as it is in English, when the idiomatic expressions for 'forgetting' such as 'it escapes my mind' or 'it's completely gone from my mind' are used or when we say 'it's coming back to me' or 'it will come to me' when we describe the involuntary process of remembering.

Impersonal verbs are *always* compound verbs. The formation and conjugation of these verbs are still regular but different from the standard Persian verb conjugation.

We can start by looking at the verb 'to feel sleepy' and 'to fall asleep' and compare these with the regular verb 'to sleep' to demonstrate the differences.

Look at the six cases of the simple past tense of the verb 'to sleep' in the table.

Singular	Plural
خوابیدم I slept	خوابیدیم we slept
خوابیدی you slept	خوابیدید you (pl.) slept
خوابید he, she, it slept	خوابیدند they slept

The subject ending is clearly different in each case, making it quite clear as to who has undertaken the action which is 'voluntary', in the sense that you can say:

I slept in the park last night. ‏من دیشب در پارک خوابیدم.‏

They slept on (lit. in) the train. ‏آنها توی قطار خوابیدند.‏

But 'feeling sleepy' and 'falling asleep' are perceived as outside our control, as if the force of sleep 'comes' (feeling sleepy) and then 'takes us away' (falling asleep). The impersonal Persian verb 'to feel sleep' describes this process exactly. Grammatically, it is the sleep that acts like the subject and the six cases will follow the pattern of 'my sleep came', 'your sleep came', 'his or her sleep came' etc. (see table). In all cases 'the sleep' is a third person singular subject so its verb component of 'came' will always be a third person singular verb and the compound 'my sleep' will be formed by using the attached, 'suffixed' possessive pronouns ‏َم، ِت، َش، ِمان، ِتان، ِشان.‏

Singular	Plural
‏خوابَم آمد‏ I was sleepy (lit. my sleep came)	‏خوابِمان آمد‏ we were sleepy (lit. our sleep came)
‏خوابَت آمد‏ you were sleepy (lit. your sleep came)	‏خوابِتان آمد‏ you (pl.) were sleepy (lit. your sleep came)
‏خوابَش آمد‏ he, she, it was sleepy (lit. his, her, its sleep came)	‏خوابِشان آمد‏ they were sleepy (lit. their sleep came)

Insight

Certain actions deemed as involuntary, impulsive or beyond our control can be expressed in alternative ways, as if they are done by someone else. The doer of the action will therefore always be a third person singular he/she.

‏مریم خیلی خسته بود و خوابش می آمد. ساعت هشت خوابید.‏
Maryam was very tired and sleepy. She slept at 8 o'clock.

‏بچه ها خوابشان می آمد و قبل از شام خوابیدند.‏ The children were very sleepy and went to bed (lit. slept) before supper.

‏امشب خوابم نمی آید.‏ I am not sleepy (lit. my sleep is not coming) tonight.

Other impersonal verbs

'To fall asleep' (lit. sleep to take someone away) خواب بُردن:

Singular	Plural
خوابَم بُرد I fell asleep (*lit.* sleep took me away)	خوابِمان بُرد we fell asleep
خوابَت بُرد you fell asleep	خوابِتان بُرد you (pl.) fell asleep
خوابَش بُرد he, she, it fell asleep	خوابِشان بُرد they fell asleep

'To like' or 'dislike' someone or something خوش آمدن – بد آمدن. In this verb it is the person's pleasure or displeasure that is derived from something. This verb requires the preposition 'of' or 'from':

مایکل از فیلمهای جدید ایرانی خوشش می آید. Michael likes (lit. his joy comes from) the new Iranian films.

ما خیلی از این رستوران خوشمان می آید. We really like (lit. our pleasure comes from) this restaurant.

آنها از بوی ماهی بدشان می آید. They dislike (or hate) (lit. their displeasure comes from) the smell of fish.

The verb 'to like' دوست داشتن is the 'regular' version of this impersonal verb.

'To forget' از یاد رفتن (lit. gone from mind) از is optional: 'I forgot' یادم رفت, 'you (sing.) forgot' یادت رفت, 'we forgot' یادمان رفت. 'To remember' به یاد آمدن (lit. to come back to one's mind) به is optional:

من یادم رفت کیف پولم را بیاورم. I forgot (lit. it slipped my mind) to bring my (money) purse.

دیشب یادشان آمد که فردا تولد مُژگان است. They remembered last night that tomorrow is Mojgan's birthday.

188

'To have a good time' is also an impersonal Persian verb, but it is formed slightly differently from the ones we have seen so far. This verb is again always in the third person singular, however, the subject is in the form of the relevant pronoun and the verb requires the preposition به 'to' as we can see from the following table.

Singular	Plural
به من خوش گذشت I had a good time	به‌ما خوش گذشت we had a good time
به تو خوش گذشت you had a good time	به شما خوش گذشت you (pl.) had a good time
به او خوش گذشت he, she, it had a good time	به آنها خوش گذشت they had a good time

در ایران به ما خیلی خوش گذشت. We had a lovely time in Iran.

اُمیدوارم به شما در مهمانی خوش بگذرد. I hope you have a nice time at the party.

Finally, چیزی بودن is another of these impersonal and also idiomatic verbs used to describe one's mood or state of being. In the negative, it is close to saying 'I am OK': چیزیم نیست is implying 'there is nothing wrong with me' or 'I am fine'.

Exercise 1
Translate into Persian using the appropriate impersonal verbs:

1 My sister went to Italy last summer and she had a very nice time.
2 I don't like this colour but that blue is pretty.
3 You forgot to call Maryam yesterday.
4 We want to watch the ten o'clock news but I am too sleepy.
5 They fell asleep on the train and didn't see the beautiful scenery.

Exercise 2
Translate into English:

١ آنها از این محلهٔ شهر بدشان می آید.

٢ تو چرا همیشه در جلسات سخنرانی خوابت می بَرَد؟

٣   هر بار که به ایران می رویم خیلی بهمان خوش می گُذَرَد.

۴   یادم رفت که فردا قرارِ دندانساز دارم یا پس فردا؟

۵   او از موسیقی ایرانی خوشش می آید.

Insight

Some actions deemed totally beyond our control can only be expressed in the impersonal way discussed in this chapter. The subject ending is always third person singular, whether it is present tense, past, future or passive.

Exercise 3

◄» CD 2, TR 11, 01:16

Practise the use of impersonal verbs in the following dialogue. Classical music and making a reservation at a restaurant will be discussed:

Amir	شما از موسیقی اصیل ایرانی خوشتان می آید؟
You	Yes, I love Persian music, why do you ask?
Amir	آخر ماه آینده یک کنسرت با چندین خوانندهٔ مشهور ایرانی در تالارِشهر خواهد بود. دوست دارید با ما بیایید؟
You	I'll definitely come. Which night is the concert on?
Amir	پنجشنبه، بیست و سوم. من همین فردا برای همه بلیط میگیرم چون میترسم که بلیط تمام شود.
You	Thank you so much. Shall we go to a nice restaurant afterwards? There is an Iranian restaurant close by.
Amir	بله، چلوکبابی یاس آنجاست و تا دیروقت هم باز است.
You	Right then. I'll book a table for eight people for 10:30.

Test yourself

1   Give three examples of Persian verbs that are not conjugated in the usual way.

2 In these verbs who seems to be the subject (doer) of the verb?

3 List the attached possessive pronouns that you need to form Persian impersonal verbs.

4 Are there regular synonyms for impersonal Persian verbs?

5 Using the appropriate Persian verbs describe the various stages from 'feeling sleepy', to 'falling asleep' and then 'sleeping'.

6 In how many ways in Persian can you express 'like' or 'dislike' for something?

7 Can you think of a comparable, 'impersonal' way in English of saying: 'I'm sorry, I forgot', or 'I'll remember her name in just a second'?

8 How do you wish someone a good time in Persian?

9 Is this verb conjugated in the same way as the other impersonal verbs?

10 Rewrite the following two sentences using an impersonal verb:

خانهٔ مریم را خیلی دوست دارم.

نامِ برادرم را فراموش کردند.

21

Grammar reference unit

Arabic influence on Persian

Owing to the influence of Islam, the Arabic alphabet is one of the most widespread writing systems in the world, found in large regions of Africa and Asia that were conquered either by the Arab or Muslim armies or, later, formed parts of the non-Arab empires that had converted to Islam. The Arabic alphabet has been adopted by users of other groups of languages, such as Persian, Pashtu, Ottoman Turkish, Urdu and Malay (Jawi), to write their own vernaculars.

The presence of Arab conquerors of the seventh century in lands such as Persia often lasted for hundreds of years, inevitably leading to the importation of numerous Arabic words into the local language. Furthermore, Arabic was the language of intellectual, scientific and philosophical discourse used by countless non-Arab writers, in the same way that Latin served as the language of scientific and religious writing in Europe.

What distinguishes Persian from the languages spoken in other conquered parts of the early Muslim Empire, such as Syria for example, is that the influence of Arabic on Persian has been limited to the expansion of vocabulary and Arabic grammar has hardly touched the *structure* of the language.

Moreover, the Arabic words that have entered Persian have become 'Persianized' to the extent that they are occasionally unrecognizable to present-day speakers of Arabic.

Since 1979 there has been a propensity on the part of the judiciary and academia to borrow more Arabic phrases and to use them in broadcasts, speeches and writings, but again this is limited to an increase in the number of loan nouns, adjectives, adverbs and prepositions and it does not affect the construction or formation of Persian words. Arabic, a Semitic language, uses a root system that does not exist in Persian, which means that even when Arabic plurals are used in Persian, they apply only to Arabic words and Persian words cannot follow the Arabic pattern to form their plurals.

Someone who is learning to speak Persian does not need to have any prior knowledge of the Arabic language to realize quite quickly that certain words used in Persian can be grouped together, as there seems to be a 'family resemblance' demonstrated by the occurence in each group of three fixed letters, appearing in different patterns. The following example should illustrate this point further. Look at these words:

درس– دروس– مدرسه– مدارس– مدرس

کتاب– کتب– مکتب– مکاتب– مکتوب

The following examples show how the Arabic root system is used to derive nouns by inserting certain vowel patterns in the blank slots in the root template.

Root form: *k_t_b*

Some words derived from the root form:

ketāb	book
kotob	books
katbi	written
kāteb	scribe
maktab	(primary) school

Insight

Arabic words and expressions used in Persian sound rather archaic or classical to speakers of modern Arabic. These are mostly Arabic expressions that came to Iran over a thousand years ago and have in many cases become quite Persianized.

These Arabic words have been imported and lexicalized in Persian. So, for instance, the Arabic plural form for *ketāb* is *kotob* obtained by the root derivation system. In Persian, the plural for the lexical word *ketāb* can be given as in Arabic (*kotob*) or it can be obtained simply by adding the Persian plural marker: *ketāb* + *hā* → *ketābhā*.

The learner of basic Persian does not need to worry about learning the rules of Arabic word formation and can merely learn the common Arabic words that have everyday usage as part of his or her vocabulary. However, in-depth study of the Persian literature and even understanding the subtleties of the common language will not be possible without some knowledge of Arabic.

◀)) **CD 2, TR 12**

The following is an example of a text that relies on many Arabic words and derivatives (and a translation can be found in the Key):

کتبی هست که می توانیم جواب سؤال های مختلف را در آنها پیدا کنیم. این کتابها را لغت نامه و دایرة المعارف می خوانیم. در این کتابها کلمه ها و اسامی به ترتیب الفبایی و با حروف سیاه درج شده و دربارهٔ هریک توضیح مفصلی با حروف نازک داده شده است.

دایرة المعارف معمولاً کتابِ قطوری است که می توانیم هر نوع اطلاعات علمی، ادبی، هنری، تاریخی، جغرافیایی و جز اینها را در آن بیابیم. برخی از دایرة المعارف ها در جلدهای متعددی فراهم آمده است.

The story of Iran

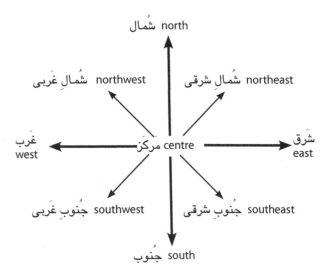

شُمال north

شُمال غَربی northwest

شُمال شَرقی northeast

غَرب west

مَرکَز centre

شَرق east

جُنوب غَربی southwest

جُنوب شَرقی southeast

جُنوب south

🔊 **CD 2, TR 13**

کِشوَرِ ایران دَر نیمکُرهٔ شُمالی و دَر جُنوبِ غَربی آسیا است. ایران یِکی اَز کِشوَرهای بُزُرگِ خاوَرمیانه است. مَساحَتِ ایران ۱۶۴۸۱۹۵ (یِک ملیون و ششصَدو چِهِل و هَشت هِزار و صَد و نَوَد و پَنج) کیلومترِ مُرَبَع است. ایران با هَفت کِشوَرِ هَمسایه اَست. دَر شُمال و شُمالِ شَرقی، ایران با جُمهوری تُرکمَنِستان و دَر شُمالِ غَربی با جُمهوری های آذَربایجان و اَرمَنِستان هَم مَرز است. پایتَختِ آذَربایجان شَهرِ باکوست. پایتَختِ جُمهوری اَرمَنِستان، شَهرِ ایرِوان اَست و عشق آباد پایتَختِ جُمهوری تُرکمَنِستان است. دَر شَرقِ ایران کِشوَرِ اَفغانِستان قَرار دارَد و پاکِستان دَر جُنوبِ شَرقی ایران است.

پایتختِ اَفغانِستان شهرِ کابُل و پایتختِ پاکِستان، اِسلام آباد است.

ایران دو هَمسایهٔ غَربی دارَد: کِشورِ تُرکیه در شُمالِ غَربی و کِشورِ عَراق در غَرب.

پایتختِ تُرکیه، آنکارا و پایتختِ عَراق شهرِ تاریخی بَغداد است.

مَرزِ بینِ ایران و هَمسایگانَش در جاهایی بِسیار کوتاه و در جاهای دیگر طولانیست.

مَثَلاً، مَرزِ ایران و جُمهوریِ اَرمَنِستان فَقَط ۳۸(سی و هَشت) کیلومتراست ولی مَرزِ بینِ ایران و عَراق ۱۶۰۹(هِزار و شِشصَد و نُه) کیلومتر است. ایران یِك کِشورِ کوهِستانی و نِسبتاً خُشك است ولی در شُمال و جُنوبِ ایران دو دریای خیلی بُزُرگ قَرار دارَد. دریای خَزَر در شُمالِ ایرانَست و خَلیجِ فارس در جُنوبِ ایران. دریای خَزَر با ۴۲۴۲۰۰ (چِهارصَد و بیست و چِهار هِزار و دویست) کیلومترِ مُرَبَّع وُسعَت، بُزُرگتَرین دریاچهٔ جَهان است. خاویارِ دریای خَزَر در دُنیا مَعروف است. مَرزِ ایران و آب های خَلیجِ فارس ۲۰۴۳ (دوهِزار و چِهل و سه) کیلومتر است. خَلیجِ فارس چه اَهَمیتی دارد؟ نَفتِ ایران و کِشورهای دیگرِ مَنطَقه از راهِ خَلیجِ فارس به اُقیانوس هند و از آنجا به کِشورهای دیگرِ دُنیا می رود.

مُروارید و ماهی های خَلیجِ فارس هَم خیلی مَعروف است.

جَمعیتِ ایران نَزدیک به شَصت و هَشت مِلیون نَفَر است. زَبانِ رَسمیِ بیشترِ مَردُمِ ایران فارسی است ولی خیلی از ایرانیان، تُرکی، کُردی یا عَربی حَرف می زَنَند.

۹۹٪ (نَوَد و نُه دَرصَد) مَردُمِ ایران مُسلمان هَستَند: ۸۹٪ (هَشتاد و نُه دَرصَد) شیعه و ۱۰٪ (ده دَرصَد) سُنّی. ولی تا پیش از قَرنِ هَفتُمِ میلادی، بیشترِ ایرانیان زَرتُشتی بودَند و هَنوز هَم زَرتُشتیان، یَهودیان و مَسیحیان در ایران زِندِگی می کُنَند.

* The population of Iran is nearer 70 million (2010)

پایتَختِ ایران شهرِ تهران است. اصفهان، شیراز، تبریز، کرمانشاه، اَهواز، رشت و مشهَد از شهرهای بُزُرگِ ایرانَند.

شَهرِ تهران در دامَنهٔ کوه است. هَوای تهران در تابِستان خیلی گَرم و در زِمستان خیلی سَرد و بَرفی است.

بَهار و پاییزِ تهران بسیار زیباست. روزِ اَوَلِ بَهار، نُوروز، و عیدِ باستانیِ ایرانیان است.

رَنگ های گِلیم، قالیچه، و قالی های ایرانی هَمان رَنگ های طَبیعَتِ ایران اَست. گِلیم، قالیچه، و قالی های ایرانی بسیار زیبا و قَشَنگَند.

شاعرانِ بُزُرگِ ایران هَم مَعروف اَند. یِکی اَز شاعرانِ بُزُرگِ ایران فردوسی نام دارد.

او بیشتَر از هزار سال پیش در شهرِ طوس، در شُمالِ شَرقیِ ایران به دُنیا آمد.

این شِعرِ فردوسی آرمانِ خوبی برای زِندِگیست:

tavānā bovad har ke dānā bovad
تَوانا بُوَد هَر که دانا بُوَد

ze dānesh del-e pir bornā bovad
زِ دانِش دِلِ پیر بُرنا بُوَد

Persepolis: the Columns

keshvar	country	کِشوَر
dar	in	دَر
nim-kore	hemisphere	نیمکُرِه
shomāli	northern	شُمالی
jonub	south	جُنوب
gharbi	western	غَربی
ast	is	اَست
yeki az	one of	یِکی اَز
bozorg	big, large	بُزرگ
khāvar-e miyane	Middle East	خاوَرِمیانه
masāhat	surface area, expanse	مَساحَت
moraba'	square	مُرَبع
bā	with, by	با
haft	seven	هَفت
hamsāye	neighbour	هَمسایه (همسایگان)
shomāl	north	شُمال
jomhuri	republic	جُمهوری
shomāl-e sharqi	northeast	شُمالِ شَرقی
ham-marz	with common border, sharing the same border	هَم مرز
pāytakht	capital city	پایتَخت
shahr	city	شَهر
qarār dārad	placed, situated قرار داشتَن from infinitive to be situated	قَرار دارَد
tārikhi	historic	تاریخی

198

jā	*place*	جا
jāhā	*places* (pl.)	جا ها
jāhā'i	*some places* (indefinite pl.)	جاهایی
besiyār	*much, very*	بسیار
kutāh	*short (brief)*	کوتاه
tulāni	*long*	طولانی
masalan	*for instance, for example*	مَثَلاً
faqat	*only*	فَقَط
vali	*however, but*	وَلی
kuhestāni	*mountainous*	کوهستانی
nesbatan	*relatively*	نسبتاً
khoshk	*dry, arid*	خُشک
daryā	*sea*	دریا
kheyli	*very, much*	خِیلی
daryā-ye kheyli bozorg	*very big sea*	دریای خیلی بزرگ
khazar	*the Caspian*	خَزَر
Khalij-e fārs	*Persian Gulf*	خَلیجِ فارس
vos'at	*expanse, surface area*	وسعت
bozorgtarin	*biggest, largest*	بُزُرگتَرین
daryāche	*lake*	دریاچه
jahān	*world*	جهان
bozorgtarin daryāche-ye jahān	*biggest lake in the world*	بُزُرگتَرین دریاچهٔ جهان
āb	*water*	آب
khāviyār	*caviar*	خاویار
dar	*in, at*	در

donyā	*world*	دُنیا
ma'ruf	*famous*	مَعروف
che?	*what?*	چِه؟
ahammiyat	*importance, significance*	اَهَمییت
naft	*oil*	نَفت
digar	*other*	دیگَر
mantaqe	*region*	مَنطقهِ
az	*from, of, through*	اَز
rāh	*way, path, road*	راه
be	*to*	به
oqiyānus	*ocean*	اُقیانوس
hend	*India*	هِند
ānjā	*there, that place*	آنجا
miravad	(*to go* رَفتَن inf.) *goes,* 3rd per. sing. present tense	می رَوَد
morvārid	*pearl*	مُروارید
māhi	*fish*	ماهی
ham	*also, too*	هَم
jam'iyyat	*population*	جَمعییَت
nazdik	*near by, close to*	نَزدیک
shast o hasht	*68*	شَصت و هَشت
nafar	*persons*	نَفَر
zabān	*language (tongue)*	زَبان
rasmi	*official*	رَسمی
bishtar	here *most of* (*more, majority*)	بیشتَر
mardom	*people*	مَردُم

harf mizanand	*they speak*	حَرف می زَنَند
mosalmān	*Muslims*	مُسلمان
hastand	*they are*	هَستَند
shi'e	*Shi'ite*	شیعِه
sonni	*Sunni*	سُنّی
pish az	*before, prior to*	پیش از
qarn	*century*	قَرن
haftom	*seventh*	هَفتُم
milādi	*Christian era (BCE)*	میلادی
zartoshti	*Zoroastrian*	زرتُشتی
budand	*they were*	بودَند
hanuz	*still, as yet*	هَنوز
yahudi	*Jewish*	یَهودی pl. یَهودیان
masihi	*Christian*	مَسیحی pl. مَسیحیان
zendegi mi-konand	*they live*	زندگی می کُنَند
dāmane	*outskirts*	دامنِه
kuh	*mountain*	کوه
havā	*weather* (also *air*)	هَوا
tābestān	*summer*	تابِستان
garm	*warm (hot)*	گَرم
zemestān	*winter*	زمِستان
sard	*cold*	سرد
barfi	*snowy*	بَرفی
bahār	*spring*	بَهار
pā'iz	*autumn*	پاییز
zibā	*pretty (beautiful)*	زیبا
ruz	*day*	روز

avval	first	اَوَل
noruz	first day of Persian New Year	نوروز
'eid	festival, feast, celebration	عید
bāstani	ancient	باستانی
rang	colour, shade	رنگ
gelim	kelim rugs	گلیم
qāliche	small rugs	قالیچِه
qāli	carpet	قالی
hamān	that very	هَمان
tabi'at	nature	طَبیعَت
qashang	beautiful	قَشَنگ
shā'er	poet	شاعِر
nām dārad	is named	نام دارَد
hezār	thousand	هِزار
sāl	year	سال
sāl-e pish	year(s) ago	سالِ پیش
be donyā āmad	was born, lit. came to the world	به دُنیا آمد
in she'r	this poem	این شِعر
ārmān	maxim	آرمان
khub	good	خوب
khubi	a good	خوبی
barā-ye	for	برای
zendegi	life	زِندِگی

[The country of] Iran is [situated] in the northern hemisphere, in southwest Asia. Iran is one of the largest countries of the Middle East. Iran's area is 1,648,195 square kilometres. Iran borders onto seven countries (lit. is neighbours with seven countries). To the north and the northeast, Iran borders onto the Republic of Turkmenistan and in the northwest it borders onto the Republics of Azerbaijan and Armenia.

The capital of Azerbaijan is the city of Baku. The capital of the Republic of Armenia is the city of Yerevan and Ashkabad is the capital of the Republic of Turkmenistan.

[The country of] Afghanistan is situated to the east of Iran and Pakistan is to the southeast [borders] of Iran. The capital of Afghanistan is Kabul and Pakistan's capital is Islamabad.

Iran has two western neighbours: Turkey in the northwest and Iraq in the west.

The capital of Turkey is Ankara and the capital of Iraq is the historic city of Baghdad.

The border between Iran and its neighbours at some points is very short and at others it is long. For example, the border between Iran and the Republic of Armenia is only 38 km but the border between Iran and Iraq is 1,609 km.

Iran is a mountainous and relatively dry country; however, two very large seas lie to the north and the south of Iran. The Caspian Sea is to the north of Iran and the Persian Gulf is to the south. The Caspian Sea, with an area of 424,200 sq km, is the biggest lake in the world. The caviar of the Caspian is world famous. The Persian Gulf and Iran share a 2,043-km long border. What is the significance of the Persian Gulf? The oil from Iran and from other countries of the region goes to other countries of the world by way of the Persian Gulf and through the Indian Ocean. The pearls and fish from the Persian Gulf are also very renowned.

The population of Iran is nearly 70 million. The official language of most people in Iran is Persian; however, many Iranians speak Turkish, Kurdish or Arabic.

Ninety-nine per cent of the people in Iran are Muslim: 89% Shi'ite and 10% Sunni. However, before the seventh century (BCE), Iranians were Zoroastrian and Zoroastrians, Jews and Christians still live in Iran.

The capital of Iran is the city of Tehran. Esfahan, Shiraz, Tabriz, Kermanshah, Ahvaz, Rasht and Mashhad are the big cities of Iran. The city of Tehran is in the foothills of mountains. The weather in Tehran is very hot in the summer and very cold and snowy in winter. The spring and autumn in Tehran are very beautiful. The first day of the spring is *noruz*, 'the new (year) day', and an ancient festival of the Iranians.

The colours of Persian kelims, rugs and carpets are the very colours of nature in Iran. Persian rugs and carpets are very pretty and beautiful.

The great poets of Iran are also famous. One of the great poets of Iran is called Ferdosi. He was born, more than 1,000 years ago, in the city of Tus, in northeast Iran.

This poem of Ferdosi is a good maxim for life:

Knowledge is Power. (*Lit.* He who has knowledge is powerful.)
It is from knowledge that the heart of an old person remains rejuvenated.

Taking it further

Persian/Iranian studies are offered at undergraduate or post-graduate level at the following universities: University of London School of Oriental and African Studies, Cambridge, Edinburgh, Oxford, Manchester, and Durham; Australian National University (ANU); Harvard, New York University, Princeton, Columbia, Texas Austin, Utah, Chicago and Toronto.

The internet will give you access to a wealth of resources on Persian culture. The Iranian Cultural and Information Center at
http://tehran.stanford.edu/

is a good place to start, with its many sections (history, literature, names, etc.).

The British Institute of Persian Studies, at the British Academy, 10 Carlton House Terrace, London SW1Y 5AH, is another fine resource.
http://www.bips.ac.uk

Language resources are available at
http://www.columbia.edu/cu/lweb/indiv/mideast/cuvlm/persian.html

News is available from the BBC at
http://www.bbc.co.uk/persian/

The following official government websites will give you valuable information:
http://www.gov.ir/

For a real treasure trove, go to
http://www.iranian.com

For the latest cultural events in the UK go to:
http://iranheritage.org

And for a list of all Iranian newspapers, radio and TV and much, much more go to
http://www.gooya.com

Appendix: complex grammar

Complex sentences in Persian

Complex sentences can mean anything from two simple sentences linked by the conjunction 'and' to very complex sentences containing subordinate and relative clauses, temporal and dependent clauses as well as indirect statements.

The purpose of this appendix is to refer to some aspects of relative clauses because although they are considered as advanced grammar they are used widely in everyday conversation and writing.

Co-ordinate sentences

When two sentences are linked by 'and' وَ they form the simplest of complex sentences:

مریم آمد و کتابم را آورد. Maryam arrived and brought my book.

The link can also be 'but' or 'however':

من ژاپنی هستم ولی در پاریس زندگی می کنم. I am Japanese but I live in Paris.

When the two actions in the two parts of the sentence follow each other in time and the agent or subject of the verb is the same person, the co-ordinate 'and' وَ can be omitted:

به بازار رفتم میوه خریدم. I went to the market (and) bought fruits.

Subordinate sentences

When the action in the second part of the sentence is somehow dependent on the action in the first part or if the first action is done 'in order' that the second action is possible, the two sentences can follow each other without a conjunction; however, the verb in the second or 'subordinate clause' is in the *subjunctive*:

به کتابخانه می روم درس بخوانم. I am going to the library to study (lit. that I may study *or* in order to study).

به ایران رفته اند فامیلشان را ببینند. They have gone to Iran to see their family.

In the last two sentences the subject of the verb is one and the same person. However, if the subjects (agents) of the two part-sentences are different people, a conjunction such as که *ke*, or تا *tā* ('in order') is used:

این کتاب ها را آوردند تا من به شما بدهم. They brought these books so that I give them to you (*or* in order that I give them to you).

در اتاق را باز کردم که صدای ما را بهتر بشنود. I opened the door (of the room) so that he could hear us better.

However, که and تا can, of course, be used in sentences where the subject does not change, so the first examples will be:

به کتابخانه می روم که درس بخوانم.

به ایران رفته اند تا فامیلشان را ببینند.

Temporal sentences: uses of 'when' که

که *ke* 'that, when, where' is used in the following sentences, in a similar way to the English use:

سه سال پیش بود که به انگلستان آمدیم. It was three years ago that we came to England.

در تهران بود که با این نویسنده آشنا شدند. It was in Tehran where they met this writer.

آنقدر خسته بودم که شام نخوردم و زود خوابیدم. I was so tired that I did not eat any supper and went to bed early.

هوا آنقدر سرد نیست که پالتو بپوشیم. The weather is not too cold for us to wear a winter coat (*lit.* that we wear a winter coat).

به خانه رسیدم که بابک تلفن زد. I got home when Babak telephoned.

Relative clause sentences with 'who, which' که

The nearest examples to the relative clause as it is understood in English are sentences that effectively select one person, place or unit from a wider selection. There is no separate equivalent of the English relative pronouns 'who' or 'which' and instead که is used. The sentences are constructed in a remarkably similar way to the English relative clause. However, every sentence must start according to one of the following patterns:

(1) antecedent + ی + که + ...

(2) antecedent + ی + را + که + ...

Look at these examples:

مردی که دیروز به خانهٔ ما آمد، ایرانی اَست.

The man who came to our house yesterday is Iranian.

The 'antecedent' here is مرد 'the man' so the pattern will be:

مرد + ی + که →

دختران جوانی که کنار پنجره نشسته اند در کوچهٔ ما زندگی می کنند.
(دخترانِ جوان + ی + که) The young girls who are sitting by the window live in our street.

کتابی را که علی خرید دربارهٔ قالیهای ایرانیست.
(کتاب + ی + را + که) The book that Ali bought is about Persian carpets. (**Note:** The verb in the first clause is transitive.)

لُطفاً نامه ای را که به خواهرم نوشته ام پست کنید.
Please post the letter that I have written to my sister.

The exceptions to this rule are when the antecedent is a proper noun, i.e. a name or a pronoun or a noun followed by a suffixed pronoun (such as 'my friend' دوستِ من or دوستم). In this case, the ی is not added to the antecedent:

مریم که طبقهٔ بالا زندگی می کند آشپزِ خیلی خوبی است.
Maryam who lives upstairs is a very good cook.

Adverbial conjunctions

as long as	تا وقتیکه
as soon as	همینکه
because	چونکه
despite the fact that	با اینکه – با وجودیکه
just as, as	همانطوریکه
since	از وقتیکه – از زمانیکه
when	وقتیکه– موقعیکه– زمانیکه
whenever	هر وقتیکه
where	جاییکه
wherever	هر جاییکه
whichever	هر کدامیکه
while	در حالیکه
whoever	هر کس که or هرکسیکه

Conditional sentences in Persian

Conditional sentences in Persian are introduced by the word اگر *agar* 'if'. The part of the sentence that contains the 'if' clause is known technically as the *protasis*. The section of the sentence that contains the 'if' clause normally precedes the section of the sentence that deals with the consequence of the condition, which is known as the *apodosis*, but we will refer to the two components of a conditional sentence as the 'if clause' and the 'subsequent' clause.

In English, it is not unusual to place the section that contains the word 'if' in the second part of the sentence and say, for example: 'I'll come to your party *if* I can get a lift.' In Persian, however, it is very unusual *not* to start a conditional sentence with the word 'if', that is اگر *agar*.

Conditional sentences are divided into two groups:

1 Sentences that offer *possible conditions*
2 Sentences that offer *impossible conditions*.

Possible conditions

The following table demonstrates the tense or mood of verbs that are needed in each of the two clauses or sections of a conditional sentence, depending on whether the condition applies to a time in the *past*, *present* or *future*.

Verb in 'if' clause (protasis)	Subsequent clause (apodosis)	Type of condition
Present subjunctive or simple past* *see notes*	Present or future	Conditionals referring to **future**
Present indicative** *see notes*	Present or future	Conditionals referring to **present**
Past subjunctive	Present or future	Conditionals referring to **past**

* If the action in the 'if clause' is a single action and takes place before the action in the main or 'subsequent' clause then *simple past* is used in the 'if' clause.

اَگَر مریم را دیدم به او می گویم. If I see Maryam I will tell her.

We can equally use present subjunctive in the 'if' clause of this same example:

اگر مریم را ببینَم به او می گویم.

** With the verb 'to be', although the present indicative can be used (e.g. هست or هستیم) it is quite common to use the present subjunctive of 'to be', such as باشد or باشیم in the 'if clause' too.

Examples of possible conditionals in future, present and past

Future

اگر به منزلِ علی بروید، من هم می روم/خواهم رفت.

If you go to Ali's house, I shall go also.
(The subjunctive is used when the outcome is quite likely.)

اگر به منزلِ علی رفتید، من هم می روم/خواهم رفت.

If you go to Ali's house, I will go too.

(The use of simple past means that I will only go if you do go to Ali's house.)

اگر قیمتِ خانه در لندن ارزان بشود، یک آپارتمان در غَربِ لندن می خرم.

If property prices come down in London I'll buy a flat in West London.

Present

اگر دارید شام می خورید، بعداً تلفن می زَنم.

If you are having (eating) supper, I'll call later.

اگر بچه ها سر و صدا می کنند، بگویید ساکت شوند.

If the children are making a lot of noise, tell them to keep quiet.

Note: In this last sentence, the use of the imperative 'tell them' means that the second verb in the subsequent clause, 'keep quiet', has to be in the subjunctive:

اگر این کتاب را دوست دارید آن را به شما می دهم.

If you like this book, I'll give it to you.

اگر خواب است، او را بیدار نکنید.

Don't wake him up if he is asleep.

Usually, the present subjunctive of 'to be' is used in conditions in the present time.

Past

اگر علی خبر را نشنیده باشد، به او می گویم/خواهم گفت.

If Ali hasn't heard the news (yet or already) I will tell him.

Note: For conditionals referring to the past, where the English uses the future perfect tense in the subsequent clause, the Persian uses the perfect, also known as the past narrative tense:

اگر تا به حال به خانهٔ ما آمده باشند حتماً گربه ام را دیده اند.

If they have ever (lit. up to now) been to our house they will have surely seen my cat.

Impossible conditionals

Impossible conditions, whether relating to the past or present take the imperfect (past continuous) in both clauses:

اگر می توانستم، حتماً می آمدم. I would have come if I could. (*or* If I could come I would (but I cannot).)

اگر زودتر می رفتید، به اتوبوس می رسیدید.

If you had gone earlier, you would have caught the bus.

اگر جوانتر بود، تا صبح می رقصید. If he had been younger he would have danced till morning. (*or* He would dance till morning if he were younger (but he is not).)

Pluperfect (or remote past tense, as it is also known) can also be used in both clauses of an impossible condition, but this is usually confined to events relating to the past. Use of this tense means that we refer to the *possibility* of an event in the past which in fact did not happen because it *could not*:

اگر تندتر رفته بودیم به اتوبوس رسیده بودیم.

If we had gone faster we would have caught the bus.

اگر در را قُفل کرده بود، دزد نیامده بود.

If he had locked the door, thieves wouldn't have come or, combining the imperfect and the pluperfect:

اگر در را قفل کرده بود، دزد نمی آمد.

Past subjunctive

Past subjunctive = present subjunctive of 'to be' + past participle forms of the main verb.

Subjunctive present of 'to be':

باشیم	باشم
باشید	باشی
باشَند	باشد

Reminder: Past participle = ـه / ه + past stem, e.g.

رفته، خورده، گفته، آمده، زندگی کرده

Spoken versus written language

If you eavesdrop on a conversation between two Persian speakers, or listen to any informal programme on the radio or television, then you will soon realize that spoken Persian is quite different from the written language. This is, of course, true of any language, especially of the vernacular of the urban population living in big cities. However, the differences between the spoken and written Persian are nothing as drastic as the differences between colloquial and written Arabic, for example. The most significant differences, apart from the accent of the speakers, are contained in pronunciation of certain vowels and verb endings. This is invariably done based on rules (of a sort) and so can be learnt. However, nothing will aid the learning process as much as some time spent listening to the colloquial conversations of native speakers or radio plays, comedies and chat shows where you will hear colloquial Persian being used.

The grammar of colloquial Persian is really not very different from that of the written language. However, the spoken everyday language is full of local colour and flavour and the presence of many regional accents and dialects makes it that much more difficult for learners of Persian to follow. It is just as mind boggling trying to work out what a Cockney taxi driver says as it is to bargain at a stall in the Tehran bazaar. However, there are certain grammatical rules that can help.

First of all, the sentence order is more arbitrary in colloquial Persian than it is in the written language. For instance, it is not uncommon to start the sentence with the verb as in the following example:

Written: دیشب به سینما رفتم.   Last night I went to the cinema.
Spoken: دیشب رفتم سینما.

The spoken Persian sentence order is that much closer to the subject–verb–object of some European languages such as English. It is worth noting that this order is most common with intransitive verbs, i.e. verbs that do not take the direct object marker را rā.

The other significant difference between the spoken and written Persian is the way in which verbs are pronounced, especially verbs whose present stem ends or begins with a vowel. The verb 'to be', in the present tense, is used mainly in its short forms. However, in spoken Persian the third person singular of this form is pronounced as just a final vowel *e* after consonants and as the letter س *s* after vowels *a* and *ā* and sometimes *u*:

بُزُرگ اَست ← بُزُرگه	سَرد اَست ← سَرده
ایرانی اَست ← ایرانیه	خوب اَست ← خوبه
مالِ ما اَست ← مالِ ماس	اینجا اَست (اینجاست) ← اینجاس
	خانه اَست ← خونَس

The following patterns should give you some idea of the spoken verbal forms. Compare the written with the spoken style. The asterisks denote the *unchanged* forms:

'to go' رَفتَن

Present tense		*Simple past*	
pl.	sing.	pl.	sing.
می رویم ← می ریم	می روم ← می رم	رفتیم ← رفتیم*	رفتم ← رفتم*
می روید ← می رین	می روی ← می ری	رفتید ← رفتین	رفتی ← رفتی*
می روند ← می رَن	می رود ← می ره	رفتند ← رفتن	رفت ← رفت*

As you see the changes in the past tense verbs are quite minor, however, *every one* of the six cases of the present tense of the verb 'to go' is pronounced differently. The same applies to the subjunctive from of the verb:

pl.	sing.
برویم ← بریم	بروم ← برم
بروید ← برین	بروی ← بری
بروند ← برن	برود ← بره

Look at the present tense forms of the verb 'to say' کُفتَن:

بگییم ← بگم بگوییم ← بگیم   می‌گویم ← می‌گم می‌گوییم ← می‌گیم

بگویی ← بگی بگویید ← بگین   می‌گویی ← می‌گی می‌گویید ← می‌گین

می‌گوید ← می‌گه بگه ← بگوید بگویند ← بگن   می‌گوید ← می‌گه می‌گویند ← می‌گن

The past tense forms are the same as in 'to go', where only the second and third person plurals change:

گُفتَند ← گُفتَن they said   گُفتید ← گُفتین you (pl.) said

Other examples:

'to come' آمَدَن

	Present			Past	
	pl.	sing.		pl.	sing.

می آیم ← می یام می آییم ← می یایم   آمَدَم ← اومَدَم آمَدیم ← اومَدیم

می آیی ← می یای می آیید ← می یاین   آمَدی ← اومَدی آمَدید ← اومَدین

می آیَد ← می یاد می آیَند ← میان   آمَد ← اومَد آمَدَند ← اومَدَن

'to give' دادَن

Present
pl.   sing.

می دَهَم ← می دَم می دَهیم ← می دیم

می دَهی ← می دی می دَهید ← می دین

می دَهَد ← می ده می دَهَند ← می دَن

'to allow' or 'to place' گُذاشتَن

Present
pl.   sing.

می گُذارَم ← می ذارَم می گُذاریم ← می ذاریم

می گُذاری ← می ذاری می گُذارید ← می ذارین

می گُذارَد ← می ذارِه می گُذارَند ← می ذارَن

The present stem of the infinitive 'to want' خواستَن changes from خواه khāh to خوا khā. The conjugation follows the pattern of 'to come'. The present stem of 'to know' دانستن changes from دان dān to دون dun and its past stem changes from توانست tavānest, to تونست tunest; the verb is then conjugated as the verbs seen earlier. In spoken Persian, the present tense stem of the verb 'to sit' نشستَن neshastan loses its initial n and becomes شین shin instead of نشین neshin.

Nouns also undergo some changes. Usually, but not always, the long vowel ā preceding an m or an n, changes to a long vowel u:

خانه ← خونه نان ← نون ایرانی ← ایرونی آن ← اون مهمان ← مهمون

حَمام ← حموم تَمام ← تموم بادام ← بادوم کُدام ← کُدوم

The numeral 'one' یک yek changes to یه ye if it comes before a noun and is on its own:

یک روز ← یه روز   یک پِسَر ← یه پِسَر   یک اُتاق ← یه اُتاق

However, it stays the same in number combinations and after nouns:

چِهِل و یک،   صد و بیست و یک،   ساعَتِ یک بَعدازظُهر

And finally, the direct object marker, or postposition را rā, also changes depending on whether it follows a vowel or a consonant. After vowels, را becomes رو ro with a short o vowel. After consonants it becomes a mere short vowel o و:

میوه را *mive rā* ← میوه رو *mive ro*   او را *u rā* ← او رو *u ro*

آقا را ← آقا رو

آن را ← اونُو (اون + و) *uno* این را ← اینُو *ino* من را ← مَنُو *mano*

کتاب را ← کتابُ *ketābo*

مَگَر *magar*, meaning 'but' (used with a negative question expecting the answer 'yes' or with an affirmative question expecting the answer 'no'), also becomes مَگه *mage* in spoken Persian:

مَگه نگفتم (But) didn't I tell you?

Grammar formulas

Before using the formulas make sure you recognize some of the basic terminology: e.g. *past stem* is formed by removing the -*an* (ﻦ) from the end of the infinitive; *present stem* is formed by dropping the complete ending of the regular verb (these are دن بدن تن) or consulting the present stem table supplied. Also, don't forget that there are only five subject endings for all past tense verbs: however, present tenses have one extra ending which is for the third person singular, making it a total of six. Finally, remember that with compound verbs you only conjugate the verb element and then put the noun or preposition component of it at the beginning.

Three verbs have been used in the grammar formulas that follow. These are:

رَفتَن 'to go', irregular single verb; past stem: رَفت, present stem: رَو

کتاب خواندَن 'to read books', regular compound verb; past stem: (کتاب) خواند, present stem: (کتاب) خوان

زندگی کردن 'to live', irregular compound verb; past stem: (زندگی) کرد, present stem: (زندگی) کُن

Present tense

1 *Present indicative*	mi (می) + present stem + subject endings*
می رَوَم (irregular) I go *or* I'll go	می+ رو + مَ
کتاب می خوانی (regular) you read (a book)	می+ خوان + ی
زندگی می کُنَند (irregular) they live	می+ کُن +نَد
*Subject endings for the present tense are: مَ یم ی یﺪ ﺪ نَد	

2 *Present progressive*	appropriate present form of 'to have'* + *mi* (می) + present stem + subject endings
دارم می رَوَم I am just coming	دارم + می + رَو + َم
داری کتاب می خوانی you are reading (a book)	داری + می + خوان + ی
دارنَد زندگی می کَنَند they are living	دارنَد + می + کُن + َند

داریم	دارم *	
دارید	داری	
دارنَد	دارَد	

3 *Imperative**	*be* (بـ) + present stem + subject endings (only for 2nd person plural [ید])
بُرو go! (singular)	بـِ + رو (but unusual to say *bero*, more common to say *boro*)
بِروید go! (plural)	بـِ + رو + ید

* There are only two forms: second person singular or second person plural.

4 *Present subjunctive*[1]	*be* (بـ) + present stem + subject endings
بِرَوَم (that) I *may go*	بـِ + رَو + َم
کتاب بِخوانی (that) you *may read* a book	بـِ + خوان + ی
زندگی بِکُنَند or زندگی کُنَند they *may live*	[2]بـِ + کُن + َند

Past tense

1 *Simple past*	past stem + subject endings*
رَفتَم I went	رَفت + مَ
کتاب خواندی you read (a book)	خواند + ی
زندگی کَردَند they lived	کَرد + َند
*Subject endings for the past tenses are: م یم ی ید ـ ند	

2 *Imperfect* (past continous)	*mi* (می) + past stem + subject endings
می رَفتَم I used to go	می + رَفت + مَ
کتاب می خواندی you were reading (a book) *or* you used to read (a book)	می + خواند + ی
زندگی می کَردَند they used to live	می + کَرد + َند

3 *Past progressive*[1]	appropriate past form of 'to have'[2] + *mi* (می) + past stem + subject endings
داشتَم می رفتَم I was *about* to go *or* just *when* I was leaving *or* I was just going *when*...	داشتَم + می + رفت + َم
داشتی کتاب می خواندی you were reading your book *when*... *or just when* you were reading your book...	داشتی + می + خواند + ی
داشتَند زندگی می کَردَند they were living there *when*...	داشتَند + می + کَرد + َند

1 This gives the sense of an ongoing action that is interrupted or immediately followed by another action.

2

داشتیم	داشتم
داشتید	داشتی
داشتَند	داشت

4 *Past participle**	past stem + final short vowel ـه / ه 'e'
رفته gone (missed)	رفت + ـه
کتاب خوانده well read	خواند + ه
زندگی کَرده lived (experienced)	کَرد + ه

* The past participle on its own could be an adjective or a noun too.

5 Present perfect	past participle of the verb + appropriate short form of present tense 'to be'*
رَفته اَم I have gone	رَفته + اَم
کتاب خوانده ای you have read books	خوانده + ای
زندگی کَرده اَند they have lived	کَرده + اَند

ايم	اَم*	
ايد	ای	
آند	آست	

6 Pluperfect	past participle of the verb + appropriate past tense of the verb 'to be'*
رَفته بودم I had gone	رَفته + بودم
کتاب خوانده بودی you had read (a book)	خوانده + بودی
زندگی کَرده بودند they had lived	کَرده + بودند

بوديم	بودم*	
بوديد	بودی	
بودند	بود	

7 _Past subjunctive_	past participle of main verb + appropriate present subjunctive form of 'to be'*
رَفته بـاشَم I might have gone	رَفته + بـاشَم
کتاب خوانده باشی you might have read (a book)	خوانده + باشی
زندگی کَرده باشَند they might have lived	کَرده + باشَند

باشَم*	باشیم
باشی	باشید
باشَد	باشَند

Future tense

Future	appropriate present form of the modal 'will'* + past stem of main verb
خواهَم رَفت I will/shall go	خواهَم + رَفت
کتاب خواهی خواند you will/shall read a book	خواهی + خواند
زندگی خواهی کَرد they will/shall live	خواهَند + کَرد

* The future tense is, technically, a verb formed from the past tense. Remember you can use the present tense for the future too. Remember no _mi_ می:

خواهَم	خواهیم
خواهی	خواهید
خواهَد	خواهَند

Passive voice

Usually only transitive verbs such as 'to eat', 'to see' and 'to buy' can have a passive form. Intransitive verbs do not have a passive form. There are two ways of forming the passive verb: (**1**) formation with single verbs; (**2**) formation with compound verbs. In either case, we need the help of the verb *shodan* شدن 'to become' in order to create a new compound, passive verb.

Passive of single verbs = past participle of main verb + شدن

For example, the passive of the single verb 'to eat' will be 'to be eaten'. 'to eat' is خوردن. Past participle of خوردن is خورده. 'To be eaten' is therefore: خورده شدن = خورده + شدن; 'to close' or 'to shut' is بستن; 'to be closed' or 'to be shut' is therefore بسته شدن.

من در را بَستَم (active) I closed the door

در بسته شد (passive) the door was shut

Various tenses of the passive compound verbs are formed like any compound verb by using the general rules listed earlier. E.g. شده است در بسته 'the door has been shut' or درِدارد بسته می شَوَد 'the door is about to be shut', ممکن است در بسته بِشَوَد 'the door may be about to be shut' (*subjunctive*).

Passive of compound verbs

In transitive compound verbs that have کردن *kardan* 'to do' as their verb part, کردن is simply changed to شدن. E.g. خاموش کردن 'to switch off' or 'to turn off' becomes خاموش شدن 'to be switched off' or 'to be turned off'. Similarly, فراموش کردن 'to forget' becomes فراموش شدن 'to be forgotten'; درست کردنِ 'to make' or 'to mend' becomes درست شدن 'to be made' or 'to be mended'.

Some compound forms, however, have their own special passive. For example, the verbal element of most compounds ending with دادن or زدن 'گول زَدَن (گرفتَن or) is changed to خوردن and یافتَن respectively: 'to deceive' becomes گول خوردن 'to be deceived'; کتک زَدَن 'to hit, to slap' becomes کتَک خوردن 'to be hit, to be slapped'.

However, سامان دادَن 'to sort someone out, to help' becomes سامان یافتن or سامان گرفتَن 'to be sorted out or helped', پرورش دادن 'to nurture' becomes پرورش یافتَن 'to be nurtured'; انجام دادن 'to do, to complete' becomes انجام یافتن (or sometimes انجام شدن).

The odd one out is شکَست دادن 'to defeat' which becomes شکَست خوردن 'to be defeated'.

These verbs are then conjugated like any other compound verb.

Remember, passive verbs *never* have a specific direct object and, therefore, never take the postposition را *rā*.

Negative

The negative of all verbs is formed by prefixing the negative sign نَ *na* or نِ *ne* to the verb. If the verb form contains the continuous or present tense prefix of می *mi*, then the negative is formed by نِ *ne*. Otherwise, all other forms are put into the negative by the prefix نَ *na*. Remember to use a buffer if the negative prefix has to latch onto a verbal element that starts with a vowel.

The only exception to this rule is the formation of the negative of subjunctive and imperative verbs in Persian. The subjunctive and imperative verbs begin with the prefix بِ *be*. The negative of these verbs is formed by replacing the بِ prefix with the negative نَ *na* prefix.

Examples:

رفتَم I went → نَرفتم I did not go

آمَدَم I came → نیامَدم (note the buffer) I did not come

زندگی کردند they lived → زندگی نَکردند they did not live

می آمَدید you were coming → نمی آمَدید you were not coming

خورده اَست he has eaten → نَخورده اَست he has not eaten

درس خوانده بودیم we had studied → درس نَخوانده بودیم we had not studied

224

می خَرَد she buys → نمی خَرَد she does not buy

(شايد) برَوَند they (may) go → (شايد) نرَوَند they (may not) go (notice *na* has replaced *be*)

بِدِه! give (it)! → نَدِه! don't give!

بِنشينيد! sit down (pl.)! → نَنشينيد! don't sit down!

Note: Although it is not necessary to use the subjunctive بـ with compound verbs, the use of negative نَـ with compound subjunctive is compulsory:

ديده باشند they may have seen → نَديده باشند they may not have seen

خواهيم گُفت we shall say → نَخواهيم گُفت we shall not say

Key to the exercises

Writing, alphabet and pronunciation

Exercise 1

۱ بابا ۲ بازار ۳ پرستار ۴ آواز ۵ ماشین ۶ هزار ۷ مرجان
۸ ناظم ۹ اژدر ۱۰ مقیاس ۱۱ استراحت ۱۲ اجاق ۱۳ وراث
۱۴ کوچک ۱۵ خیابان ۱۶ گاری ۱۷ موقع ۱۸ سوسک
۱۹ لاکپشت ۲۰ موشک ۲۱ اصفهان ۲۲ ضرر ۲۳ ظهر
۲۴ طاووس ۲۵ یواشکی ۲۶ کتابخانه ۲۷ همسایه ۲۸ قهوه
۲۹ رادار ۳۰ سفیر

Exercise 2

*pā – pāru – sup – kāshi – ketāb – kuche – mikh – sābun – maryam – āqā
– shirāz – afghān – emruz – izad – ashk – tāqche – kushesh – ārāmgāh
– kāghaz – esfahān – ijāb – 'oghāb*

Exercise 3

۱ فَرد 2 پلَنگ 3 بُشقاب 4 آچار 5 آتش 6 واجِب 7 نمَک 8 کوچکِ 9 اَکبَر
10 ظهر 11 گوشتِ 12 خانه 13 قهوه 14 زَرد 15 هوا 16 اِمشب 17 ایرلند
18 شیرین 19 دختر 20 بیستَ 21 بیمارِستان 22 شما 23 هَدف 24 عمو
25 خاله

Unit 1

Exercise 1

صُبح بِخیرِ خانم، سَلام اَحمَد جان، سَلام، عَصریبخیر آقا
خداحافظ مَریَم، شَب‌بخیر بابِک، سَفَربخیر آقای شَمس

Exercise 2

(a) ‫۱ صبح بخیر مهری، خوش آمدی! ۲ بله، لطفاً، بی‌زحمت چای.‬

‫۳ ببخشید بابک. ۴ نه مرسی، پری. ۵ سفر بخیر رضا و متشکرم.‬

‫خواهش می‌کنم.‬

(b) 1 Hello sir, if you please. 2 One tea and a Danish pastry, please.
3 Forgive me, madam, I am very sorry. 4 No thanks, dear Babak.
5 You are welcome, goodbye (*lit.* God keep you).

Exercise 3

‫۱ ۱ یکشنبه – سه‌شنبه – پنجشنبه – جمعه ۲ بهار – تابستان –‬

‫زمستان 2 آبان – آذر – تیر – مرداد – شهریور – شهریور 4 فروردین –‬

‫تیر 5 31‬

Unit 2

Exercise 1

‫1 ۶ ۱۲ ۲۵ ۳۴ ۷ ۰ ۱۰۷ ۳۵۸ ۸۱۹ ۴۸ ۹۸۷ ۱۰۴۶ ۲۶۹۰۳‬

‫2 چهل و دو یازده هشت سیزده، چهل شصت و نه‬

‫یکصدو پنجاه و یک دویست یکهزارو ششصدو بیست و پنج‬

3 7, 12, 23, 1998, 591, 183, 9,212

‫4 سه کتاب یک پسر هشت ماشین دو مرد چهارده روز‬

Exercise 2

‫1 یازدهم – بیست و سوم – چهل و یکم – صدو بیست و پنجم – نودو چهارم –‬
‫دوم – ششم – دهم‬

2 fourth, 26th, third night, 1,000th, 11th day of Farvardin, 1st Khordad, 31st.

Exercise 3

‫1 خواهران، خواهرها – ماشین‌ها – پسران، پسرها – کتابخانه‌ها –‬

‫پنجره‌ها – روزها – استادان، استادها – زنان، زنها‬

شهرها – پسران – گلها – گربه‌ها – زَنان، زَنها، زَنان، زنان – روزها –
تابستانها – قَلَمها – تَرَنها– جَوانان، جَوانها – عاقلان –
سه خواهَر – دَه پَرَنده – دو ساعَت

2

Unit 3

Exercise 1

صبح بخیر، عصربخیر مریم، خیلی متشکرم رضا، خدانگهدار علی،
سفر بخیر، خانمها و آقایان، شب بخیر

Unit 4

Exercise 1

۱ این قالیچه گرانست.   ۲ آن اُتاق خیلی بزرگ نیست ولی تَمیزَست.
۳ آنها در اُتوبوسَند.   ۴ آن دُخترَها خواننده نیستَند.   ۵ شُما با
مریم دوستید؟

Exercise 2

۱ این هُلو خوشمَزه است.   ۲ مریم نَقاش است.   ۳ شما خسته هَستید
/ خسته اید.   ۴ من جوانَم / جوان هَستَم.   ۵ ما در تِهران هَستیم.

Exercise 3

۱ نه، آن پسَر اِسکاتلَندی نیست.   ۲ نه، ما با ایرَج دوست نیستیم.
۳ نه، تو ورزشکارنیستی.   ۴ نه، آنها خیلی خسته‌نیستَند.   ۵ نه، ما
نَقاش نیستیم.

228

Exercise 4

ب   مریم جان، سلام!

م   به! بابک جان، سلام، صبح بخیر. چطوری؟

ب   مرسی، قُربانَت، بد نیستم، تو چِطوری؟ خوبی؟

م   خیلی خوبم، مرسی.

ب   مریم جان تنهایی؟

م   نه، بابک، با دوستمَم. با دوستم، یاسمَن. یاسمن این
بابکَست. بابک نقاشَست.

ی   سلام.

ب   سلام، یاسمن خانم. خوشوقتم. شما ایرانیید؟

ی   بله من از ایرانیَم ولی مادرم روسَست. شما اَهلِ کجایید؟

ب   من شیرازیَم. شما مثلِ مریم دانشجویید؟

ی   نه، من دانشجو نیستم، من عَکاسَم.

ب   به! چه خوب! مریم، امشب منزلی؟

م   بله من و یاسمن امشب منزلیم.

Unit 5

Exercise 1

1- شُما، ایشان   2- تو   3- شما – ایشان   4- تو – او   5- شما، ایشان

Exercise 2

(a) 1 large garden 2 Maryam's Persian book 3 Iranian man
4 my friend's daughters 5 delicious food 6 dark, cold night
7 London University *or* University of London 8 old house
9 china teapot of Babak's kind sister

(b)

۱ اَنگورِ شیرین   ۲ دوستِ روسِ مریم   ۳ ماشینِ آقای اَحمَدی

۴ اُتاقِ قشَنگِ بُزُرگ   ۵ قالیهای دستباف کاشان   ۶ شَهرِ تاریخی

قَدیمی   ۷ روزِ سردِ آفتابی   ۸ همسایهٔ او   ۹ چَترِ سَبزِ من

۱۰ مردانِ پیرِ مِهربان

(c)

نامِ من علیست. من ایرانی هَستَم. من در تِهران دانِشجو هَستَم. این،
خواهرِ من مریم اَست. روزِ تَوَلد مریم در دسامبر اَست. برادرِ دوستِ
او هَمکِلاسِ من اَست. اِسمِ او مِهرداد اَست. موی مِهرداد قَهوه‌ایست.
خانهٔ او در خیابانِ اَفشار است.

(d)

خانه   گران   غَذای سَرد   میوه   خوشمزه   موی سیاه   کَفشِ
ناراحت   صَندلی راحت   چشمِ سیاه   هوای گرم   موی طلایی
کَفشِ اَرزان   گربه   سیاه

Exercise 3

۱ مادربزرگم ۹۲ ساله اَست.   ۲ او دخترخالهٔ من است.
۳ عَموی من دوستِ پدرِ توست.   ۴ برادرِ ما پِزشک (دکتر) است.
۵ خواهرشوهرِ آنها و خواهرِ ما اِمروز در لندن هَستند.

Exercise 4

۱ برادرِ من – برادرش   ۲ اَسبِ آنها – اسبشان   ۳ خانهٔ ما –
خانه‌مان   ۴ سگِ سیاهِ شما – سگِ سیاهتان   ۵ چَترِ آنها –
چَترِشان   ۶ دوستِ او – دوستش   ۷ کتابِ تو – کتابت   ۸ عَموی
مهربانِ من – عموی مهربانم   ۹ مادربزرگِ او – مادربزرگش
۱۰ شَهرِ ما – شَهرِ مان

Exercise 5

1 hungry man 2 good weather 3 good, sunny weather 4 clever girl
5 young student 6 young Irish student 7 sour lemon 8 open window
9 old house 10 these two open doors 11 open doors 12 these
open (and) large doors 13 that pretty (and) white cat 14 green,
sour apples 15 mother of those two boys 16 young mother of
those two small boys 17 kind grand father 18 Shirazi sweet apples
19 green apple and sweet orange 20 warm day and cold night
21 country of Iran 22 British Isles 23 Tehran–Esfahan bus ticket
24 cities of Iran 25 Parisian shops

Exercise 7

۱ برادرم – برادرِ من ۲ ماشینِ کوچکت – ماشینِ کوچکِ تو
۳ خانهٔ بزرگِ گران ۴ اُتاقِ راحتِ او – اُتاقِ راحتش ۵ فنجانِ
چایِ سرد ۶ قلمِ طلاییِ ما ۷ کفشِ سیاهِ ارزان ۸ سیبِ شیرینِ
خوشمزه ۹ پسرِ جوانِ گرسنه ۱۰ کشورِ زیبایِ من

Unit 6

Exercise 1

۱ خانهٔ آنها به مغازه نزدیکتر است. ۲ برادرِ مریم خیلی از برادرِ
من بلندتر است. ۳ بلندترین (بلند–قدترین) دخترِ اتاق برزیلی است.
۴ خانهٔ او خیلی از خانهٔ من بزرگتر است ولی باغِ من بزرگتر است.
۵ آنها خیلی سختتر از تو کار می‌کنند. ۶ تو از ماریا بهتر فارسی
حرف می‌زنی. – تو بهتر از ماریا فارسی حرف می‌زنی.
۷ امشب از دیشب گرمتر است. ۸ این بلندترین شبِ سال است.
۹ بهترین دوستِ من نزدیکِ پارک زندگی می‌کند. ۱۰ این فیلم
خیلی طولانی است، طولانیتر از دکتر ژیواگو.

Exercise 2

1 Today is warmer than yesterday, but it's still very cold. 2 My sister's youngest child is called Roya. 3 Does chicken (meat) or fish (meat) have less fat? 4 You got to the restaurant earlier than us. 5 Today he is feeling better than yesterday.

Exercise 3

تهران بزرگتر است یا اصفهان؟ ۱ لندن از تهران بزرگتر است ولی هوای تهران گرمتر است. ۱ خانهٔ من به مرکز شهر نزدیکتر است ولی خانهٔ اَفسانه نزدیکترین به پارک است. ۱ فیلم «خانه ای از ماسه و مه» خیلی خوب است، «بازگشت پادشاه» بهتر است ولی بهترین فیلم «مثل بکهام شوت بزن» است.

Exercise 4

مریم، چه لباس قشنگی!

Thank you, very kind of you. It's my sister's dress.

خواهرت از تو بزرگتر است یا کوچکتر؟

My sister is four years younger (*lit.* smaller than me). She is the youngest child in the family.

Unit 7

Exercise 1

M	Whose glasses are these?
D	Which glasses?
M	These sunglasses. Are they yours Dariush?
D	No, these glasses are not mine, they are Amir's. Whose books and key are these?
M	The books belong to my brother and the key is mine.
D	Where is your brother today? Why is he not here?
M	My brother is at Reza's house today.
D	Who is Reza?
M	Reza is my brother's colleague. Reza is a photographer.
D	Is your brother a photographer too?
M	No, my brother is a graphic artist.

Exercise 2

۱ اسم من ... مریم (for example) است. ۲ اسم فامیلِ من ... بهبودی (for example) است. ۳ خانۀ من در شمالِ لندن است.
۴ اسم مـادرم مِهری و اسم پدرم رازی است. ۵ تولد من آبان ۱۳۴۰ است. ۶ من در تهران بدنیا آمدم. ۷ من روزها در یک کتابفروشی کارمیکنم. ۸ نه، من دانشجو نیستم. ۹ من دو تا خواهر دارم ولی برادر ندارم. ۱۰ ساعت الآن ... دو و نیمِ بعدازظُهر(for example)است.

Unit 8

Exercise 1

۱ مریم و علی یک خانۀ کوچکِ خیلی قَشَنگ دارند. ۲ من غذای ژاپنی دوست ندارم ولی غذای لبنانی دوست دارم. ۳ فردا خیلی کار دارند. ۴ آیا در پاریس دوستی or دوستانی داری؟ ۵ زنِ برادرم شش دایی دارد.

Exercise 2

I have a small cottage in the mountains near the Caspian Sea. This cottage has neither electricity nor a telephone, but has very beautiful views (lit. its views are very beautiful). There is a spring near the cottage. This cottage has two or three chairs, a wooden table, a large bed, a small kitchen and an open fireplace. This far-from-the-city cottage is the best place for resting (or relaxation).

Exercise 3

۱ ما در ایران دو تا ماشین داشتیم. ۲ او در خانه‌اش در ترکیه یک اسب، دو تا گربه، جوجه و خرگوش داشت. ۳ آنها چندین دوست در تهران داشتند. ۴ دیروز چِقَدر پول داشتی؟ ۵ من تلویزیون نداشتم ولی یک رادیوی قدیمی داشتم.

Exercise 4

۱ داشتم. ۲ شما ۳ او ۴ نداشتیم. ۵ داشتند؟

Exercise 5

کِشوَری شَبی پَرَنده‌ای میزی صُبحی اُستادی کوهی
هَفته‌ای مَردی کِتابی آقایی همسایه‌ای دوستانی پایی
خوابگاهی قَلَمی جَزیره‌هایی گُربه‌ای صَندَلی‌ای راهی
شَهری دَری ماهی‌ای اَسب‌هایی روزی سِتاره‌ای خانه‌ای

Exercise 6

مردی خانه‌ای پسرهایی گربه‌ای ستاره‌ای گلی شهرهایی
میوه‌هایی بچه‌ای

Unit 10

Exercise 1

۱ رفتید – ۲ رفتَند – ۳ خوردیم – ۴ آمدی – ۵ دیدیم –
۶ بودَند – ۷ ماندَم – ۸ داشتیم – ۹ بود – ۱۰ رسیدید؟–

Exercise 2

۱ دیشب به خانهٔ ما آمد. ۲ سه سال در شیراز بودم. ۳ دو روز
پیش به لندن رسیدیم. ۴ مریم و علی روز شنبه یک فیلم خیلی
خوب دیدند. ۵ آیا امروز صبح چیزی از بازار خریدی؟

Unit 11

Exercise 1

۱ غذایمان را خیلی تند خوردیم. ۲ آنها اغلب نامه‌های تَشَکُّرِ
قشنگی می‌نوشتند. ۳ خوشبختانه همسایهٔ خیلی مهربانی بود.
۴ همیشه مریم را صبح‌ها می‌دیدیم. ۵ او معمولاً با خانواده‌اش در
آن خانهٔ بزرگ زندگی‌می‌کرد. ۶ ما ماه پیش به شیراز رفتیم ولی
متاسفانه هوا خوب نبود. ۷ ماریا قشنگ می‌رقصد. ۸ آنها آهسته
صحبت کردند و ما خوب فهمیدیم. ۹ آیا آنها را فوراً صدا زدید؟
۱۰ خوشبختانه من یک چتر داشتم.

Exercise 2

1 I suddenly woke up at 3 a.m. and came out of the room quietly. آهسته – ناگهان – ساعت سه صبح 2 He was very worried. خیلی 3 Luckily, they got to the airport quickly. خوشبختانه – زود 4 He is still in London. هنوز 5 We came home very late last night. دیر خیلی – دیشب 6 Have you only got $10? فقط 7 I like Persian food, especially broad bean rice. مخصوصاً 8 All the restaurants were closed at that time of night. آنوقت شب 9 Your letter arrived at least three days ago. نزدیک 10 Our house is close to the park. اقلاً – سه روزِ پیش

Unit 12

Exercise 1

۱ مریم در آن اتاق خوابیده‌است.   ۲ ما هیچوقت به ایران نرفته‌ایم.
۳ شما قبلاً در آفریقا زندگی کرده‌اید.   ۴ دوستانشان از پاریس
رسیده‌اند or آمده‌اند.   ۵ من در این هتلِ کوچک مانده‌ام.

Exercise 2

1 He hasn't been to the office since yesterday. 2 I have been in the park since this morning. 3 I have cooked chicken and vegetables for supper. 4 How long have you lived in Iran? 5 They have gone (been) to Esfahan three times.

Exercise 3

الو منزلِ آقای اَفشار؟ / شما نسرین خانم هستید؟ من پدرامم. /
خیلی ممنون، خوبم، بد نیستم. خانم هم حالشون خوبست. الآن
فرانسه است، پیشِ مادرش است. / برای یک هفته رفته است. چهار
ماه است که مادرش را ندیده. برادرش هم از آمریکا آمده است. همهٔ
فامیل حالا آنجا جمع هستند. / ببخشید، علی منزل است؟ /
خداحافظ شما نسرین خانم. به امیدِ دیدار انشالله.

Unit 13

Exercise 1

۱ او در خانهٔ ما در شیراز زندگی‌می‌کرد.   ۲ من صبح‌ها درس می‌خواندم و عصرها کار می‌کردم.   ۳ تو غذای مارا دوست‌نداری ولی چای ما را دوست داری.   ۴ امروز صبح به رادیو گوش کردیم. ۵ فکر کردند امروز دوشنبه است.   ۶ تو وقتیکه مریم را دیدی تَعَجب‌کردی.   ۷ او تصمیم دشواری گرفت.   ۸ آیا ماشین را درست کردی؟   ۹ از سه‌شنبه تا حالا کار نکرده‌ام.   ۱۰ اَمیر و مریم در عروسی پری آواز خواندند.

Exercise 2

Three years ago we used to live in Bordeaux, in France. My father was working in a commercial bank and my mother taught piano at the local school. I met several Iranian boys and girls at school. Every weekend we used to either ride bicycles in the side streets or swim in the pool. The mother of one of the Iranian boys used to make us supper every Sunday night. I like Persian food very much. However, my father's job in France came to an end and this summer we returned to London.

Exercise 3

نخیر. شنبه صبح تمامش کار کردم، بعد شب به منزلِ پسرعمویم کنارِ دریاچه رفتم. / نه، حدود ساعتِ نُه و نیم رسیدم. شام خوردیم و کمی صحبت کردیم و رفتیم خوابیدیم. / یکشنبه صبح رفتیم به یک بازارِ محلی و بعد گُلف بازی کردیم. من نزدیکِ ساعتِ شش برگشتم منزل. / پسرعمویم همیشه آنجا زندگی می کند.

Unit 14

Exercise 1

۱ صدایش را شنیدم.   ۲ دوستم این کتابها را از مغازه خرید. ۳ بسته را به منزلمان آوردند.   ۴ این گلها را به او داد.   ۵ مادرِ

مریم را دیروز ندیدم. ۶ همهٔ آن سیبها را خوردیم. ۷ کمی غذا
برای او بردم. ۸ آنرا به برادرَش داد. ۹ دیروز تو را در نانوایی
دیدم. چه خریدی؟ ۱۰ این کتاب را نمی‌خواستی؟ ۱۱ دوستِ مرا
دیدی؟ ۱۲ من آنها را نمی‌شناسم. ۱۳ آیا اخبار را شنیده‌ای؟
۱۴ من آن یکی ماشین را می‌خواهم. ۱۵ کی این گلها را آورد؟
۱۶ آدرس شما را به شاگردها دادم. ۱۷ دیروز خوب غذا خوردم.
۱۸ دیروز در خانهٔ خواهرت غذا خوردم. ۱۹ آن شکلات در یخچال
را خوردم. ۲۰ آیا فیلم را دوست داشتی؟

Exercise 2

Three years ago I met an Iranian girl at a party in London. Her
name is Maryam. Maryam is a photographer and on Tuesdays and
Wednesdays she works in a photographic studio. She travels a lot
and I don't see her much. Yesterday, after a long time, I saw her at a
party at my friend's house. After the usual exchange of niceties and
how are you chitchat she said that she has moved (lit. changed) house
and lives in West London now. She said that she loves her new flat.
Maryam gave me her new address and telephone number. Maryam
and her friend Omid have found this flat together. They have painted
the walls, changed the wall-to-wall carpet, cleaned the kitchen and
planted flowers in its small garden. The window in the bathroom was
broken and they have mended that too. Then, they brought Maryam's
thing to the flat. Omid was also at the party and she introduced him
to me. Maryam and Omid had not brought their car and I gave them a
lift home after dinner.

Exercise 3

سلام خانم، صبح بخیر. من این کتاب را پنجشنبهٔ پیش خریدم،
برای یک دوستم بود ولی این کتاب را دارد. / بله. از همینجا خریدم.
/ بسیارخوب. دراین صورت آن را با این دو کتاب عوض میکنم. این
کتاب دربارهٔ ایران را هم میخواهم. قیمتش چقدر است؟

Unit 15

Exercise 1

۱ من هر شنبه به خانهٔ مادرم می‌روم و او را به سوپرمارکت
می‌برم.   ۲ او در یک آپارتمان بزرگِ قشنگ با دو تا گربه زندگی
می‌کُنَد.   ۳ ما هر روز صبح دخترخاله‌ات را توی اتوبوس می‌بینیم.
۴ آیا برای مریم یک نامه می‌نویسی؟   ۵ آنها روز چهارشنبه به
مهمانی ما می‌آیند.

Exercise 2

نشست می نشینیم	آمدند می آیند	گفتم می گویم
نوشتند می نویسند	خوردیم می خوری	گرفتید می گیرم
رفت می روید	خریدیم می خرد	ماندی می مانند
	آوردی می آوری	دیدم می بینم

Unit 17

Exercise 1
The shop of Cyrus's father-in-law

Cyrus's father-in-law has a greengrocer's and fruit shop. His shop is
in Ferdosi Avenue. In front of the shop there is a narrow pavement
and a (water) gutter. Several tall trees and a newspaper kiosk are
also in front of the shop. On the right-hand side of the shop there is a
patisserie and on the left-hand side there is a shoe shop. Opposite the
shop, on the other side of the road, there is a hairdresser, a bank and
a foreign language teaching college. Above the shop there is a doctor's
surgery and behind the shop there is a petrol station. Cyrus's father-
in-law works in this shop from early morning till night; however, he
sometimes goes to a rice kebab restaurant near the cinema for lunch.
Ferdosi Avenue is always busy. It is only quiet in the early morning.
There are all sorts of shops in this street: bookshops, photographers,
tailors, carpenters, clothes boutiques, jewellers, bakers, butchers,
chemists and other shops. Cyrus's father-in-law sells all sorts of
vegetables (herbs) and fruits in his shop: parsley, mint, spinach,

garlic, pumpkin, onions, aubergines, tomatoes, potatoes, oranges, bananas, grapes, pomegranates, apples, peaches, pears and melon.

Exercise 2

۱ مریم دیشب به خانهٔ ما آمد. ۲ ما با اتوبوس به خانهٔ علی رفتیم. ۳ او گلدان را روی میز گذاشت. ۴ کفشهایش زیرِ میز است. ۵ این آخرِ هفته میخواهم پیشِ مادربزرگم بروم. ۶ کمی غذا در یخچال هست. ۷ فرم را با مداد پُر نکن. ۸ برای تعطیلات (به) کجا میروی؟

Unit 18

Exercise 1

Mr Absent-minded: When Mr Absent-minded was leaving his house in the morning his wife gave him a letter and said: 'Make sure you post this letter today. It's a very important letter. Don't forget!' Mr Absent-minded, however, forgot what his wife had said and did not post the letter (lit. did not throw the letter into the letter box). When he was getting off his bus and rushing off to his office (lit. going to office by running) a gentleman suddenly tapped him gently on the shoulder and said: 'Don't forget the letter!' Mr Absent-minded was very surprised and put the letter in the postbox and went on towards his office. En route, a beautiful woman suddenly said to him: 'Sir, don't forget your letter.' This time Mr Absent-minded stopped and said in astonishment: 'Dear God! How do these people know that I have to post a letter? I posted it a few minutes ago!' The woman laughed in response and said: 'In that case, please remove this note from your back.' On the note was written: 'Please tell my husband not to forget the letter.'

Exercise 2

۱ میخواهند شما را فردا شب ببینند. ۲ نمیتوانم امشب به کلاسِ فارسیم بروم. ۳ اَمیدواریم که تابستانِ آینده یک خانهٔ بزرگتر بخریم. ۴ او هم میخواست به شیراز سفربکُند (سفرکُند). ۵ لطفاً پیشازاینکه به منزلش بروید تلفن بکنید.

Unit 19

Exercise 1

۱ فردا شب شما را خواهم دید. ۲ آیا با اتوبوس مسافرت خواهندکرد یا با ترن؟ ۳ او هفتهٔ آینده این نامه را خواهدنوشت و آنرا به من خواهدداد. ۴ وقتیکه از پاریس برگردند به ما تلفن خواهندزد. ۵. بزودی یک خانهٔ بزرگتر خواهیمخرید.

Exercise 2

1 I will go to Iran next week and will stay in Tehran for three months. 2 They will definitely write this letter this afternoon. 3 When will you go to your sister's house? 4 We will give your message to Babak. 5 In how many hours' time will you finish your work with the computer (*lit.* will your work finish with the computer)?

Exercise 3

سعی میکنم فرداشب آنرا تمام کنم، ولی نمیتوانم قول بدهم. شما فرداشب منزل هستید؟ / آن واقعاً کمک بزرگی خواهد بود. من حدود ساعتِ نه و نیم، بعداز شام میآیم پیشتون.

Unit 20

Exercise 1

۱ خواهرم پارسال به ایتالیا رفت و خیلی به او خوش گذشت. ۲ از این رنگ خوشَم نمیآید ولی آن آبی قَشنگ است. ۳ یادت رفت که دیروز به مریم تلفن بزنی. ۴ ما میخواهیم اخبار ساعتِ دَه را نگاهکنیم ولی من خیلی خوابَم میآید. ۵ آنها توی ترن خوابشان بُرد و مناظرِ زیبا را ندیدند.

Exercise 2

1 They dislike (loathe) this part of the city. 2 Why do you always fall asleep at talks? 3 Whenever we go to Iran we have a lovely time.

4 I can't remember (it has slipped my mind) whether I have a dentist's appointment tomorrow or the day after. 5 He likes Persian music.

Exercise 3

بعـــله! من عاشقِ موسیقی ایرانی هستم. چطور مگر؟ / من حتماً میآیم. کنسرت کدام شبست؟ / یکدنیا ممنون. بعداز آن برویم یک رستورانِ خوب؟ یک رستوران ایرانی آن نزدیکیهاست. / بسیارخوب، پس من یک میز برای هشت نفر، برای ساعت ده و نیم رزرو میکنم.

Unit 21

There are books in which we can find the answers to different questions. We call these books dictionaries and encyclopaedias. In these books, phrases and names are printed in bold letters in alphabetical order and each one is given a detailed explanation in ordinary print. Encyclopaedias are usually textbooks in which we can find all sorts of scientific, literary, art, historical, geographic and other information. Some encyclopaedias are published in several volumes.

Persian–English glossary

الف

water	آب
pomegranate juice	آب اَنار
they extract the juice	آب می‌گیرَند
fruit juice	آب میوه
cloud	ابر
eyebrow	ابرو
cloudy	ابری
silk	ابریشم
blue	آبی
apartment	آپارتمان
room	اُتاق
bedroom	اُتاق خواب
bus	اُتوبوس
rent	اِجاره
to rent	اِجاره کردن
they have rented out	اِجاره دادن
permission	اِجازه
brick	آجر
respect	اِحترام

hello, how are you, exchange of niceties	احوالپرسی
last, in the end	آخر
the last	آخرین
office	اداره
manners, politeness	اَدَب
literary, formal prose	اَدبی
address	آدرس
gradually, 'slowly, slowly', 'calmly, calmly'	آرام آرام
mausoleum	آرامگاه
beauty salon	آرایشگاه
cheap	ارزان
maxim	آرمان
informal yes, 'yup'	آره
from, of, through	اَز

since	از وقتیکه، از زمانیکه	mistake	اشتباه
		to make mistakes	اِشتباه کردن
to get married	ازدواج کردن	tears	اشک
experiment, test	آزمایش	familiar	آشنا
easy	آسان	to become acquainted	آشنا شدن
horse	اَسب	information	اطلاعات
equipment, furniture	اسباب	often	اَغلَب
Spain	اسپانیا	sun	آفتاب
is	اَست	sunny	آفتابی
master, teacher	اُستاد	gentleman, sir	آقا
rest	استراحت	period of stay, residence	اقامت
to use, to benefit from	استفاده کردن	economy	اقتصاد
		ocean	اَقیانوس
hour glass-shaped tea glasses	اِستِکان	now	اکنون
		now	الآن
studio	استودیو	of course	اَلبَته
spinach	اسفِناج،	Germany	آلمان
name, title	اسم	bangles	اَلَنگو
(lit. family name) surname	اِسم فامیل	now	اما
		examination	اِمتحان
sky	آسمان	to come, arrive	آمدَن
cook, chef	آشپز	order, command, request	اَمر
kitchen	آشپزخانه		

today	امروز	he or she	او
this year	امسال	to sing	آواز خواندن
tonight	امشب	to bring, fetch	آوردن
college	آموزشگاه	first	اَوَل
hope	اُمید	stop (as in bus stop), station	ایستگاه
I hope	اُمیدوارَم		
that	آن	they	ایشان
the other one	آن یکی دیگر	this	این
pomegranate	اَنار	here	اینجا
to choose	اِنتخاب کردن	future, next	آیَنده
there, that place	آنجا		
			ب
fig	اَنجیر	with, by	با
size, amount	اَندازه	despite the fact that	با اینکه
little, a bit	اندک		
as if	انگار	despite the fact that	با وجودیکه
finger (or toe)	اَنگشت		
ring	اَنگشتر	loyal, faithful	با وفا
grape	اَنگور	father	بابا
they (their, them as possessor)	آنها	to lose	باختن
		wind	باد
slow, slowly	آهسته	aubergine, eggplant	بادنجان
native of; to have a liking for something	اَهل	rain	باران
		rainy	بارانی
importance, significance	اَهَمیت	narrow, slender	باریک

open	باز	revolting (in taste)	بدمزه
to open	باز کردن	without	بِدونِ
bazaar, market	بازار	to return	بَرگَشتَن
game, play	بازی	brother	برادر
ancient	باستانی	for	برای
garden	باغ	some	برخی
zoo	باغ وحش	to take, carry away	بردن
small garden	باغچهِ	snow	برف
up	بالا	snowy	بَرفی
further up	بالاتر	electricity	برق
clever, bright	باهوش	electric	برقی
excuse me, forgive me	ببخشید!	bronze	برنز
tiger	بَبر	large, big, great	بُزُرگ
childhood, childlike behaviour	بچگی	bigger	بُزُرگتَر
child	بچه	biggest, largest	بُزَرگتَرین
fireplace, open fire	بخاری دیواری	to tie up, wrap; to close, shut	بستن
bad	بد	ice cream	بَستَنی
unfortunate, unlucky	بدبخت	parcel	بسته
unfortunately	بدبختانه	to your health	بسلامتی
smelly, pungent	بدبو	many, much, very	بسیار
nasty, mean, deceitful	بدجنس	plate	بُشقاب

then, next	بَعد	unfaithful, disloyal	بی وفا
later	بعداً	rude, uncouth	بی ادب
afternoon	بَعدازظُهر	for no good reason, pointlessly	بی خود– بی خودی
next	بعدی	if it's no trouble, please	بی زحمت
grocer's shop	بقالی		
tall, high	بُلَند	unemployed; not busy	بی کار
yes	بَله	undoubtedly	بیتردید
ticket	بلیط	poor thing, wretched	بیچاره
purple	بَنَفش	outside	بیرون
to	به	outside	بیرون–خارج
instead of	به جایِ		
with difficulty	به دشواری	most of, many of [following by an *ezafe* (*e*)]	بیشتَرِ
to be born	به دُنیا آمدن		
by force, forcibly, grudgingly	به زور – به زحمت	more	بیشتَر
as pretty as	به قَشَنگی	sick, unwell; patient	بیمار
sign of exclamation (meaning wonderful, lovely)	به! به!	hospital	بیمارستان
		nose	بینی
spring	بَهار		
better	بِهتَر		پ
to be	بودن	foot; leg	پا
kiss	بوسه		

lit, favourite meeting-up place, where people hang out	پاتوق	chatterbox	پرحرف
		obnoxious, bolshy	پررو
cloth, material	پارچه	question	پرسش
last year	پارسال	bird, fowl	پَرَنده
park	پارک	to fly	پرواز کردن
car park	پارکینگ	butterfly	پروانه
answer, reply	پاسخ	to jump	پریدن
overcoat, winter coat	پالتو	day before yesterday	پریروز
capital city	پایتَخت	physician, doctor	پزشک
autumn	پاییز	so, in that case, therefore, then	پَس
down, below	پایین		
to cook	پختن	to take back, get back, retrieve	پس گرفتن
father	پدر	day after tomorrow	پس فردا
grandfather	پدربزرگ	to post	پست کردن
father-in-law (wife's father)	پدرزن	postman	پستچی
father-in-law (husband's father)	پدرشوهر	post office	پستخانه
full of	پُر اَز	boy, son	پسر
to fill	پر کردن	back, behind	پشتِ
oranges	پرتقال	one after the other	پشتِ سرِ هم
chatting too much	پرچربی		

plaque, door number	پِلاک	before, prior to	پیش از
window	پنجره	message	پیغام
Thursday	پنجشنبه		ت
cheese	پَنیر	until, up to	تا
next to, beside	پَهلوی	as long as	تا وقتیکه
wide	پَهن	theatre	تئاتر
winter snowboots	پوتین	summer	تابِستان
skin	پوست	date; history	تاریخ
to wear	پوشیدن	historic	تاریخی
money	پول	dark	تاریک
rich, wealthy	پولدار	fresh	تازِه
continuously	پیاپی	hill	تپه
on foot	پیاده	trade	تجارت
sidewalk, pavement	پیاده رو	bed	تختخواب
going for a walk	پیاده روی	reduction, discount	تخفیف
onion	پیاز	to give discount	تخفیف دادن
message	پیام	eggs	تُخم مُرغ
to find	پیدا کردن	wet	تر
old	پیر	scales	ترازو
shirt; dress	پیراهن	order	ترتیب
to (used for people: going to s.o.); at	پیشِ	hesitation, reluctantly	تردید
		fear	ترس
		coward, scared	ترسو

sour	تُرش	lazy	تنبَل
to leave; give up	ترک کردن	spicy, hot	تند
thirsty	تِشنه	fast, quick; fast, quickly	تُند
to decide (lit. take decisions)	تَصمیم گرِفتَن	alone	تَنها
exchange of niceties	تَعارُف	to; you (sing.)	تو
to be surprised	تَعَجُب کردن	to be able to	توانستن
to describe, give detailed account	تعریف کردن	ball	توپ
		to explain	توضیح دادن
closed, shut	تعطیل	birth (also birthday)	تَوَلُد
holidays, vacation	تعطیلات	inside, into	توی
approximately, nearly	تَقریباً		
bitter	تَلخ		ث
telephone	تلفن	seconds	ثانیه
to make a call, telephone	تلفن کردن / زدن		
			ج
television	تلوزیون	place	جا
to watch, look at	تماشاکردن	places (pl.)	جا ها
all of the . . .	تَمام	spacious	جادار
to finish, complete	تمام کردن	vacuum cleaner	جاروبرقی
stamp	تمبر	interesting	جالب
practice, exercises	تمرین	soul, life, term of endearment after proper names	جان
to practise	تمرین کردن		
clean	تَمیز	some places (indefinite pl.)	جاهایی
to clean	تمیز کردن		

where	جاییکه	world	جَهان
really, seriously	جِداً	tourist	جهانگرد
new	جدید	reply	جواب
apart	جز	young; youth (person)	جوان
island	جَزیره	jewellery	جواهر
party, celebration	جشن	chicken, baby bird	جوجه
festival	جشنواره	type, kind	جور
box	جعبه	socks	جوراب
parsley	جَعفری		
geography	جغرافی	**چ**	
pair; mate	جفت	fat	چاق
cover for book; volume	جِلد	kitchen or other types of knife	چاقو
meetings, sessions (pl.)	جلسات	chin	چانه
meeting, one session	جلسه	tea	چای
front	جلو	left	چپ
prevention	جلوگیری	umbrella	چتر
in front of, by	جلوی	why?	چرا؟
Friday	جمعه	light, lamp	چراغ
population	جمعیَت	stuck down	چَسباندن
republic	جمهوری	eyes	چشم
war	جنگ	ophthalmic physician	چشمپزشک
forest	جنگل	spring	چشمه
south	جُنوب	how was it?	چطور بود؟

why? why do you ask? (idiomatic)	چِطور مَگَر	because	چونکه
how? how come?	چطور؟	what	چی؟
how are you?	چطوری؟	something	چیزی
how	چقدر		
how much? how long?	چقدر؟		ح
hammer	چَکُش	now, presently	حالا
several, a few	چند	definitely	حتماً
how many?	چند تا	even	حتی
a few weeks ago	چَند هَفته پیش	letters of alphabet; spoken word	حرف
how many?	چَند؟	to speak, talk	حرف زدن
several	چَندین	profession	حِرفه
fork	چنگال	letters (pl.)	حروف
what kind?, sort?	چِ جور؟	bath, bathroom	حَمام
what year?	چه سالی؟	what a pity, what a shame	حیف
what did you do?	چِ می کردید؟	animal	حِیوان
what!; how . . .!	چه!		خ
what?	چه؟	outside	خارج از
four	چهار	foreign, foreigner	خارجی
Wednesday	چهار شنبه	dust, earth, soil	خاک
fourth	چهارم	grey	خاکستری
wooden	چوبی	maternal aunt	خاله
because	چون	switch off, silent, dark	خاموش

private, confidential	خُصوصی	home made	خانگی
line	خط	lady, madam, term of address for women	خانم
danger	خطر	house, home	خانه
dangerous	خطرناک	family	خانواده
quiet, free of people	خلوت	Middle East	خاورمیانه
Persian Gulf	خَلیجِ فارس	caviar	خاویار
toothpaste	خمیردندان	news	خبر
smilingly, cheerfully	خندان	to have news	خبر داشتن
funny (lit. with laughter)	خنده دار	funeral	خَتم
cool	خُنَک	goodbye, farewell	خداحافظ
dormitory, hall of residence	خوابگاه	god bless, goodbye, farewell	خدانگهدار
to sheep	خوابیدن	to go off; to break down	خراب شدن
singer	خواننده	sweet melon	خربزه
sister	خواهر	small change	خُرد
to ask politely, request	خواهش کردن	a bit, just a little, a touch	خُرده
good, nice, pleasant	خوب	rabbit	خرگوش
biro, ballpoint pen	خودکار	to buy	خریدن
fountain pen	خودنویس	the Caspian Sea	خَزَر
to eat; to drink	خوردن	tired	خسته
to have had a good time	خوش گذشتن	dry, arid	خُشک
		with enmity, angrily	خصمانه

252

polite, pleasant exchanges	خوش و بش	story, account of	داستان
welcome	خوش آمد	hot	داغ
you are welcome	خوش آمدید	bridegroom	داماد
kind, honest, decent	خوش جنس	vet	دامپزشک
fortunate, happy	خوشبَخت	skirt	دامن
luckily, fortunately	خوشبختانه	outskirts	دامَنه
I'm happy to meet you	خوشبَختَم	to know	دانستن
		student	دانشجو
		university	دانشگاه
fragrant, nice smelling	خوشبو	circle	دایره
happy, cheerful	خوشحال	encyclopaedia	دایره المعارف
pretty	خوشگل	maternal uncle	دایی
delicious, tasty	خوشمَزه	girl, daughter	دختر
blood	خون	cousin; daughter of maternal aunt	دخترخاله
street, avenue	خیابان	in, at, inside	دَر
tailor's, dressmaker's	خیاطی	door, gate	دَر
mind, imagination	خیال	to get or take something out, bring out	درآوردن
much, very, many	خیلی		
very good	خیلی خوب	while	در حالیکه
		to knock	در زدن
	د	percentage	در صد
inside, within	داخِل	long	دراز
to give	دادن	about	دربارهٔ
chemist, pharmacy	داروخانه		

to be printed, published	درج شدن	teeth	دندان
tree	درخت	dentist	دندانپزشک
lesson	درس	dental technician	دَندانساز
to study	دَرس خواندَن	world	دُنیا
correct, right, exact	درست	mouth	دهان
to fix, mend	دُرُست کردن	tenth	دهم
greetings	درود	two or three hours	دو سه ساعَت
inside	درون – داخل	Monday	دو شنبه
sea	دریا	again	دوباره
lake	دریاچه	bicycle	دوچرخه
very big sea	دریای خیلی بُزُرگ	far, faraway	دور
hand	دست	binoculars	دوربین
bracelet	دستبند	photographic camera	دوربین عکاسی
difficult	دُشوار	friend	دوست
to tell off, rebuke, argue	دعوا کردن	to like	دوست داشتن
to invite	دَعوَت کردن	friendly	دوستانه
stand, kiosk	دکه	government	دولت
brave	دلیر	second	دوم
next to, near	دَم	to see	دیدن
time to time	دمادم	yesterday	دیروز
to look for, search for	دنبالِ...گشتن	late	دیروقت
		last night	دیشَب

no longer (with negative verb), no more	دیگَر	to dance	رقصیدن
		colour, shade, dye	رَنگ
other	دیگَر	to paint, colour in	رنگ زدن\ کردن
	ر	visa	روادید
(direct object marker)	را	river	رودخانه
comfortable	راحت	day	روز
to be relieved, become comfortable	راحت شدن	daily	روزانه
		good day	روزبخیر
radio	رادیو	newspaper	روزنامه
straight, true, right	راست	newsagent's	روزنامه فروشی
to drive	رانندگی کردن	Russian	روس
way, path, road	راه	light, bright, switched on	روشن
corridor, hallway	راهرو		
name of legendary horse	رَخش	oil	روغن
		on, on top of	روی
to pass by; to fail	رد شدن	beard	ریش
rose	رز		ز
to deliver; to give a lift	رساندن	language (tongue)	زَبان
official	رَسمی	rough	زِبر
to arrive; to reach	رسیدن	Zoroastrian	زرتشتی
to go	رفتن	yellow	زرد
pal, close friend, comrade	رفیق	clever	زِرَنگ

ugly	زِشت	quiet, silent	ساکت
earthquake	زلزله	year	سال
winter	زِمِستان	year(s) ago	سالِ پیش
ground, floor, earth, land	زمین	healthy	سالِم
surface, land	زمینی	(lit. salon) hall, big room	سالُن
wife, woman	زن	basket	سبد
wasp	زنبور	green	سبز
honey bee	زنبورعسل	herbs	سبزی
life	زِندِگی	greengrocer's	سبزی فروشی
to live	زندگی کردن	vegetables	سبزیجات
soon, early	زود	vegetarian	سبزیخوار
much, very	زیاد	moustache	سبیل
pretty (beautiful)	زیبا	grateful	سپاسگزار
olives	زیتون	then	سپس
under, beneath	زیرِ	star	ستاره
ashtray	زیرسیگاری	difficult	سخت
		speech, delivered lecture	سخنرانی
	س	at the head of, at the top of, at	سرِ
question	سؤال	head	سر
building	ساختمان	red, crimson	سرخ
to build, make, construct	ساختن	cold	سرد
(here) o'clock, hour of	ساعت	speed	سرعت
four o'clock	ساعتِ چهار		

hobby	سرگرمی		ش
cold (noun)	سرما	branch, stem	شاخه
embassy	سفارت	happy	شاد
special, registered	سفارشی	poet	شاعر
travel, journey	سفر	supper, dinner	شام
to travel	سفر کردن	comb; shoulders	شانه
bon voyage	سفربخیر	perhaps	شاید
white	سفید	night	شَب
dog	سگ	goodnight	شب بخیر
hello	سلام	brave, courageous	شجاع
hairdresser's, barber	سلمانی	personal, private	شَخصی
heavy	سَنگین	to become; to happen	شدن
Sunni	سُنی	to begin, start	شروع شدن
Tuesday	سه شَنبه	to wash	شُستن
riding	سواری	poetry	شعر
needle	سوزن	sugar	شکَر
beetle	سوسک	to break	شکستن
political	سیاسی	broken	شکسته
black	سیاه	chocolate	شکلات
apple	سیب	trousers	شلوار
potato	سیب زمینی	busy, crowded	شُلوغ
garlic	سیر	you (pl.)	شُما
full, satiated	سیر	number	شماره
cinema	سینَما	telephone number	شمارهٔ تلفن
tray	سینی		

north	شُمال	hundred	صَد
northeast	شُمالِ شَرقی	sound, noise	صدا
northern	شُمالی	peace	صُلح
to recognize	شناختن	chair	صَندَلی
to swim	شناکردن	pink	صورتی
Saturday	شنبه		
to hear	شنیدن		ط
city, cities	شهر (.pl) شَهرها	melon	طالبی
salty, savoury	شور	level, floor	طبقه
husband	شوهَر	nature	طَبیعَت
milk	شیر	designer	طَراح
sweet	شیرین	side, direction	طَرَف
confectionery	شیرینی	supporter	طرفدار
glass	شیشه	golden	طلایی
(lit. Satan) naughty	شیطان	long	طولانی
Shi'ite	شیعه		
			ع
		excellent, superb	عالی
	ص	bride	عروس
owner; landlord/landlady	صاحبخانه	doll	عروسک
morning	صُبح	wedding	عروسی
good morning	صبح بخیر	dear	عزیز
breakfast	صبحانه	my dear	عزیزم
stage	صحنه	honey	عسل
		love	عِشق

258

romantic, lovey-dovey	عشقی		ف
angry	عصبانی	French	فرانسه
anger	عصبانیت	to provide; to bring together	فراهم آمدن
afternoon tea, snack	عصرانه		
good afternoon	عصربخیر	tomorrow	فردا
back	عقب	to send	فرِستادن
photographer	عَکاس	carpet	فرش
photography	عکاسی	form	فرم
photograph	عکس	to sell	فروختن
scientific	علمی	airport	فرودگاه
paternal aunt	عَمه	store, department store	فروشگاه
paternal uncle	عمو		
public	عمومی	only	فَقَط
		poor	فقیر
to change, exchange, replace	عَوض کردن	thought, idea	فکر
		to think	فکر کَردَن
religious or traditional celebration	عید	pepper	فلفِل
		cup	فنجان
glasses	عینک	film	فیلم

غ

food	غذا		ق
west	غرب	spoon	قاشق
western	غَربی	carpet	قالی
sorrow, grief	غصه	small rugs	قالیچه
et al., etc., and others	غیره	old (not for people)	قدیمی

appointment arrangement	قرار	postcard	کارت پستال
red, crimson	قرمز	factory	کارخانه
century	قَرن	knife (cutlery)	کارد
beautiful	قَشَنگ	workshop	کارگاه
butcher's	قصابی	worker, labourer	کارگر
train	قطار	employee (here cashier)	کارمند
thick	قَطور	bowl	کاسه
lock	قُفل	if only, would that . . .	کاش
heart	قلب	to plant, sow	کاشتن
pen	قَلَم	paper	کاغذ
coffee	قهوه	sufficient, enough	کافی
brown	قَهوه ای	garlic sausage, mortadella	کالباس
coffee house	قهوه خانه	matches	کبریت
teapot	قوری	book	کتاب
scissors	قیچی	library	کتابخانه
price, value	قیمت	books	کتب
		kettle	کتری
	ک	where?	کجا؟
present, gift	کادو	where in?	کُجای؟
jobs, work, things that keep one busy	کار	from where? (re nationality)	کجایی؟
to be busy, to have things to do	کار داشتن	which?	کُدام؟
to work	کار کردن	marrow, courgette	کَدو
card	کارت	pumpkin	کَدو تنبل

260

butter	کَره	short (brief)	کوتاه
sphere	کُره	smaller	کوچَکتَر
someone; no one (with negative verb)	کسی	side street	کوچه
		tiny, very small	کوچولو
ship	کَشتی	child	کودک
country	کِشوَر	mountain	کوه
shoe shop	کفاشی	mountainside	کوهستان
hat	کلاه	mountainous	کوهستانی
cottage, a small house	کلبه	when?	کی؟
thick	کُلُفت	who, whom?	کی؟
word	کلمه	bag	کیف
key	کلید	cake	کیک
church	کلیسا		
little	کم		گ
low-fat	کم چربی	sometimes	گاهی
comedy	کُمدی	to put, place; to allow	گذاشتن
belt	کمربند		
shy, bashful	کمرو	to pass by	گُذَشتن
to help, assist	کمک کردن	cat	گُربه
a little	کمی	neck	گردن
rare	کمیاب	hungry	گُرسنه
edges of, next to, on the banks of	کنارِ	to grab, catch, take	گِرفتن
that	که	warm (hot)	گَرم
old (as in rags)	کُهنه	heat	گرما

necklace	گردنبند	clothing	لباس
in tears, tearfully	گریان	please	لطفاً
tears	گریه	dictionary	لغتنامه
to cry	گریه کردن	lemon	لیمو
to say, tell	گفتن	glass, tumbler	لیوان
flower (arch. roses)	گُل		
to plant flowers	گل کاشتن		**م**
rosewater	گُلاب	we, us	ما
pear	گُلابی	noisy kiss	ماچ
flowerpot, vase	گلدان	grandmother	مادربزرگ
florist	گلفروشی	mother-in-law (wife's mother)	مادرزن
throat	گَلو	mother-in-law (husband's mother)	مادرشوهر
kelim rugs	گلیم		
tomato	گوجه فرنگی	yoghurt	ماست
sheep	گوسفَند	car	ماشین
ear	گوش	mama, mummy	مامان
to listen	گوش کَردن or گوش دادن	to remain, stay	ماندن
		mouth; moon	ماه
meat; flesh	گوشت	honeymoon	ماه عسل
earring	گوشواره	fish	ماهی
		tuna fish	ماهی تُن
	ل	congratulations!	مبارک!
thin, skinny	لاغر	grateful	متشکر
tulips	لاله	various	مُتعَدِد
lip	لب		

like, similar to	مثل	surface area, expanse	مَساحَت
example, for instance	مَثَلا	traveller, passenger	مسافر
triangle	مُثَلَث	to travel	مُسافَرَت کردن
free	مجانی	equal	مساوی
statue	مجسمه	mosque	مسجد
magazine	مجله	Muslim	مُسَلمان
well equipped	مُجَهَز	toothbrush	مسواک
area, neighbourhood, district	محله	Christian (pl. of مسیحی)	مَسیحیانِ
varied, different	مختلف	alcoholic drinks	مشروب
pencil	مداد	difficult; problem	مشکل
duration	مدت	to consult	مشورت کردن
for a long while	مدتها	surgery	مطب
school	مدرسه	certain, sure	مطمئن
jam	مربا	temple	مَعبد
square	مربع	to introduce	معرفی کردن
related, connected	مربوط	famous	معروف
man	مرد	teacher, instructor	مُعَلم
people	مردم	usual	معمول
merci, thank you	مرسی	common	معمولی
bird, hen, chicken	مرغ	shop	مغازه
centre	مرکز	detailed	مُفَصَل
marble	مرمر	shrine	مقبره
pearl	مروارید	but	مگَر

nationality	ملیت	Christian era (BCE)	میلادی
possible	ممکن	Monkey	میمون
grateful	ممنون		
me, mine, my	مَن		ن
to be waiting for s.t.	منتظر بودن	uncomfortable	ناراحت
		orange colour	نارنجی
home, house	مَنزِل	thin, fine	نازک
house warming	منزل مبارکی	to be called sth., named sth.	نام داشتن
region	مَنطقه		
view	منظره	fiancé(e)	نامزد
moonlight	مَهتاب	letter	نامه
kind	مهربان	bread	نان
important	مُهِم	bakery	نانوایی
party	مِهمانی	lunch	ناهار
hair	مو	not to be	نَبودَن
to be careful, cautious	مواظب بودن	carpenter's	نجاری
		thread	نخ
ant	مورچه	polite no	نَخیر
banana	موز	rate, price	نرخ
museum	موزه	narcissus	نرگس
music	موسیقی	soft, smooth	نرم
mouse	موش	near by, close to	نَزدیک
wall-to-wall carpet	موکت	relatively	نسبَتاً
carnation	میخک	directions, address	نِشانی
desk, table	میز		

to sit	نشستن	half	نیم...
half	نَصف	hemisphere	نیمکُره
saucer	نَعلبکی		**و**
mint	نَعناع	to enter	وارد شدن
oil	نَفت	wild	وحشی
persons	نَفَر	sport	ورزش
painter	نقاش	athlete, sporty person	ورزشکار
painting	نقاشی		
cash	نَقد	entrance; arrival	ورود
silver	نُقره ای	weight	وزن
to look at	نگاه کردن	expanse, surface area	وُسعَت
anxious, worried, concerned	نگران	means, tools	وسیله
		time	وَقت
salt	نَمَک	to have time	وَقت داشتن
no	نه	when, at the time that	وقتی
neither ... nor ...	نه... نه...	when	وقتیکه – موقعیکه – زمانیکه
light	نور		
first day of Persian New Year	نوروز	punctual	وقتشناس
		lukewarm	ولَرم
drink	نوشابه	however, but	ولی
to write	نوشتن	visa	ویزا
to drink	نوشیدن		
type	نوع		**ه**
grandchild	نوه	present	هدیه
writer	نویسنده	wherever	هر جاییکه

all sorts, kinds	هر جور	spouse	همسر
both of us	هر دو	fellow traveller	همسفر
whichever	هر کدامکه	fellow citizen	همشهری
whoever	هر کس که or	colleague	همکار
	هرکسیکه	classmate	همکلاس
whenever	هر وقتیکه	all	همه
as soon as possible	هرچه زودتر	always	همیشه
		as soon as	همینکه
everyday	هرروز	India	هند، هندوستان
never	هرگز	water melon	هندوانه
thousand	هزار	art	هنر
seven	هفت	artistic	هنری
seventh	هفتم	still, as yet	هنوز
week	هفته	weather (also air)	هوا
peach	هلو	aeroplane	هواپیما
also, too	هم	air	هوایی
roommate	هم اتاق	never	هیچوقت
with common border, sharing the same border	هم مرز		
			ی
that very	همان	either . . . or	یا . . . یا
there (and then)	همانجا	to teach	یاد دادن
just as, as	همانطوریکه	to learn	یاد گرفتن
companion	همراه	eleven	یازده
neighbour	همسایه (pl. همسایگان)	ice	یخ

frozen	یخ زده	one of	یکی اَز
fridge	یخچال	one by one	یکی یکی
each other	یکدیگر	jewish	یَهودی pl. یَهودیان
lit. one day	یکروز	slowly, quietly	یواش
one year	یِکسال	Greece	یونان
Sunday	یکشنبه		

English–Persian glossary

a little	کمی – یک کم	ant	مورچه
about	دربارهٔ	anxious	نگَران
address	آدرس – نِشانی	apart	بِغیر از
aeroplane	هواپیما	apartment	آپارتمان
afternoon	بَعدازظُهر – عَصر	apple	سیب
afternoon tea, snack	عصرانه	appointment, arrangement	قرار – قرارِ ملاقات
again	دوباره	approximately, nearly	تَقریباً – نَزدیک به
air	هوا	area, neighbour-hood, district	مَحَله – همسایگی
airport	فُرودگاه		
alcoholic drinks	مَشروب	art	هُنَر
all	همه	artistic	هُنَرمَند
all of the ...	همهٔ – تَمامِ	arrive, reach (to)	رِسیدَن
all sorts, kinds of	همه جور – همه نوع	as if	انگار
alone	تَنها	as long as	تا وقتیکه – تا زمانیکه
also, too	همچِنین، نیز		
always	همیشه	as pretty as	به قَشَنگیِ
ancient	قَدیمی – باستانی	as soon as	تا – به محضِ اینکه
anger	خَشم – عَصبانیت		
angry	خَشمگین – عَصبانی	as soon as possible	هرچه زودتر
animal	حیوان – جانوَر		
answer, reply	پاسُخ – جواب	ashtray	زیرسیگاری

English	Persian
ask politely, request (to)	خواستَن
at last, in the end	آخر – بالاخره
at the head of, at the top of, at	سرِ
athlete, sporty person	ورزِشکار
aubergine, eggplant	بادِنجان
autumn	پاییز – خَزان
back	پُشت – عَقَب – تَه
back, behind	پُشتِ سرِ
bad	بَد
bag	کیف
bakery	نانوایی
ball	توپ
banana	موز
bangles	اَلَنگو
basket	سَبَد
bath (tub)	وانِ حَمام
bathroom	حَمام
bazaar, market	بازار
be (to)	بودَن
be able to (to)	توانِستَن
be born (to)	به دنیا آمَدَن
be busy, have things to do (to)	کارداشتَن
be called something, be named something (to)	نام داشتَن

English	Persian
be careful, cautious (to)	مُواظِب بودن
be printed, be published (to)	چاپ شدن – منتَشر شدن
be relieved, become comfortable (to)	راحَت شُدن
be surprised (to)	تَعَجُب کردن
be waiting for something (to)	مُنتَظِر شُدَن
beard	نان
beautiful	زیبا – قَشَنگ – ناز
beauty salon	آرایشگاه – سالن زیبایی
because	زیرا – چونکه – برای اینکه
become, happen (to)	شُدن
become acquainted (with)	آشنا شُدن
bed	تختخواب
bedroom	اُتاق خواب
beetle	سوسک
before, prior to	پیش از اینکه – قبل از اینکه
begin, start (to)	شُروع کردن
belt	کَمَربَند
better	بهتر – خوبتر
bicycle	دوچرخه
bigger	بُزُرگتَر
biggest, largest	بزرگترین

binoculars	دوربین	bridegroom	داماد
bird, fowl	پَرَنده – مُرغ	bring, fetch (to)	آوَردَن
bird, hen, chicken	مرغ – جوجه	broken	شِکَسته
biro, ballpoint pen	خودکار	brother	بَرادَر
birth (also birthday)	تَوَلُّد	brown	قهوه‌ای
bitter	تَلخ	build, make, construct(to)	ساختن
black	سیاه	building	ساختمان – بنا
blood	خون	bus	اُتوبوس
blue	آبی	busy, crowded	شلوغ
bon voyage	سَفَر بِخیر	but	أما – ولی
book	کتاب	butcher's	قَصاب
books	کُتُب – کتاب ها	butter	کَره
both of us	هر دو – هردوی ما	butterfly	پَروانه
bowl	کاسه – پیاله	buy (to)	خَریدن
box	جعبه	by force, forcibly (also grudgingly)	به زور
boy, son	پسر		
bracelet	دَستبَند		
branch, stem	شاخه	cake	کیک – شیرینی
brave	شُجاع – دَلیر	capital city	پایتخت
bread	نان	car	ماشین – اتومبیل – نَفَربَر
break (to)	شکَستَن		
breakfast	صبحانه	card	کارت
brick	آجُر	carnation	گل میخک
bride	عروس	car park	پارکینگ

carpenter	نَجّار	chin	چانه
carpentry	نَجّاری	chocolate	شکُلات
carpet	فَرش – قالی	choose (to)	انتخاب کردن
carpet (wall to wall)	موکت	Christian	مَسیحی
cash	پولِ نقد	Christian era (BCE)	میلادی
Caspian	خَزَر	church	کلیسا
cat	گُربه	cinema	سینَما
caviar	خاویار	circle	دایره – مَحفِل
centre	مَرکَز	city, cities	شهر – شَهرها
century	قَرن	classmate	همکلاسی
certain, sure	مُطمَئِن – حتم داشتَن	clean	پاک – پاکیزه – تَمیز
		clean (to)	تمیز کردن
chair	صَندَلی	clever	باهوش – زرَنگ
change, exchange, replace (to)	عَوض کردن	closed, shut	بَسته
		cloth, material	پارچه
chatterbox	پُرحَرف – وِراج – پرچانه	clothing	لباس
		cloud	اَبر
cheep	اَرزان	cloudy	اَبری
cheerful	شادمان – خوشحال	coffee	قهوه
		coffee house	قهوهخانه – کافه
cheese	پَنیر	cold	سَرد
chemist, pharmacy	داروخانه		
chicken, baby bird	جوجه	cold (noun)	سَردی
child	بَچه – فَرزَند	colleague	همکار
childhood	بَچگی	college	کالِج – دانشکَده – آموزشگاه
childlike behaviour	بَچگانه		

colour, shade, dye	رَنگ	cry (to)	گریه کردن
comb; shoulders	شانه	cup	فنجان
come, arrive (to)	آمَدَن	knife (cutlery)	کارد
comedy	کُمِدی		
comfortable	راحَت	daily	روزانه
common	عادی – مَعمولی	dance	رقصیدن
companion	مونِس – همنِشین	danger	خطَر
confectionery	شیرینی	dangerous	خطَرناک
congratu-lations!	تَبریک – مُبارک	dark	تاریک – تیره
		date; history	تاریخ
consult (to)	مَشوِرَت کردن	day	روز
continously	مُدام – پیوَسته – یکبَند	day after tomorrow	پَس‌فَردا
cook, chef	آشپَز	day before yesterday	پریروز
cook (to)	پُختن– آشپَزی کردن	dear	عَزیز
cool	خُنک	decide (lit. take decisions) (to)	تَصمیم گِرِفتن
correct, right, exact	دُرُست	definitely	حَتماً
corridor, hall	راهرو– هـال	delicious, tasty	خوشمَزه
cottage, a small house	کُلبه– آلونک	deliver; give a life (to)	رِساندَن
country	کشوَر	dental technician	دَندانساز
cousin, daughter of maternal aunt	دُختَرخاله	dentist	دَندانپِزشک
cover for books; volume	جِلد	describe, give detailed account (to)	تَعریف کردن
coward, scared	ترسو– بزدل	desk, table	میز

272

despite the fact that	با وجودیکه – باوجود اینکه
detailed	مُفَصَّل
dictionary	فَرهَنگ – لُغتنامه
difficult	سَخت – دشوار – پیچیده
difficult; problem	مُشکِل
(direct object marker)	را
directions, address	نِشانی – آدرس
dog	سَگ
doll	عَروسک
door, gate	دَر
dormitory, hall of residence	خوابگاه
down, below	زیر – پایین
drink	نوشابه – آشامیدَنی
drink (to)	نوشیدن – آشامیدن
drive (to)	راندن – رانَندگی کردن
dry, arid	خُشک
duration	دوران – طول
dust, earth, soil	خاک
each other	دیگَری – هَمدیگَر
ear	گوش
earring	گوشواره
earthquake	زَلزِله – زمینلرزه
easy	ساده – آسان
eat; drink (to)	خوردن
economy	اقتصاد
edges of, next to, on the banks of	لَب – کنار – لَبۀ
eggs	تُخمِمرغ
either . . . or	یا... یا
electric	بَرقی
electricity	بَرق
eleven	یازده
embassy	سِفارَت
employee	کارمَند
encyclopaedia	دایرۀالمَعارِف
enter (to)	وارِد شدن
entrance; arrival	وُرود – وُرودیه
equal	بَرابَر – مُساوی
equipment, furniture	اَساس – اَسباب – وسایِل
et al., etc.; others	و غیره
even	حَتی
everyday	هَرروز

examination	اِمتِحان
excellent, superb	عالی
exchange of niceties	تَعارُف
exclamation (meaning 'wonderful, lovely')	به! به!
excuse me, forgive me	بِبَخشید
expanse, surface area	وُسعَت
experiment, test	آزمایِش
explain (to)	توضیح دادن
eyebrow	اَبرو
eyes	چَشم
factory	کارخانه
familiar	آشنا
family	خانواده – فامیل
family name, surname	اِسم فامیل
famous	مَعروف
far, faraway	دور
fast, quick; fast, quickly	تُند – سَریع
fat	چاق – پَروار
father	پِدَر
father-in-law (husband's father)	پِدرشوهَر

father-in-law (wife's father)	پِدَرزَن
favourite meeting place where people hang out	پاتوق
fear	تَرس
fellow citizen	هَمشَهری
fellow traveller	هَمسَفَر
festival	جَشنواره – فِستیوال
fiancé(e)	نامزَد
fig	اَنجیر
fill (to)	پُر کردن
film	فیلم
find (to)	پیدا کردن
finger (or toe)	اَنگُشت
finish, complete (to)	تَمام کردن
fireplace, open fire	بُخاری دیواری – شومینه
first	اَوَل
fish	ماهی
florist	گُلفُروش
flower (arch. roses)	گُل
flowerpot, vase	گُلدان
fly (to)	پرواز کردن

food	غذا– خوراکی	friend	دوست – رَفیق
foot; leg	پا	friendly	دوستانه
for	برای	from, of, through	از
for a long while	مُدَتها	from where?	کُجایی؟
for example, for instance	مَثَلاً	(re nationality)	اهلِ کجا؟
		front	جلو
for no good reason, point- lessly	بیخود – بیخودی – بیدلیل	frozen	یخزده
		fruit juice	آبمیوه
foreign, foreigner	خارجی	full, satiated	سیر
forest	جَنگَل	full of	پُر از
fork	چَنگال	funeral	خاکسپاری
form	فُرم–شکل	funny	خَندهدار
formal prose	نَثرِ ادبی	(lit. with laughter)	
fortunate, happy	خوشبخت	further up	بالاتَر
fountain pen	خودنِویس	future, next	آیَنده
four	چَهار		
four o'clock	ساعتِ چَهار	game, play	بازی
fourth	چَهارُم	garden	باغ
fragrant, nice smelling	خوشبو	garlic	سیر
free	آزاد – رایگان	garlic sausage, mortadella	کالباس
French	فَرانسه – فَرانسَوی	gentleman, sir	آقا
fresh	تازه	geography	جُغرافی
Friday	جُمعه – آدینه	Germany	آلمان
fridge	یخچال	get married (to)	ازدِواج کردن

get or take something out, bring out (to)	درآوردَن	grandchild	نَوه
		grandfather	پدَربُزُرگ
girl, daughter	دُختَر	grandmother	مادَربُزُرگ
give (to)	دادن	grape	اَنگور
give discount (to)	تَخفیف دادن	grateful	مَمنون
glass	شیشه	Greece	یونان
glass, tumbler	لیوان	green	سَبز
glasses	عِینک	greengrocer's	سَبزی فروش
go (to)	رفتن	greetings	درود – سلام و اَحوالپُرسی
go off, break down (to)	خراب شدن		
		grey	خاکستَری
god bless, goodbye, farewell	خُداحافظ	grocer's shop	بَقالی
going for a walk	پیاده‌روی	ground, floor, earth, land	زمین
golden	طَلایی		
good afternoon	عَصربِخِیر	hair	مو – زُلف – گیسو
good, nice, pleasant	خوب	hairdresser's, barber	سلمانی
good day	روزبِخِیر	half	نیم – نِصف
good morning	صُبح‌بِخِیر	hammer	چکُش
good night	شَب‌بِخِیر	hand	دَست
goodbye, farewell	خُداحافظ – بدرود	happy	خوشحال – شاد
government	دولَت	hat	کُلاه
grab, catch, take (to)	گِرِفتن	have had a good time (to)	خوش گذشتن
gradually, 'slowly, slowly', 'calmly, calmly'	یواش یواش	have news (to)	خبَر داشتن

have time (to)	وقت داشتن – فُرصَت داشتن	horse	اَسب
		hospital	بیمارِستان
he or she	او	hot	گَرم – داغ
head	سَر	hour glass-shaped tea glasses	اِستِکان
healthy	سالِم		
hear (to)	شَنیدَن	house warming	مَنزِل مُبارَکی
heart	قَلب	house, home	خانه– مَنزِل
heat	گَرما – حَرارَت	how . . .!	چِقَدر...
heavy	سَنگین	how are you? (informal)	چِطوری
hello	سَلام		
help, assist (to)	کُمَک کَردَن	how? how come?	چِطور؟
hemisphere	نیم‌کُره	how many?	چَند تا؟
herbs	سَبزی	how much? how long?	چِقَدر؟
here	اینجا	how was it? (idiomatic)	چِطور بود؟
hesitation	مَکث– تَأمُل		
hill	تَپه	however, but	وَلی – اَما
historic	تاریخی	hundred	صَد
hobby	سَرگَرمی	hungry	گُرُسنه
holidays, vacation	تَعطیلات	husband	شوهَر
home, house	خانه – مَنزِل		
home made	خانگی	I hope	اُمیدوارَم
honey	عَسَل	I'm happy to meet you	خوشبَختَم
honey bee	زَنبورِ عَسَل		
honeymoon	ماهِ عَسَل	ice	یَخ
hope	اُمید	ice cream	بَستَنی

if it's no trouble, please	لُطفاً – بی زَحمَت	Jewish	یَهودی
if only, would that . . .	کاش – کاشکی	jobs, work, things that keep one busy	کار
importance, significance	اَهَمییَت	jump (to)	پَریدن
important	مُهِم	just as, as	هَمانطورکه
in front of, by	جلوی – روبروی	kelim rugs	گلیم
in tears, tearfully	گِریان	kettle	کِتری
in, at, inside	دَر	key	کِلید
India	هِندوستان	kind	مِهرَبان
information	اِطلاعات	kiss	بوسه – ماچ
inside	داخِل– دَرون	kitchen	آشپَزخانه
inside, into	تو– توی	kitchen or other types of knife	چاقو
instead of	به جای– عَوضِ	knock (to)	دَر زَدن
interesting	جالِب	know (to)	دانِستَن
introduce (to)	مُعَرفی کردن – آشنا کردن	lady, madam, term of address for women	خانُم
invite (to)	دَعوَت کردن	lake	دَریاچه
is	اَست	language (tongue)	زَبان
island	جَزیره	large, big, great	بُزُرگ
		last	آخِر – آخَری
jam	مُرَبا	last night	دیشَب
jewellery	جَواهِر	last year	پارسال

late	دیر – دیروقت	lock	قُفل
later	دیرتر	long	طولانی
lazy	تَنبَل	look at (to)	نگاه کردن
learn (to)	یادگِرفتن – آموختن	look for, search for (to)	دنبال... گَشتن
leave, give up (to)	رها کردن – ول کردن	lose (to)	گُم کردن
left	چپ	love	عِشق – مُحَبَت
lemon	لیمو	low fat	کم چربی
lesson	درس	loyal, faithful	با وفا
letter	نامه	luckily, fortunately	خوشبختانه
letters of alphabet; spoken word	حُروف اَلفبا	lukewarm	وِلَرم
level, floor	طَبقه	lunch	ناهار
library	کتابخانه		
life	زِندِگی	magazine	مَجَله
light	نور – روشنایی	make a call, telephone (to)	تِلفن کردن
light, bright, switched on	روشَن	make mistakes (to)	اِشتباه کردن
light, lamp	چراغ	mama, mummy	مامان – ماما
like (to)	دوست داشتن	man	مرد
line	خَط	manners, politeness	اَدَب – تَربیت
lip	لَب	many, much, very	خیلی – بِسیار
listen (to)	گوش دادن		
little	کوچک – کوچولو	marble	مَرمَر
little, a bit	کمی	marrow, courgette	کَدو
live (to)	زِندِگی کردن		

master, teacher	اُستاد	morning	صُبح
matches	کِبریت	mosque	مَسجِد
maternal aunt	خاله	most of, many of	خیلی از– بِسیاری از
maternal uncle	دایی		
mausoleum	آرامگاه– مَقبَره	mother-in-law (husband's mother)	مادرشوهَر
maxim	آرمان	mother-in-law (wife's mother)	مادرزَن
me, mine, my	مَن		
means, tools	وَسایِل – اَسباب	mountain	کوه
meat; flesh	گوشت	mountainous	کوهِستانی
meeting, one session	جَلسه	mountainside	کوهِستان
meetings, sessions	جَلسات	mouse	موش
melon	طالِبی	moustache	سِبیل
mend, fix (to)	دُرُست کردن	mouth	دَهان
message	پَیام – پیغام	much, very	خیلی – بِسیار
Middle East	خاوَرِ میانه	museum	موزه
milk	شیر	music	موسیقی
mind, imagination	تصَوُر – خیال	Muslim	مُسَلمان
mint	نَعناع	my dear	عَزیزَم
mistake	اِشتِباه		
Monday	دوشَنبه	name, title	نام – لَقَب
money	پول	narcissus	گُلِ نَرگِس
monkey	میمون	narrow, slender	باریک
month; moon	ماه	nasty, mean, deceitful	بدجِنس
moonlight	مَهتاب		
more	بیشتر	nationality	مِلیَت

280

native of; have a liking for something	اَهلِ	now	حالا – الآن – اکنون
nature	طَبیعَت	number	عَدَد – شُماره
near by, close to	نَزدیک	obnoxious, bolshy	پُررو
neck	گَردَن	ocean	اُقیانوس
necklace	گَردَنبَند	of course	اَلبَته
needle	سوزَن	office	اداره – دَفتَر
neighbour	هَمسایه	official	رَسمی
neither . . . nor . . .	نه... نه...	often	اَغلَب – بیشتَرِ اوقات
never	هَرگِز	oil (as in cooking or motor)	روغَن
new	نو – جَدید – تازه	oil (as in petroleum)	نَفت
news	اَخبار	old	پیر
newsagent's	روزنامهفروشی	old (as in rags)	کُهنه
newspaper	روزنامه	old (not people)	قَدیمی
next	بَعدی	olives	زیتون
next to, beside	کِنارِ – پَهلوی	on, on top of	رویِ – بالایِ
night	شَب	on foot	پیاده
no	نه – نَخیر	one after the other	یکی پَس اِز دیگَری – پُشتِ سَرِ هَم
no longer, no more (with negative verb)	دیگَر	one by one	یکی یکی
noisy kiss	ماچ	one by one	یکی یکی
north	شُمال	one day	یکروز
northeast	شُمالِ شَرقی	one of	یکی اِز
northern	شُمالی	one year	یک سال
nose	بینی – دَماغ	onion	پیاز
not to be	نَبودَن	only	فَقَط – تَنها

open	باز- گَشوده	park	پارک - باغِ ملی
open (to)	باز کردن- گُشودن	parsley	جَعفَری
ophthalmic physician	چِشمپزِشک	party	مهمانی
		party, celebration	جَشن
orange (colour)	نارنجی	pass by (to)	گُذَشتَن
oranges	پُرتُقال	pass by; fail (to)	رد شدن
order	تَرتیب	paternal aunt	عمه
order, command, request	دَستور – فرمان	paternal uncle	عَمو
		peace	صُلح
other	دیگر	peach	هُلو
outside	بیرون	pear	گُلابی
outskirts	دامَنه	pearl	مُروارید
overcoat, winter coat	پالتو	pen	قَلَم
		pencil	مداد
owner, landlord/lady	صاحبخانه	people	مَردُم
		pepper	فلفل
		percentage	درصد
paint, colour in (to)	رَنگ کردن/زدن	perhaps	شاید
painter	نَقاش	period of stay, residence	اقامَت
painting	نَقاشی	permission	اجازه
pair; mate	جُفت	Persian Gulf	خلیجِ فارس
pal, close friend, comrade	رَفیق	personal, private	شَخصی – خُصوصی
paper	کاغَذ	persons	نَفَر
parcel	بَسته	photograph	عَکس

photographer	عَکاس	post (to)	پست کردن
photographic camera	دوربینِ عکاسی	post office	پُستخانه
		postcard	کارتپستال
photography	عَکاسی	postman	پُستچی
physician, doctor	پِزِشک- دُکتُر	potato	سیبزمینی
		practice, exercises	تَمرین
pink	صورتی	practise (to)	تمرین کردن
place	جا	present	حاضر
places (pl.)	جاها	present, gift	هَدیه – کادو
plant, sow (to)	کاشتن	pretty	زیبا – قَشَنگ
plaque, door number	پلاک – شمارهٔ	prevention	پیشگیری– جلوگیری
plate	بُشقاب	price, value	قیمَت – بَها
please	لُطفاً – خواهش میکُنَم – بی زَحمَت	private, confidential	خصوصی – مَحرَمانه
poet	شاعِر	profession	شُغل
poetry	شِعر	provide, bring together (to)	فَراهَم کردن
polite, pleasant exchanges	خوش و بِش	public	عُمومی
political	سیاسی	pumpkin	کَدو
pomegranate	اَنار	punctual	وَقتشِناس– سَرِ وقت
pomegranate juice	آب نار	purple	بَنَفش
poor	بیچاره – بینَوا	put, place; allow (to)	گُذاشتن
poor thing, wretched	بیچاره– بَدبَخت		
population	جَمعیَت	question	پُرسِش – سؤال
possible	مُمکِن	quiet, free of people	خَلوَت

quiet, silent	ساکِت
rabbit	خَرگوش
radio	رادیو
rain	باران
rainy	بارانی
rare	کَمیاب – نایاب
rate, price	نِرخ – قیمَت
recognize (to)	شناختن
red, crimson	سُرخ – قِرمِز
reduction, discount	تَخفیف
region	مَنطقه
related, connected	مَربوط
relatively	نِسبَتاً
religious or traditional celebration	عید
remain, stay (to)	ماندن
rent	اجاره– کرایه
rent (to)	اجاره کردن
reply	پاسُخ– جَواب
republic	جمهوری
respect	اِحترام
rest (to)	اِستراحَت کَردَن
return (to)	برگَشتن
revolting (in taste)	بَدمَزه

rich, wealthy	پولدار – ثروتمند – توانگر
riding	سواری
ring	اَنگُشتَر
river	رودخانه
romantic, lovey, dovey	عاشقانه
room	اُتاق
room (as in space)	جا – فضا
room mate	هم اُتاقی
rose	گُل سُرخ – صورتی
rose water	گُلاب
rough (to touch)	زِبر
rude, uncouth	بی تَربیت
Russian	روس
salon, hall, big room	سالُن
salt	نَمک
salty, savoury	شور
Satan (meaning naughty)	شِیطان
Saturday	شَنبه
saucer	نَعلبکی
say, tell (to)	گُفتن
scales	ترازو
school	مَدرِسه

scientific	علمی	sidewalk, pavement	پیاده‌رو
scissors	قیچی	silk	اَبریشَم
sea	دَریا	silver	نُقره
second	دُوم	since	اَز – اَز وَقتیکه
seconds	ثانیه	sing (to)	آواز خواندن
see (to)	دیدن	singer	خواننده
sell (to)	فُروختن	sister	خواهَر
send (to)	فرِستادن	sit (to)	نِشَستن
seriously	جدی	size, amount	اَندازه
seven	هَفت	skin	پوست
seventh	هَفتُم	skirt	دامَن
several	چندین	sky	آسمان
several, a few	چند	sleep (to)	خوابیدن
sheep	گوسفَند	slow; slowly	آهسته – یَواش
Shi'ite	شیعه	small change	پولِ خُرد
ship	کَشتی	small garden	باغچه
shirt; dress	پیراهَن	small rugs	قالیچه
shop	مَغازه – دُکان	smaller	کوچکتَر
short (brief)	کوتاه	smelly, pungent	بَدبو
shrine	امامزاده – مَقبَره	smilingly, cheerfully	خَندان
shy, bashful	کَمرو – خِجالَتی	snow	برف
sick, unwell; patient	بیمار – مَریض	snowy	بَرفی
side, direction	جَهَت – طَرَف	so, in that case, therefore then	پَس– بَنابراین
sidestreet	کوچهٔ فرعی	socks	جوراب

soft, smooth	صاف – نَرم	spoon	قاشُق
some	بَعضی	sport	وَرزِش
some places (indefinite pl.)	جاهایی	spouse	همسَر
		spring	بَهار
someone; no one (with negative verb)	کَسی – (هیچکَس)	square (shape)	مُربَع
		stage	صحنه
something	چیزی	stamp	تَمبر
sometimes	گاهی – بعضی وقتها	stand, kiosk	گیشه – کیوسک
		star	ستاره
soon, early	زود	statue	مُجَسمه
sorrow, grief	غَم – اَندوه	still, as yet	هَنوز
soul, life, term of endearment after proper names	جان	stop (as in bus stop), station	ایستگاه
		store, department store	فُروشگاه
sound, noise	صدا		
sour	تُرش	story, account of	داستان
south	جُنوب	straight, true, right	راست
spacious	جادار	street, avenue	خیابان
Spain	اسپانیا	stuck down	چسبیده
speak, talk (to)	حَرف زدن	student	دانشجو
		studio	استودیو
special, registered	سفارشی	study (to)	درس خواندن
speech, delivered lecture	سُخَنرانی	sufficient, enough	کافی
speed	سُرعَت	sugar	شِکَر
spicy, hot	تُند	summer	تابستان
spinach	اسفِناج	sun	خورشید – آفتاب

Sunday	یکشَنبه	tears	اَشک
Sunni	سُنی	teeth	دَندان
sunny	آفتابی	telephone	تِلِفُن
supper, dinner	شام	telephone number	شَماره تِلِفُن
supporter	طَرَفدار – هَوادار – پشتیبان	television	تِلویزیون
surface	سَطح	tell off, rebuke, argue (to)	دَعوا کردن – پَرخاش کردن
surface area, expanse	مَساحَت	temple	مَعبَد
surgery (doctor's)	مطَب	tenth	دَهُم
surgery (operation)	جَراحی	thank you	مُتشَکِرَم – مَمنونَم – سِپاسگزارم
sweet	شیرین		
sweet melon	خَربُزه	that	آن
swim (to)	شنا کردن	that very	هَمان
switched off, silent, dark	خاموش	theatre	تِناتر – نَمایشخانه
		then	سپَس
		then	آنوقت
tailor's dressmaker's	خیاط	there (and then)	هَمانجا
take back, get back, retrieve (to)	پَس گِرفتن	there, that place	آنجا
		they (their, them as possessor)	آنها – ایشان
take, carry away (to)	بُردن		
tall, high	بلَند	thick	کلُفت
tea	چای	thin, fine	نازُک
teach (to)	درس دادن	thin, skinny	باریک – لاغَر
teacher, instructor	مُعَلِم – آموزگار	think (to)	فِکر کردن
		thirsty	گرُسنه
teapot	قوری	this	این

this year	امسال
thought, idea	فِکر – نَظَر
thousand	هِزار
thread	نَخ
throat	گلو
Thursday	پَنجشَنبه
ticket	بلیط
tie up, wrap, close, shut (to)	بَستن
tiger	بَبر
time	وَقت – زَمان
time to time	گاه گاه
tiny, very small	کوچولو – کوچک – ریز
tired	خَسته
to	به
to (used for people: going to s.o.); at	پیشِ
to your health	به سلامَتی
today	اِمروز
tomato	گوجهفَرَنگی
tomorrow	فَردا
tonight	اِمشَب
toothbrush	مِسواک
toothpaste	خَمیردَندان
tourist	توریست – جَهانگَرد

trade	تِجارَت
train	تِرَن – قَطار
journey travel,	سَفَر – مُسافِرَت
travel (to)	سَفَر کردن– مُسافِرَت کردن
traveller, passenger	مُسافِر
tray	سینی
tree	دِرَخت
triangle	مُثَلَث
trousers	شَلوار
Tuesday	سهشَنبه
tulips	لاله
tuna fish	ماهی تُن
two or three hours	دو سه ساعَت
type	نوع – جور
ugly	زِشت – بدتَرکیب
umbrella	چَتر
uncomfortable	ناراحَت
under, beneath	زیر
undoubtedly	بدونِ شَک – بیتَردید
unemployed; not busy	بیکار

unfaithful, disloyal	بی‌وَفا	watch, look at (to)	نگاه – تَماشا کردن
unfortunate, unlucky	بدبَخت – بدشانس	water	آب
unfortunately	بدبَختانه	water melon	هِندوانه
university	دانشگاه	way, path, road	راه
until, up	تا	we, us	ما
up	بالا	wear (to)	پوشیدن
use, benefit from (to)	اِستفاده کردن	weather (also air)	هَوا
		wedding	عروسی
usual	مَعمول	Wednesday	چهارشنبه
		week	هَفته
vacuum cleaner	جاروبرقی	weight	وَزن
varied, different	مُتِفاوِت – مُختَلِف	welcome	خوش‌آمد
		well equipped	مُجَهَز
various	گوناگون	west	غَرب
vegetables	سَبزیجات	western	غَربی
vegetarian	سَبزیخوار	wet	خیس
very good	خیلی خوب	what; how . . .!	چه!
vet	دامپزشک	what a pity, what a shame	چه بد! چه حیف!
view	مَنظَره		
visa	ویزا – روادید	what kind, sort?	چه نوع؟ چه جور؟
		when	کی؟
war	جَنگ	when, at the time that	وَقتیکه – هنگامیکه
warm (hot)	گَرم		
wash (to)	شُستن		
wasp	زَنبور	whenever	هَروَقت

worker, labourer	کارگَر
workshop	کارگاه
world	دُنیا – جَهان
write (to)	نِوِشتَن
writer	نِویسَنده
year	سال
year(s) ago	سال(ها)پیش
yellow	زَرد
yes	بَله
yes (informal), 'yup'	آره
yesterday	دیروز
yoghurt	ماست
you are welcome	خوش آمدید
you (pl.)	شُما
you (sing.)	تو
young; youth (person)	جوان
zoo	باغِ وَحش
Zoroastrian	زَرتُشتی

where?	کُجا؟
wherever	هَرجا
which?	کُدام؟
whichever	هَرکُدام
while	در حالیکه
white	سِفید
who, whom?	کی؟
whoever	هَرکه – هَرکَس– هَرکسیکه
why? why do you ask? (idiomatic)	چرا؟
wide	پَهن
wife, woman	زَن
wild	وَحشی
wind	باد
window	پَنجَره
winter	زِمِستان
winter snowboots	پوتین
with, by	با
with common border, sharing the same border	هَم‌مَرز
with difficulty	به سَختی
without	بدونِ– بی
wooden	چوبی
word	لُغَت – کَلِمه
work (to)	کار کردن